Banking Crises
in Latin America

Edited by
Ricardo Hausmann and Liliana Rojas-Suárez

Published by the Inter-American Development Bank
Distributed by The Johns Hopkins University Press

Washington, D.C.

1996

Acknowledgements

The authors would like to thank Deborah Davis and Michael Treadway for their contribution during the editorial process; Ivan Sergio Guerra and Erik Wachtenheim for their very able research assistance; and Norelis Betancourt for coordination support. Transcription and word processing support of Cecilia Coder and Luisa Choy-Luy are also gratefully acknowledged.

The views and opinions expressed in this publication are those of the authors and do not necessarily reflect the official position of the Inter-American Development Bank.

Banking Crises in Latin America

Distributed by
The Johns Hopkins University Press
2715 North Charles Street
Baltimore, Maryland 21218-4319

Library of Congress Catalog Card Number: 96-77938
ISBN: 1-886938-12-1

Contents

iv

Introduction

Enrique V. Iglesias

This volume grew out of a conference held jointly by the Inter-American Development Bank and the Group of Thirty. We became a partner in this venture because of the special opportunity it afforded us to learn from distinguished representatives of the public and private sectors in Latin America and the rest of the world who have had experience managing economic crises. One might think that the conference was prompted purely by recent events in Latin America. While these developments were discussed, they were not the main reason for the meeting. Rather, we talked mainly about what the new economic environment means for Latin America and how we can expect it to impact our banking systems. The purpose of this volume is to give policymakers the benefit of recent experience, as well as a sense of the profound changes underway in our economic systems.

Banking crises are nothing new. They go back as far as the seventeenth century, to the crisis in Holland. Nor are they limited to one country or region: the banking crisis that struck the United States in 1929 was a worldwide phenomenon by 1930. Recurring crises are in the nature of capitalism. In recent times, even industrialized nations with highly advanced financial systems and solid banking oversight agencies have experienced severe crises.

Financial systems today are different, however. Financial activity has expanded and diversified, driven by globalization, deregulation, new financial instruments, and computerized transactions, all of which have created a financial world beyond past imagining.

Within the region, certain factors have emerged that are very much a product of our times. The first is the introduction of stabilization programs in most Latin American countries. We know what the crisis of the 1980s meant for our financial systems. The vigorous response of our countries brought these systems out of inflationary crises and into the period of stability in which they now operate. This transition involved major changes that should be part of our discussion of the problem.

The second factor is the macroeconomic environment and its effect on exchange rate and interest rate policies. In the latest five-year period, these have become crucial elements in macroeconomic policy and have inevitable consequences for the way banking is done in our countries. The third factor is the frame for economic policy decisions of the monetary authorities, which have a tremendous impact on banking.

The fourth factor that has transformed economic systems is that most countries have adopted new mechanisms for deregulation and financial openness. These mechanisms raise the issue of pacing, which involves the quality of the bank supervision instruments and regulatory mechanisms, and the manner in which openness and deregulation are carried out. In particular, inappropriate pacing has enabled some operators with little technical or professional experience and low ethical standards to make their way into financial markets, creating problems such as misappropriation of bank funds for speculation and personal profit.

The recent crises have also revealed the political constraints to financial reorganization. In weak countries with few resources, financial crises become systemic. Simply allowing market forces to correct critical processes sometimes leads to serious political issues, with the result that appropriate solutions cannot be applied in practice.

These new considerations will no doubt underlie our discussions over the next several years. We need to understand why banking crises occur in the context of stability, globalization, openness, regulation, and privatization. We also should look at some of our successes; if there is anything to be learned from recent developments, it is that the monetary and economic authorities were able to manage the crises. In addition—and this is of primary importance—we need to understand how to prevent new crises by reforming our regulatory, insurance, and reporting systems. One particularly important issue is the type of regulatory systems needed for our regional and worldwide banking systems at this economic juncture. New instruments are needed to adapt volume regulation, portfolio quality regulation, and risk policies to current realities.

Other issues to be debated include deposit insurance mechanisms, such as those recently applied by Argentina; rules of competition and ownership; and international relations as a means of securing and expanding our markets and sharing risks. A further issue concerns reporting systems and transparency as they affect consolidated banking systems—reporting systems need to provide a true picture of ownership and of banking system risks. Until recently, financial data were thought to be finely tuned and transparent, but recent experience at both the international and national levels has shown that some data are not entirely reliable—and, as we know, inadequate information can take markets by surprise and compound the problems that come with crises.

Finally, we need to consider the importance of ensuring the professional and technical caliber and ethics of bankers, and ways to reorganize banking systems to increase their efficiency. In recent years, the Inter-American Development Bank has addressed this issue in concert with the International Monetary Fund and the World Bank. Our policies now include support for financial systems, technical support for reorganizing banking systems, and, more recently, support for the overhaul of major banking systems, for example, in Argentina and Mexico.

A new culture of financial systems and banking structures is materializing: a culture of stability, competition, openness, and flexibility. Monetary authorities must fully understand the implications that macroeconomic policies have for efficient and well-run national banking systems. For our part, we must understand that we can win the battle at the macroeconomic level but still lose it at the microeconomic level, unless we have efficient regulatory mechanisms that enable us to limit crises, or better yet, prevent them from happening.

Enrique V. Iglesias, President
Inter-American Development Bank

Paul Volcker

The Group of Thirty's involvement in this volume, and the conference on which it is based, arise out of a longstanding interest in the smooth functioning of the international financial system. In earlier times, thinking about the international financial system generally meant concentrating on exchange rate management and cross-border financial flows. While sound national financial systems were considered important, they were simply not part of the international agenda.

When I went into banking fifty years ago, ten or fifteen years after the Depression, banks dominated the financial system and there was little worry about the weakness of the system, certainly not in the United States. U.S. banks were risk averse to a fault, and heavily invested in government securities. Banks were thought to be bastions of propriety and stability, barriers against crises and emergencies, not themselves sources of instability. They were certainly not seen as weak links in the chain of finance if pressures should arise from external events.

But times have changed. The health of the banking sector has assumed a more prominent role in the thinking about both economic development and global finance. In part, this is because of the succession of financial crises that have erupted in the United States, Europe, Japan, and a number of Latin American countries. While most banking systems have made it to safer shores, and we have survived without the sort of crisis that became the Great Depression, a few countries still exhibit a sense of crisis regarding their banking systems.

The change is also due to increasing globalization, the speed and complexity of finance, and the shift to openness and deregulation in emerging markets. The financial system, as the cardiovascular system of the market economy, has had difficulty meeting the new demands. If information, goods and services are to flow through markets efficiently, people must have confidence in the payments process and in the intermediation of savings and investment for which banks are responsible. This is ever more complicated as individual economies become integrated into a global economy.

In this new world of global finance, it is popular to argue that governments ought to play a smaller role in the economic system, to be less intrusive. But an interesting byproduct of the crises of the recent period is that world governments have been doing more, not less, in this vital area. In fact, recent banking crises have been managed only through extensive and continuing government intervention.

There have been substantial government bailouts of national systems in the United States, Scandinavia, a number of Latin economies, and now in Japan. In the Latin American debt crises of the 1980s, government money in the form of external loans was involved to the tune of several billion dollars, in the face of a real threat to the international banking system. A decade later, the U.S. and the IMF quickly pledged $40 billion or more for Mexico alone, some of it on extended terms, in a case in which mainly Mexican banks were threatened. That episode certainly raises the question of whether we are now on a sustainable course.

Increased attention by governments to financial systems and their supervision is everywhere apparent. The communiqué of the Halifax Summit in June 1995 called for strengthening financial market supervision and regulation. It called upon international supervisory bodies to address issues of systemic risk, and it encouraged the international financial institutions to assist the process of putting adequate supervisory, regulatory, and policy structures in place for countries in the process of financial liberalization. The Hemispheric Summit held in Miami in December 1994 recognized the importance of strengthening national banking systems in promoting regional integration in the Americas. It called upon all countries in the hemisphere to establish sound, comparable supervision and regulation of banking and securities markets.

The Group of Thirty itself has devoted considerable energy to improving the safety and soundness of the international financial system through its work on clearance and settlements systems and derivatives, and has published a considerable body of work on the banking sector and the Latin American economies. This conference and the collaboration between the Group and the Inter-American Development Bank reflect a recognition that as much as we have learned about supervision and regulation, and despite our efforts to restore our banking systems as bastions of stability, these problems simply will not go away. Nor can the recent rate of expansion of assistance be sustained.

What these developments imply for the next international crisis is difficult to predict. The global financial system is increasingly operating outside of traditional channels, calling the effectiveness of traditional supervisory mechanisms into question. The Mexican crisis has made clear that the pressures may well be focused outside the banking system. Therefore, we face large and unresolved questions about the role of banks and nonbanks in the global financial system, and of appropriate methods of government support, as we approach the twenty-first century.

In planning this conference, we recognized that a good deal of experience in crisis management has accumulated, that the nature of the problems has changed with economic liberalization and financial reform, and that perhaps it was time to take stock of the collective experience inside and outside the region. The conference has been a useful step in answering some of the questions we face, but clearly only a first step.

The Group of Thirty is grateful to those who contributed to the success of the conference. Many distinguished academics, policymakers, and bankers lent their expertise to the proceedings, especially those who were on the program and wrote the papers that appear in this volume. And, finally, the Group wishes to acknowledge its debt to its cosponsor, the Inter-American Development Bank, for its disproportionate effort in hosting and organizing the conference and for subsequently producing and publishing this book.

Paul Volcker, Chairman
Group of Thirty

The Plan of the Book

This book is organized in six parts and a concluding section. Major aspects of banking crises in Latin America are analyzed in the first five papers, followed by commentaries from distinguished policymakers, academicians and participants from the private sector. The authors address four questions:

- What are the salient features of banking crises in Latin America?
- What are the main causes of banking crises in the region?
- How can governments manage banking crises effectively?
- How can banking crises be prevented?

Part I focuses on the salient features of Latin American banking systems, identifying the major sources of fragility and evaluating the severity of recent banking crises in the region, relative to those in industrial countries. The discussion also addresses issues associated with the ongoing process of financial liberalization in Latin America.

Part II analyzes the macroeconomic causes of banking crises. By focusing on banks' risk-taking incentives, it connects periods of economic expansion with the lending booms that so often end in banking crises. Part III concentrates on the microeconomic factors leading to bank difficulties. A combination of weak regulatory and supervisory procedures and undercapitalized banks with publicly guaranteed deposits are identified as a key element behind bank problems.

Part IV identifies particular constraints that make the management of banking crises more complicated in Latin America than in industrial countries. It outlines the principles needed to resolve bank problems and offers suggestions for applying them within the region.

The discussion of how to avoid crises, in Part V, offers policy recommendations at both the macro- and the microeconomic level aimed at improving the resilience of banking systems to unanticipated shocks. This reflects policy issues that run through the entire book. For example, Part II analyzes the appropriate fiscal, monetary, and exchange rate policies to maintain healthy banking systems. Similarly, Part III discusses how to strengthen regulatory procedures and supervisory practices in Latin America.

Part VI turns the focus to experiences of individual countries. Leading policymakers discuss their experiences in dealing with banking crises, assess various policy recommendations proposed and derive lessons for avoiding future crises in the region. In conclusion, Part VII summarizes the policy debate and suggests future areas of research.

Part I

Banking Crises
in Latin America:
Experiences and Issues

Liliana Rojas-Suárez and Steven R. Weisbrod

Commentary

Ruth de Krivoy

Banking Crises in Latin America: Experiences and Issues

Liliana Rojas-Suárez and Steven R. Weisbrod

Since the early 1980s, major financial crises have occurred with increasing frequency in both industrial and developing countries. Because banks play a special role in the economy as issuers of monetary liabilities and providers of clearing services for noncash payments, these crises have provoked serious concern among policymakers and regulators everywhere. Developing effective policies to reduce the severity of banking problems and to restructure banking systems has thus become a priority for bank regulators.

In Latin America, banking problems emerged in the wake of the external debt crisis in 1982. Where policymakers did not respond with stringent fiscal and monetary policies and bank regulators did not establish disciplined bank restructuring programs, the effects of crisis were prolonged, in some cases lasting almost a decade. Moreover, even where policymakers managed the crisis by following appropriate policies, resolving banking crises took four or five years and required major adjustments in the real economy.

This paper argues that the experiences with banking crises in Latin America have been different from those in the industrial world because of the peculiarities of Latin American financial systems. Lessons derived from crisis resolution in the industrial world do not always apply to Latin America's banking problems. If future crises in the region are to be managed or avoided, the unique experiences of Latin American regulators must be considered.

The remainder of the paper is divided into five sections. In the next section, we discuss the features that distinguish Latin American financial systems from those in the industrial world. Latin American financial markets are characterized by a lower ratio of financial intermediation relative to GDP, less investor willingness to commit long-term funds, and higher volatility in deposit markets. These differences result from weaknesses in the structural foundations of Latin American financial markets: the legal framework for financial markets is not fully developed and their accounting standards are weak. In addition, sharp fluctuations in policies have increased uncertainty about the stability of economic and financial conditions in these countries.

The third section discusses how the fragility of Latin American financial systems contributes to the relative severity of banking crises in the region. Moreover, inexact accounting standards make it difficult for the authorities to assess banking problems.

The fourth section discusses the performance of Latin American financial systems under the liberalized environment of the early 1990s compared to their performance under the highly regulated environment of the 1980s. While crises have occurred under both policy regimes, highly regulated regimes generally experience greater volatility in financial markets than do more liberal policy environments. Under the liberal rules of the 1990s, market discipline has played a significant role in controlling the growth of risky institutions and therefore in ameliorating the severity of banking crises.

The fifth section considers the role of the authorities in improving the performance of liberalized financial systems. Regulators have an important role in complementing private market discipline. Latin American regulators lack the tools of their counterparts in developed countries, so they often rely more heavily on reserve requirements than on supervising individual banks to control the growth of risky bank credit. Nevertheless, because reserve requirements impose costs on both strong and weak banks, these measures should be applied only until the conditions for strong supervision are present. In conclusion, we present some policy options for reducing financial market fragility.

Latin American Financial Systems: Key Features

In Latin America, depository institutions—banks and savings institutions issuing deposit-like liabilities—are the only major vehicles for institutional savings, except in Chile, where pension and insurance funds

Figure 1.1 Deposits in the Banking Sector, 1994
(Percent of GDP)

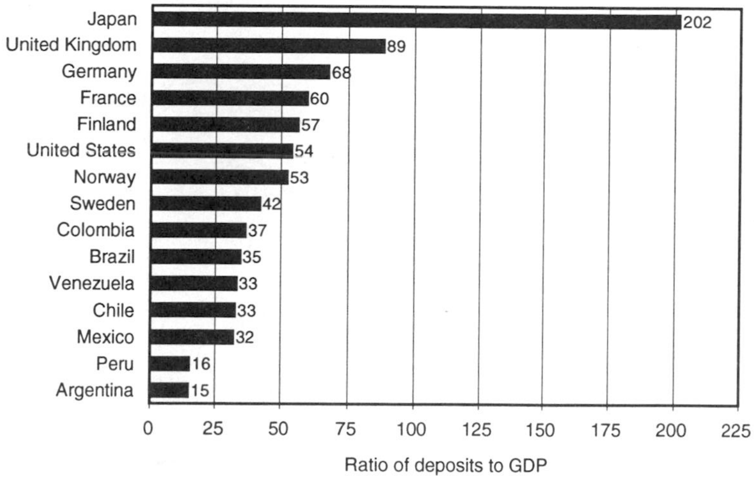

Country	Ratio of deposits to GDP
Japan	202
United Kingdom	89
Germany	68
France	60
Finland	57
United States	54
Norway	53
Sweden	42
Colombia	37
Brazil	35
Venezuela	33
Chile	33
Mexico	32
Peru	16
Argentina	15

Ratio of deposits to GDP

Note: Data for Chile and Brazil are for September 1994.
Data for United Kingdom are for March 1994.
Source: IMF, *International Financial Statistics.*

account for 44 percent of institutional savings. By contrast, savings institutions in the major industrial countries issue substantial amounts of nondeposit liabilities, which are long term, even when these institutions are classified as banks.

In the United States, depository institutions account for less than one third of institutional savings. In Germany, where depository institutions account for most of institutional savings, 45 percent of the domestic private liabilities of these institutions are medium and long-term bonds. In Japan, another bank-dominated system, 34 percent of financial institutions' private domestic liabilities are bonds, insurance reserves, and trust accounts.

Even though the deposit liabilities of banks and other depository institutions play a much more significant role in Latin American than in industrial economies, deposit liabilities to the private sector of all banking institutions are a lower percentage of GDP in Latin America than in major industrial countries (Figure 1.1). That is, relatively few funds are held in financial intermediaries.[1]

---

[1] In many Latin American economies, important segments of financial markets are informal. This fact also reflects a low degree of confidence in the financial system.

Figure 1.2a Real Interest Rates in Five Latin American Countries, 1980-94
(Percent)

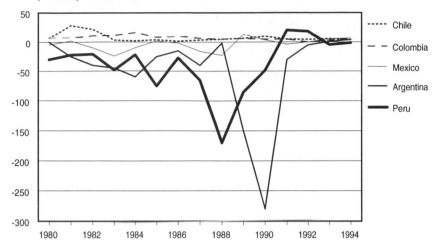

Source: IMF, *International Financial Statistics.*

Figure 1.2b Real Interest Rates in Three Industrial Countries, 1980-94
(Percent)

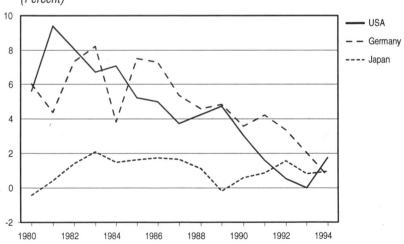

Source: IMF, *International Financial Statistics.*

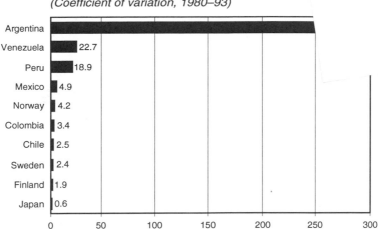

Figure 1.3 Change in Ratio of Deposits to GDP
(Coefficient of variation, 1980–93)

Argentina	
Venezuela	22.7
Peru	18.9
Mexico	4.9
Norway	4.2
Colombia	3.4
Chile	2.5
Sweden	2.4
Finland	1.9
Japan	0.6

Source: IMF, *International Financial Statistics.*

The relatively small size of the financial institution sector and the short maturity of liabilities of these institutions suggest that investor confidence that financial assets will yield a positive long-term rate of return is weaker in Latin America than in industrial countries. Investor concerns are verified in Figures 1.2a and 1.2b, which present real interest rates on deposits in selected industrial and Latin American countries between 1982 and 1993.

In contrast to the evidence for industrial countries, interest rates remained negative for substantial periods of time in several Latin American countries. This lack of investor confidence causes high volatility in the ratio of deposits to GDP in the region, as indicated in Figure 1.3.[2]

The features of Latin American financial systems delineated above are the outcome of several factors. First, accounting standards are not sufficiently developed to permit depositors to evaluate the quality of bank balance sheets, and it is difficult for banks to evaluate the income statements of borrowers. Second, the legal environment makes it difficult for creditors to predict their prospects for gaining possession of collateral in the event of default. Third, there is a legacy of destabilizing economic policies, including hyperinflation, large currency devaluations, and na-

---

[2] Indeed, many of the policies that generated a lack of investor confidence in banking systems also contributed to the large capital outflows experienced in many Latin American countries in the 1980s.

Figure 1.4 Ratio of Deposits to GDP Prior to Crises
(Percentage change)

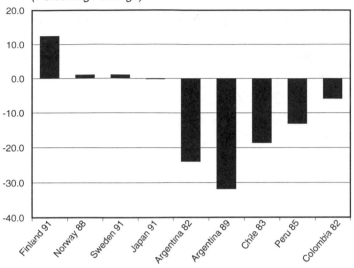

Note: Includes deposit banks only.
Source: IMF, *International Financial Statistics.*

Figure 1.5 Brady Bond Index, Argentina and Mexico, Dec. 94-May 95
(Dec. 1st 1994=100)

Note: Gaps indicate missing data.
Source: Bloomberg Business News.

tionalization of important segments of the economy, which erodes investor confidence.

As a result of these factors, investors prefer to hold short-term financial assets, and banks prefer to make short-term loans. Borrowers must remain fairly liquid in case bankers are forced to curtail lending when investors withdraw their funds. If borrowers cannot prove their liquidity, they appear insolvent because legal and accounting obstacles make other forms of credit evaluation difficult. Therefore, in Latin America liquidity crises cannot easily be differentiated from solvency crises.

The Severity of Banking Crises in Latin America

Due to the fragility of Latin American financial systems, even relatively mild shocks to the banking sector can quickly result in sharp reductions in the deposit base. For example, Figure 1.4 displays the percentage change in the ratio of deposits to GDP for selected Latin American and industrial countries during the early phases of a banking crisis. Depositors in Latin America are much more prone than depositors in industrial countries to flee the banking system when bank borrowers' capacity to pay is adversely affected. These data suggest that depositors in Latin America fear they will suffer a real financial loss following a banking crisis, whereas depositors in industrial countries believe that even in a crisis, the real value of their deposits will be preserved. That is, most investors in industrial countries expect banking crises to be temporary, and believe that the long-run viability of the system will soon be restored.

The sharp drop in confidence in Latin American financial systems following initial signals of distress is common to both domestic and foreign investors.[3] As a result, periods of banking difficulties are also associated with loss of access to international capital markets. In the 1980s, during periods of banking crisis, countries in Latin America were not able to raise sufficient funds in international capital markets to cover current account deficits, and their overall balance of payments position became sharply negative. In late 1994 and early 1995, falling confidence in the financial systems of Argentina and Mexico was reflected in a 30 percent drop in their Brady bond indexes (see Figure 1.5).

In contrast, during the Nordic banking crises in the late 1980s and early 1990s, the overall balance of payments positions of these countries

---

[3] In Latin America, initial distress is often signaled by macroeconomic disequilibrium. For a discussion of macroeconomic causes of banking crises, see Gavin and Hausmann in this volume.

Figure 1.6 Government Bond Prices in Norway and Sweden, 1988–94

(1988=100)

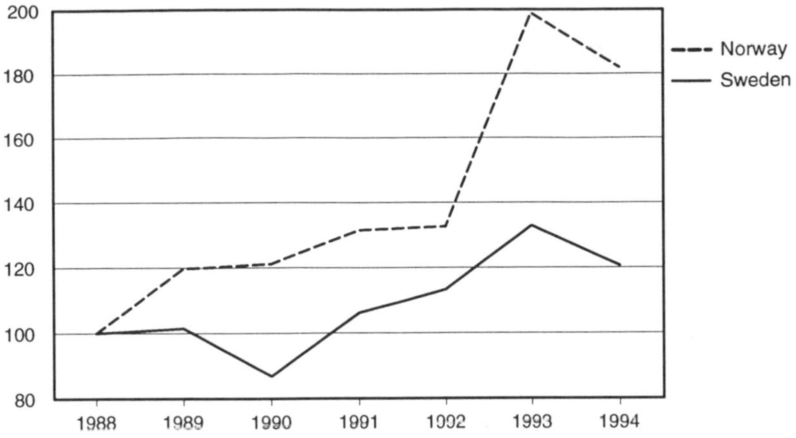

Source: IMF, *International Financial Statistics.*

were relatively stable. Moreover, long-term government bond prices in Norway and Sweden were largely unaffected by the crises[4] (see Figure 1.6).

The fragility of Latin American banking systems is also reflected in the high costs associated with restructuring banking systems after a crisis. Table 1.1 shows the cost of restructuring banking systems, excluding recoveries from future sales of assets and from future bank earnings, as a percent of GDP and as a percent of bank loans, for selected industrial and Latin American countries.[5] For industrial countries, the cost-to-loan ratio ranges from a low of about 4 to 6 percent for Norway and Sweden to a high of almost 10 percent for Finland. In Latin America, the cost ranges from a low of about 23 percent in Chile to a high of 57 percent for Venezuela. Relative to GDP, the immediate cost of bank restructuring is substantially higher in Latin America than in the industrial countries, with the exception of Colombia.

---

[4] There is no domestic long-term government bond rate available for Finland. In the fall of 1992, during an attack on the exchange rate, short-term interest rates in the Nordic countries increased sharply. Rates quickly fell after devaluation, however.

[5] We use the outlays at the time of the program as the measure of severity because it best represents the information that depositors and regulators have about the worst case magnitude of the problems faced by banks—that is, it presumes no future recoveries. It also represents the amount of funds that regulators must raise at the time of the crisis to rescue banks. For specific definitions of costs, see Table 1.1.

Table 1.1 The Cost of Restructuring Banking Systems

		Cost as Percent of	
Year	Country	GDP	Total Loans
1982	Argentina	13.0	42.5
1985	Chile	19.6	22.5
1985	Colombia	6.0	40.0
1994	Venezuela	13.0	57.2
1991–93	Finland	8.2	9.7
1988–92	Norway	4.5	5.5
1991–93	Sweden	4.5	3.7
1991	United States	5.1	7.8
1989	U.S. Commercial Banks	1.5	3.9

Note: For Argentina, the cost is estimated as the increase in central bank lending to banks in real terms between 1981 and 1982. For Chile, the cost is net central bank loans to private domestic banks in 1985. For Colombia, the cost, measured for commercial banks only, is the real change in central bank lending to banks between 1982 and 1985 plus the decline in the real value of bank capital over the same period. The U.S. estimate includes the cost of the savings and loan restructuring program up to 1991 plus total FDIC payouts between 1984 and 1989.

Sources: IMF, *International Financial Statistics;* Superintendencia de Bancos e Instituciones Financieras (Chile); Banco de la República (Colombia); Drees and Pazarbasioglu, 1995; FDIC, *Annual Report*, 1989; *Federal Reserve Bulletin*, 1992.

The extreme differences in restructuring costs between Latin American countries and industrial countries indicate the burdensome task faced by regulators in the region during a crisis. The authorities' problems are compounded by weaknesses in accounting standards. Indeed, accounting data used to describe the quality of bank balance sheets do not reflect the marked differences in the severity of crises between Latin America and industrial countries, as is evident by comparing tables 1.1 and 1.2. Table 1.2 presents a standard accounting measure of the riskiness of bank loan portfolios—the ratio of nonperforming loans to loans— at the onset of banking crises in four Latin American countries, as well as in Finland and the United States.[6]

---

[6] Differences in country coverage between tables 1.1 and 1.2 merely reflect the availability of data.

Table 1.2 Ratio of Nonperforming Loans to Total Loans

Year	Country	Ratio
1980	Argentina	9.1
1982	Chile	4.1
1993	Venezuela	9.3
1994	Mexico	10.6
1989	United States	4.8
1992	Finland	9.3

Note: All data are year end, except Mexico, which is as of September 1994. U.S. data are for commercial banks only.

Sources: Sundararajan and Balino, 1991; Superintendencia de Bancos e Instituciones Financiera (Chile), December 1982; Drees and Pazarbasioglu, 1995; Comisión Bancaria y Valores; Federal Reserve Bulletin, July 1992.

Table 1.3 Ratio of Loan Loss Reserves to Total Loans

Year	Country	Banking Segment	Loan Loss Reserves to Loans
1982	Chile	Domestic Private	4.17
1994	Argentina	Small Private	4.34
1994	Mexico	Government Assisted (1995)	4.39
1989	United States	Ten Largest	4.36

Source: See Table 1.2.

On the eve of a banking crisis, the ratio of nonperforming loans to loans for Chile at year end 1982, 4.1 percent, was less than half that reported in Finland at year end 1992, 9.3 percent. In Argentina at year end 1980 and Venezuela at year end 1993, they are about equal to those in Finland (see Table 1.2). Although the costs of resolving bank crises were substantially higher in Latin America, that is not reflected in higher ratios of nonperforming loans to loans as reported by banks in the region. In 1989, U.S. commercial banks reported their proportion of nonperforming loans at 4.8 percent, about half the ratio reported by banks in Latin American countries discussed above. However, the cost of rescuing U.S. commercial banks between 1984 and 1989 was approximately 1.5 percent of GDP, about one-tenth the relative cost of rescuing Venezuelan banks.

Because Latin American financial markets are relatively fragile, loan loss reserves as a percentage of loans should be higher in Latin America than in the industrial countries, given the severity of past crises. However, as Table 1.3 indicates, Latin American banks had a loan loss reserves-to-loans ratio very similar to that of the largest banks in the United States. In 1989, the ten largest commercial banks held loan loss reserves equal to 4.36 percent of loans. In Chile, the riskiest segment of the banking industry in 1982 was domestically owned private banks, which had loan loss reserves equal to 4.17 percent of loans. In Mexico, banks that required government assistance during the crisis had loan loss reserves to loans of 4.39 percent in December 1994. In Argentina, small private banks, which are relatively risky, had loan loss reserves to loans equal to 4.34 percent in late 1994.

The rather lax accounting standards in many Latin American countries are reflected in banks' income statements. When reporting standards are adequate, net income should appear negative in a banking crisis, because provisions for loan loss (the funds for loan loss reserves) exceed net income. When that happens, banks are forced to reduce their capital account. Yet during previous banking crises, many of Latin America's banking systems have reported positive net income to assets, whereas banking systems in industrial countries have reported significant negative net income to assets.

Chilean banks' accounting systems did improve significantly after its banking crisis in 1982, however. Argentina and Mexico have used the recent crisis to improve their reporting procedures as well.[7]

Has Financial Liberalization Worked?

By the early 1990s, many Latin American countries had instituted policies of financial liberalization. Whether such policies are appropriate for the region is questioned by many analysts, including policymakers in industrial countries, where markets are much less volatile. In the industrial world, some view the former times of interest rate regulation, high reserve requirements, and segmented financial markets as far superior to the risky world of today, following deregulation.

---

[7] For example, large provincial banks in Argentina reported losses during the first quarter of 1995.

Newly deregulated banking systems have certainly fallen into crises in Latin America. This occurred in Argentina and Chile in the early 1980s and Argentina and Mexico in 1995. However, severe banking difficulties also occurred during the mid 1980s in the highly controlled banking systems of Mexico, Peru, and Argentina, all of which were subject to high reserve requirements, credit allocation restrictions, and in Argentina and Peru, to interest rate ceilings.

These three banking crises of the mid 1980s resulted from mismanagement of banking crises earlier in the decade. Instead of adopting policies to strengthen their banking systems, authorities responded to these earlier crises by imposing credit allocation schemes that were used to finance government and government-sponsored programs. In Argentina and Peru, when the authorities were unable to pay off their debts to the banks, they imposed interest rate controls on banks and resorted to highly inflationary policies, which resulted in major reductions in the ratio of deposits to GDP as depositors' real wealth declined and capital flight took hold.

The experiences of Argentina, Mexico, and Peru in the mid 1980s strongly indicate that financial regulation in Latin America often leads to instability rather than stability. Indeed, in the 1980s and early 1990s, these countries experienced extremely high volatility in their deposit to GDP ratios compared to Chile and Colombia (Figure 1.3). As indicated in Figure 1.2, real interest rates were substantially negative in Argentina, Mexico, and Peru, in the 1980s, reflecting regulations.

Throughout the early 1990s, most Latin American countries have shown great determination in moving toward financial liberalization. As demonstrated by the recent experiences in Mexico and Argentina, these policies have allowed market discipline to work: risky banks have been forced to pay a premium for funds in an environment in which interest rates fluctuate freely.

For example, in Mexico as far back as 1992, investors had identified many of the banks that are currently experiencing the largest capital deficiencies.[8] In 1992, the two largest banks in the market were able to raise funds for 11.8 percent, whereas other riskier banks had to pay 14.5 percent. Similar evidence has been found for Venezuela before its banking crisis. In this country, banks that were later resolved paid substantially more for deposits than other banks several years before the crisis.

In the Argentine market, deposit costs were substantially higher at

---

[8] This argument is developed in detail in Rojas-Suárez and Weisbrod (1995a).

large provincial banks—a segment of the banking market with particularly high proportions of nonperforming loans—than at large private banks. In addition, in 1994, before the banking crisis, large provincials had difficulty raising funds in the dollar interbank market. Between March 1993 and November 1994, these banks' dollar liabilities to other banks declined by more than 10 percent, compared to a growth in dollar interbank liabilities of about 30 percent at large private banks.

As the Mexican data demonstrate, if the interest rate is high enough, investors are sometimes quite willing to supply short-term funds to risky banks in the hope of being able to withdraw their funds quickly when a crisis appears possible. For example, in 1993, deposits at small banks grew by about 35 percent whereas deposits at large banks grew by 2 percent. Between January 1994 and September 1994, small bank deposits grew 20 percent, compared to 5 percent at large banks.

However, as in Argentina, it became more difficult for risky banks in Mexico to raise funds as a crisis approached. Between September and December 1994, small bank deposits grew 10 percent while large bank deposits grew 17 percent. A similar phenomenon was observed in Venezuela. Banks where intervention occurred had a deposit market share that increased from 10.3 percent in 1988 to 19 percent in 1991. After 1991, they found it much harder to expand. Their deposit share increased only slightly, to 21.5 percent of deposits at year end 1993. The banking crisis began in late 1993.

Thus, past and recent experiences with regulation of financial markets in Latin America provide strong support for liberalization policies. Controls have been associated with a high degree of instability and have caused credit to be directed toward uneconomic projects. In addition, they have prevented markets from acting as automatic stabilizers by choking off funds to weak institutions.

How Regulators Complement Market Forces

The previous section emphasized the role of markets in differentiating between strong and weak banking institutions, but the evidence presented there also indicates that markets are often willing to supply credit to risky banks if the price is right. Because regulators are concerned with the stability of the economy and the preservation of the payments system, their objectives are not always the same as those of the market. Thus, even though investors in Latin America differentiate between risky and sound banks, effective supervision is still necessary to complement and strengthen the role of markets.

Figure 1.7 Ratio of Liquidity to International Reserves versus Reserve Requirements on Demand Deposits, 1994

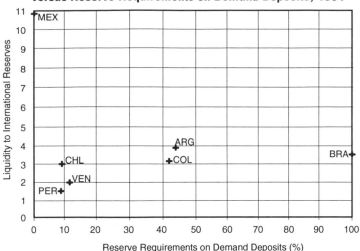

Source: Banco Central de la República, Boletín Estadístico Mensual (Argentina); Superintendencia de Bancos e Instituciones Financieras, Información Financiera (Chile); Comisión Bancaria y Valores, Boletín Estadístico de Banca Múltiple (México); Superintendencia de Banca y Seguros, Información Financiera Quincenal (Perú), Banco Central de Venezuela, Boletín Mensual (Venezuela).

Because of the fragility of Latin American financial systems, regulators may need some tools from past experience—specifically, high reserve requirements. The first argument for high reserve requirements in Latin America is that, because of the extreme volatility of the Latin American environment, banks need liquidity to meet the surprise demands for deposit withdrawals. The second is that reserve requirements tend to limit the expansion of risky credit when bank supervision is ineffective.[9] Liquidity is important because in Latin America, systemic withdrawals occur simultaneously with capital flight; hence, reserve requirements are effective only if central banks invest deposits in international reserve assets.[10] Whether reserve requirements can provide adequate liquidity

---

[9] The second argument has been developed in Fernandez and Guidotti (1994) and Rojas-Suárez and Weisbrod (1995a).

[10] International reserves are necessary to protect the stability of the banking system when a country follows a targeted or fixed exchange rate policy, which is the case in most of Latin America. Even if the financial system is dollarized, international reserves are necessary because a loss in confidence in the stability of the banking system leads to withdrawals from the system, regardless of the currency denomination of deposits.

during capital flight raises another issue: even if reserve requirements are high and properly invested so that bank deposits remain liquid, they cannot provide liquidity to other short-term financial markets, which in Latin America are primarily government and central bank paper. That is, if the lack of confidence extends to both bank and nonbank paper, the stock of reserves will leave some assets uncovered. Figure 1.7 presents the relationship between reserve requirements on demand deposits and the ratio of liquid assets to international reserves for selected Latin American countries. The countries with high reserve requirements, such as Brazil, obviously do not have lower ratios than those with low reserve requirements, such as Chile.

Even when government and central bank paper is held on bank balance sheets, reserve requirements have several other drawbacks. Because they are a tax on bank intermediation, banks find ways to avoid them, like creating off-balance-sheet markets *(mesa de dinero)*. In addition, banks move business to more liberal offshore environments.

But when effective, reserve requirements can restrain credit expansion, as well provide liquidity. To expand their balance sheets, banks must first acquire reserves, the quantity of which can be controlled by the central bank. This policy tool does not discriminate between expansion of sound and weak banks, so it may be of limited use in restricting the growth of riskier forms of credit. If possible, bank regulators would prefer to target policies that restrain banks' portfolio decisions to risky segments of the banking system. Were supervision more effective, it could be a more targeted tool for managing bank risk and liquidity. More effective supervision could be a tool for managing bank risks and liquidity.

In industrial countries, policy tools to restrict credit expansion are increasingly based on supervisory standards, which constrain banks differentially, rather than on reserve requirements, which affect all banks in similar ways.[11] For example, while capital-to-risk-weighted-asset requirements are applied across the board in the sense that all banks must meet a standard ratio, the accounting procedures by which the requirement is met can force risky banks to be more constrained than less risky ones. If supervisors pressure a bank to increase its reserves for potential loan loss, they are, in fact, forcing a bank to write down the value of its capital. Hence, the capital-to-risk-weighted-asset constraint relies much more heavily on an effective supervisory process than does the reserve require-

---

[11] Even in Germany, a market known for high reserve requirements, the reserve-to-deposit ratio has recently averaged less than 6 percent, which is low compared to many Latin American markets.

ment constraint. Thus, while regulators may not have better information than the market, they have tools to complement market discipline in controlling the growth of risky banks.

These tools are effective only if supervisors can identify nonperforming loans. In fact, several banking crises in Latin America have been preceded by capitalization of unpaid interest into new loans to make nonperforming loans look performing. However, a regulator should be able to observe whether loans to a single borrower are expanding at the rate of interest due. The ability to identify this behavior depends on establishing proper procedures for reviewing banks' loan files.

In this connection, there is a debate as to whether Bank for International Settlements (BIS) asset classification rules and capital standards are appropriate for Latin America. A more urgent issue would seem to be developing the supervisory skills needed to classify assets appropriately.

Evidence that strong supervision can be effective in reducing the impact of a crisis is provided by the differences in net income-to-asset ratios for savings and loans and commercial banks in Texas in 1988. In that year, savings and loans, which were generally recognized as lacking adequate supervision, experienced a loss equal to almost 11 percent of assets. Yet commercial banks in the Dallas Federal Reserve District, operating under the same economic conditions but well supervised, experienced a loss of about 1.5 percent of assets.

Of course, it would be difficult to duplicate the experience of U.S. commercial banks in Latin America. While it is not hard to identify whether a loan is nonperforming, it can be difficult to determine whether the borrower receiving a new loan has a business relationship with a borrower having a nonperforming loan. In other words, Latin America's less exact accounting and legal standards mean that procedures for loan documentation are less rigorous than those in the United States. Nevertheless, because the market can clearly identify potential problem banks in Latin America, regulators can focus on pressuring these banks to improve their procedures. The evidence for the effectiveness of reserve requirements versus supervision for controlling bank risk is dealt with in Rojas-Suárez and Weisbrod (1995b).

Latin America is still moving toward the conditions that make effective supervision possible. In the transition period, reserve requirements may be necessary. However, these should be viewed only as a temporary device; they should not impede the process of creating an environment in which supervision can be effective. Fragility is also not a viable reason to view reserve requirements as permanent, since fragility itself is an outcome of the same forces that make effective supervision difficult. The policy goal should be to build the proper structure for healthy financial markets, and that will take time.

Conclusion

Banking crises in Latin America are more severe than in the industrial world, and have a greater impact on local economies, because the region's financial systems are more fragile. This fragility results from frequent periods of destabilizing economic policies and structural problems in the market, which include inexact legal and accounting standards and weak supervision. Despite these factors, Latin American financial systems have been more stable under liberalized financial policies than under highly regulated regimes.

In contrast to industrial countries, the necessary conditions for effective supervision are not fully developed in most Latin American countries. Hence, some regulation, such as high reserve requirements, can be justified on a temporary basis. Nevertheless, the long-run goal must be to build legal, regulatory, and policy structures in which liberalized financial markets can flourish.

As a result of frequent changes in the direction of economic policies, authorities in Latin America face the challenge of overcoming a lack of credibility in policy announcements. In this connection, indexation and dollarization, which guarantee the value of financial contracts in real terms, are popular tools for achieving credibility in the region. Indeed, some observers attribute Chile's success in creating a stable financial system to the introduction of indexation. It is argued that Chile was able to build a long-term bond market by indexing the principal of financial contracts and mandating the development of a pension fund industry that absorbed indexed long-term bonds.

Clearly, both sound institutions and strong contractual commitments are important in developing domestic long-term bond markets. However, Chile's experience demonstrates that the road to making both these elements believable is a gradual one. For example, indexation first became an important element in the Chilean financial system during the banking crisis in the early and mid 1980s, when the central bank mandated that the principal of restructured loans would be indexed to inflation. However, when the program began, the central bank, rather than depositors, provided most (70 percent) of the indexed liabilities of the financial system. Investors were initially skeptical that banks would, in fact, be able to maintain the real value of deposits.[12] Likewise, pension funds, which are private institutions in Chile, only gradually became willing to invest in long-term assets. As late as 1988, over half of pension fund assets were still invested in bank deposits.

Thus, Chilean domestic investors had to be coaxed into providing long-term funds to the government and monetary authorities. To gain the confidence of investors, the authorities had to demonstrate their full commitment to the stability of the financial system.

As in the case of indexation, dollarization, which permits borrowers and investors to freely write their contracts in U.S. dollars, ensures that the value of principal will not be eroded by domestic currency inflation. When a banking system is sound, dollarization can help prevent capital flight if a crisis of confidence in the announced exchange rate regime emerges; bank runs can be avoided since investors can merely change the currency denomination of their deposits. However, if the banking system is weak, depositors will flee the system in a balance of payments crisis, regardless of the currency denomination of deposits, thus creating a run both on banks and on the foreign exchange reserves of the central bank. During the crises of the 1980s, Latin American investors had ample experience with dollar-denominated bank deposits being forcibly converted to local currency deposits at unfavorable exchange rates when international reserves were scarce. Building confidence that such confiscation policies will not be repeated is an additional challenge for policymakers.

While banking crises in Latin America are particularly severe, they also provide opportunities to build credibility. The commitment of the Argentine government to a stable policy course in the midst of banking difficulties is a good example. Only through such commitments will investors gain confidence in a government's pledge to uphold contractual obligations.

Liliana Rojas-Suárez is Principal Advisor, Office of the Chief Economist, Inter-American Development Bank. Steven R. Weisbrod is Consultant, Office of the Chief Economist, Inter-American Development Bank.

---

[12] The difficulty in getting investors to believe this is indicated by the fact that in 1985, the indexed interest rate on deposits of 90 to 365 days was 8.2 percent, whereas the real interest rate on unindexed short-term deposits was 4.1 percent.

References

Banco de la República (Colombia). *Revista* (various issues). Bogotá, Colombia.

Bloomberg Business News.

Comisión Bancaria y Valores (Mexico). 1994. *Boletín Estadístico de Banca Múltiple* (December). Mexico City, Mexico.

Drees, Burkhard, and Ceyla Pazarbasioglu. 1995. "The Nordic Banking Crisis: Pitfalls in Financial Liberalization?" IMF Working Paper (June). Washington, D.C.

FDIC (Federal Deposit Insurance Corporation). 1989. *Annual Report.* Washington, D.C.

Federal Reserve. 1992. *Federal Reserve Bulletin* (July). Washington, D.C.

Fernandez, Roque B., and Pablo E. Guidotti. 1994. "Regulating the Banking Industry in Transition Economies: Exploring Interactions between Capital and Reserve Requirements." Paper prepared for the Conference on Economic Reform: Latin America and the Transition Economies, Georgetown University, May 12–13, Washington, D.C.

IMF (International Monetary Fund). *International Financial Statistics* (various issues). Washington, D.C.

Rojas-Suárez, Liliana, and Steven R. Weisbrod. 1995a. "Financial Fragilities in Latin America: the 1980s and 1990s," IMF Occasional Paper No. 132 (October). Washington, D.C.

Rojas-Suárez, Liliana, and Steven R. Weisbrod. 1995b. "Achieving Stability in Latin American Financial Markets in the Presence of Volatile Capital Flows." IDB Working Paper No. 304 (April). Washington, D.C.

Sundararajan, V., and Tomas J. T. Balino, eds. 1991. *Banking Crises: Cases and Issues.* Washington, D.C.: IMF.

Superintendencia de Bancos e Instituciones Financieras (Chile). *Información Financiera* (various issues). Santiago, Chile.

Commentary to Part I

Ruth de Krivoy

The paper by Rojas-Suárez and Weisbrod brings together macroeconomic and microeconomic issues and discusses their interaction in banking crises. The authors demonstrate that Latin American banking crises are different from those in industrial countries: in Latin America the effects of banking crises last longer, banks are hurt more severely, the costs are significantly higher, crisis management is more burdensome for regulators and supervisors, and, finally, the consequences for local economies are graver than in similar episodes in the industrial world.

The authors analyze the causes of these dismal results, focusing on the key structural features of Latin American financial systems that make them so fragile: small financial sectors, a predominance of short-term deposits and deposit-like liabilities, extreme volatility in deposit-GDP ratios, and the rapid spillover of shocks to the banking system into capital flight. These features reflect certain underlying realities in the region. Investors lack confidence that long-term market rates of return will reward their risk. There is a lack of confidence in accounting standards—which causes depositors to lack trust in the banks and the banks to lack trust in prospective borrowers. Policy announcements lack credibility. Appropriate alternative vehicles to bank deposits for long-term saving are unavailable. And supervisors are prone to delaying remedial actions when problems develop: as the authors point out, the markets usually recognize weak banks long before supervisors intervene.

A number of interrelated facts support these conclusions. Investors have little confidence in long-term rates of return because a tradition of interest rate controls has led to persistently negative real rates. Traditionally, negative real rates have been used throughout Latin America as a means to foster private investment and to lower the cost of debt service to the domestic public sector.

The authors point to the weakness of bank accounting standards, as measured by two indicators. First, accounting measures do not accurately gauge the risk of loan portfolios, as evidenced by the fact that the share of nonperforming loans in the loan portfolios of Latin American banks is too low to explain the high cost of bank failure. The failure to enforce strict rules regarding loan portfolios is the consequence of lax rules and weak supervision. Authorities have not effectively addressed the issues of so-called evergreen loans (loans that never mature but are perpetually rolled over), careless practices with respect to collateral, or insider lending.

The second piece of evidence pointing to lax accounting standards is bank income statements. Latin American banks are allowed to report positive net income in times of crisis, whereas banks in industrial countries must report negative net income under similar circumstances. Artificially high reported incomes have led to weak banks and to the myth of seemingly endless profits. In effect, this politically validates the controls on interest rates and spreads, and compulsory loan portfolio allocations at subsidized rates—all part of a system of indirect subsidies channeled through the banking system. These subsidies further harm the banks by allowing governments to frequently build up arrears and sometimes not pay at all. Such policies weaken banking systems and impair their trustworthiness.

Bank ownership in Latin America is concentrated; incentives for safe, sound banking have not been in place; and banking supervision has been weak. Real interest rates have been persistently negative, leading to credit rationing to nonaffiliated borrowers and imprudent lending to affiliates. The redistributive effects of these practices have had economic, social, and political consequences.

Improper crisis management is another major source of problems. The authors mention the consequences of earlier bank crisis management in Latin America, when governments responded by imposing credit allocation schemes to finance government and government-sponsored programs, instead of adopting policies to strengthen the banking system. Under such circumstances, lack of confidence becomes a core problem. Banks don't trust borrowers; depositors don't trust banks. Investors have little confidence in long-term returns. Policy announcements lack credibility. Finally, banking supervisors have limited capacity to enforce rules and therefore are not respected. This situation can be attributed to the cultural and political milieu, which has created both controls and corruption.

What is needed to solve these problems and foster sound and safe banking throughout Latin America? The critical element is the political will to address the sources of fragility. The main task is to build credibility and establish the accountability of all players. Banks should be accountable to supervisors and to the markets. Supervisors should be accountable to the markets and the judicial system. Policymakers should be accountable to the markets and ultimately to the citizenry. To this end, strong and independent banking supervisors are crucial. Appropriate regulation to encourage sound and safe banking must be implemented promptly and synchronized with deregulation. Investment vehicles should be developed that allow for long-term financial savings in nondeposit instruments. Good economic policies and a commitment to monetary stability must lay the groundwork for a stable, sustainable banking industry. The role of early warning systems should be enhanced, and authorities should take a proactive stance and be prepared to take prompt remedial action when it is needed. We cannot change the past, but we can influence the future by supporting better policies that will help reduce the burden of banking crises on future generations.

Ruth de Krivoy is President of Síntesis Financiera in Caracas, Venezuela.

Part II

The Roots of Banking Crises: The Macroeconomic Context

Michael Gavin and Ricardo Hausmann

Commentary

Guillermo A. Calvo
Morris Goldstein
Roberto Zahler
Sebastian Edwards

The Roots of Banking Crises:
The Macroeconomic Context

Michael Gavin and Ricardo Hausmann

Most discussions of banking crises begin, not unreasonably, with an examination of the special characteristics of financial institutions that have failed. Often we find that the bankrupt institutions were poorly managed and, in some instances, even vehicles for outright fraud. With the benefit of hindsight, it is typically possible to point to specific failures of the regulatory system that permitted the mistakes or malfeasance that were the proximate cause of the failures. From inquests of this sort, valuable lessons can be drawn about the design of regulatory mechanisms for the prevention, or early detection, of dangerous or malfeasant behavior by managers of individual banks.

This is a sensible and necessary line of investigation. There can be no doubt that many bank failures are due in large part to bad decisions by bankers that are possible to understand after the fact—that may even be predictable and thus preventable by competent bank supervision and regulation. And in cases of isolated failures, such as those of Barings and BCCI, this may even be the whole story.

However, when trying to understand a major crisis in which a substantial fraction of the banking system is endangered, this focus on the characteristics of institutions that happened to fail is incomplete and potentially misleading. The question arises whether observed shortcomings of the failed banks actually explain the crisis, or merely which banks failed as a result of the crisis. A metaphor may be useful here. Chains break at their weakest link, but that does not mean that the specific flaws in the weakest link fully explain why the chain broke: one needs also to understand what caused the tension on the chain. Indeed, strengthening weak links in the chain only works if one succeeds in identifying the weakest link before it snaps, and even then another link may break if the tension on the chain is sufficiently high.

In our metaphor, the individual links in the chain represent the specific institutions that comprise the domestic financial system. Their strength is determined by their investment and funding decisions, which can be influenced by supervisory and regulatory structures. Tension is placed on the chain by economy-wide factors including, in particular, macroeconomic developments. When macroeconomic forces place great strain on the banking system, the weakest banks are most likely to fail, but it is macroeconomic tension, as much as the weakness of individual banks, that causes the failures.

As with a chain, the quality of the institutional and regulatory regime and macroeconomic factors clearly interact: to the extent that regulation and supervision strengthen each bank in the system, they permit the system to withstand larger macroeconomic stresses without falling into crisis. But institutional arrangements and supervisory systems that *eliminate* the risk of bank failure and financial crisis do not exist in any region, certainly not in Latin America, and would probably be counterproductive if they did. No matter how well regulated and supervised, banking systems are likely to remain vulnerable to macroeconomic shocks. So the question arises, how should policy respond to this vulnerability?

This paper discusses the ways in which macroeconomic developments can put stress on banks, and in extreme cases lead to banking crises.[1] Macroeconomic developments can contribute to financial crisis in many ways, and we do not argue for the special importance of any specific mechanism. Adverse macroeconomic shocks may make it difficult for bank borrowers to pay their debts in full and on time, thus threatening the solvency of banks. Adverse shocks to domestic money demand or international capital flows may undermine domestic banks' ability to fund their lending commitments, leading to crisis through another channel. A sudden increase in demand for bank deposits or a surge of foreign capital may trigger a bank lending boom, at the end of which banks may

---

[1] While macroeconomic developments can lead to financial vulnerability, it is equally true that imperfections in financial intermediation can contribute to macroeconomic instability. This important point is not discussed in this paper, but deserves more attention. See Goldfajn and Valdéz (1995) for a theoretical treatment of one linkage, and Calvo and Mendoza (1995) for discussion in the context of the recent Mexico crisis.

find themselves holding a large number of doubtful loans, making the system highly vulnerable to even a small shock.

These macroeconomic causes of bank vulnerability and crisis have important implications for regulatory regimes, and for macroeconomic policy itself. The major implications that we discuss are as follows:

- The recognition that macroeconomic shocks are an important source of bank crisis raises questions about the appropriate framework for bank regulation and supervision in Latin America. Is a regulatory environment that is adequate for banks in the relatively stable industrial countries, sufficient for a region as volatile as Latin America? Are the Bank for International Settlements (BIS) standards for bank capitalization conservative enough for Latin America? Are industrial country practices regarding bank reserve or liquidity requirements appropriate for Latin America?

- Volatile fiscal policy is an important source of shock to the financial system. Fiscal shocks can create destabilizing increases in domestic interest rates, and through their effects on expectations of inflation, can create equally destabilizing fluctuations in domestic deposit demand. The structure of domestic public debt has also proven highly destabilizing in some countries. This raises the question of how fiscal and public debt policy can be structured to avoid creating large strains on the domestic banking system.

- While macroeconomic policy cannot do much to prevent shocks to the terms of trade or world interest rates, the impact of a shock on the banking system will depend on the macroeconomic policy regime, particularly the monetary and exchange rate regime, in place when the shock arrives. We highlight the role of monetary and exchange rate policy, and argue that when banking systems are fragile, some degree of exchange rate flexibility will reduce the likelihood that an adverse shock will be transformed into a highly disruptive banking crisis. Financial fragility is, then, an important factor in the choice of exchange rate regime.

- Bank lending booms often end in failure. We suggest some reasons why rapid loan growth can generate financial system vulnerability, and argue that regulatory oversight may not be suited to coping with the problem of lending booms, even if well designed and effectively implemented. Monetary policy instruments—and specifically management of bank reserve or liquidity requirements—may be better suited to the task.

- A serious credit crunch, such as may be created by a rapid decline in demand for bank deposits or other sources of funding, can be equally disruptive. While commercial banks will hold liquidity to avoid the private costs of illiquidity, they may not have incentives to remain sufficiently liquid. This provides a policy interest in establishing standards for bank liquidity, and in managing required liquidity levels as needed to offset the disruptive economic impact of aggregate liquidity shocks.

Much of the discussion in this paper will emphasize the need for monetary policy to be set with an eye on the state of the domestic banking system—not always, and not as the main preoccupation, but as an occasionally very important consideration. In this, the discussion has the ring of unconventionality—"textbook" discussions of monetary policy seldom focus on the health of the domestic banking industry as either an objective of or a constraint on policy. But in fact monetary policy is already influenced by these considerations. It is widely believed, for example, that in the United States during the late 1980s, monetary policy was made less contractionary, and the speed of disinflation was thereby reduced, in part because of concerns that high interest rates were threatening the health of the domestic banking industry—already vulnerable because of losses on international lending that went bad in the debt crisis of the 1980s. Similarly, the failure by Mexican authorities to raise interest rates by enough to compensate for the external and political shocks of 1994 is partly attributed to their concerns about the impact of higher rates on fragile domestic banks. One aim of this paper is therefore to promote a discussion of how weak banking systems can be better incorporated into macroeconomic policy management.

The paper is organized as follows. We describe some relevant characteristics of banks and the banking industry, giving reasons why the banking industry is so vulnerable to crisis, and why it must be regulated. While much of this material is well understood, our review of the underlying market failures that beset the industry highlights the importance of prudential regulation, as well as certain limitations that are relevant for the role of macroeconomic policy toward the banking sector. The next section provides a general overview of alternative explanations for how banking crises arise, focusing on the role of shocks and vulnerability. We consider the role of macroeconomic shocks in the creation of crises, and some ways in which the macroeconomic policy response to such shocks can either reduce or increase the likelihood that the shocks will lead to banking crisis. We then take up the macroeconomic sources of banking system vulnerability, focusing on the role of bank lending booms, and conclude with a discussion of some policy implications.

Relevant Characteristics of Banks

What is special about banks? Why is the banking industry so prone to crisis, and why is there a special policy interest in preventing and dealing with such crises?

Banks Are Leveraged

The incentive problems that make banks special stem ultimately from the fact that they are leveraged; when managing their investments they are putting other people's money at risk. In addition, the nature of banks' liabilities renders ineffective the normal mechanisms for controlling the implied incentive problems.

Bank leverage has two important implications. First, capital is the cushion between adverse shocks and bankruptcy, and because that cushion is relatively thin for banks, relatively small shocks can drive a bank to insolvency. Capital is, then, a crucial buffer stock for banks; as with other buffer stocks, the amount of capital that should be held depends on the volatility of the environment in which the bank is embedded. Thus, in volatile regions such as Latin America, the problems generated by leverage may be larger than would be the case in more stable regions.

Second, leverage, combined with limited shareholder liability, generates incentives for bank managers—acting rationally on behalf of shareholders—to hold an excessively risky portfolio. This arises from the fact that shareholders receive the entire benefit of good outcomes, while debtors pay the price of outcomes sufficiently bad to drive the bank to insolvency.

Banks are not unique in being leveraged, of course. Nonfinancial firms are leveraged as well, and are therefore subject to similar conflicts of interest between shareholders and debt holders. Creditors generally address the problem by: (i) demanding higher interest rates when lending to firms that engage in riskier activities, (ii) attempting to control subsequent risktaking by negotiating and enforcing loan covenants and other contractual restrictions, and (iii) standing ready to assert control over the firm's assets in the event of bankruptcy.

While not unique to banks, these problems created by leverage are more serious for them. First, banks are much more leveraged than the typical nonfinancial firm. The value of a bank's equity typically totals about a tenth the value of its debt, making banks an order of magnitude more leveraged than the typical nonfinancial enterprise.[2] Second, for reasons that will be discussed below, bank depositors are in a poor position to perform the functions of corporate governance that are typically performed by creditors of a nonfinancial corporation.

Banks Are Illiquid

In most economies, banks perform an explicit transformation of maturities, taking relatively short-term deposit liabilities and holding longer-term loan assets. In Latin America, bank lending tends to be relatively short term, but the banking system is nonetheless illiquid. First, while Latin American bank lending tends to be short-term, loans are nevertheless longer-term than are deposits. More importantly, even though loans are written as short-term contracts, they are in fact longer-term commitments because enterprises count on the loans being rolled over, and use the resources to finance activities that cannot abruptly be terminated, except at high cost. If loans are not rolled over, firms will be forced into actions that undermine their own profitability, and perhaps that of their business partners, resulting in a decline in the quality of banks' loans. Thus, whatever the stated maturity of its loan portfolio, the banking system is illiquid in the sense that an attempt to rapidly liquidate its portfolio would sharply reduce the value of its assets.

This illiquidity has important ramifications, especially in volatile regions such as Latin America, where, as discussed in more detail below, macroeconomic shocks to banks' funding sources are very large. To prevent such shocks from disrupting the flow of credit upon which the real economy depends, banks hold buffer stocks of liquid reserves which allow them to partially insulate lending from shocks to deposits and other funding sources. Below we will ask whether banks face incentives to be sufficiently liquid, or if instead there is a justification for enforcing minimum liquidity requirements at levels higher than banks would choose if unconstrained.

---

[2] In the United States in the mid 1980s, commercial bank debt was about 11 times its equity, compared with a ratio of 1.20 in the manufacturing sector (Dewatripont and Tirole, 1994, p. 23).

Banks Manage Information Problems

A third and crucial feature of banks is their role in resolving the information problems that beset financial markets everywhere. This is what financial intermediation is all about.[3] Over time, banks learn about their borrowers through a variety of mechanisms, including periodic liquidity tests of borrowers' ability to service short-term credits. In Latin America, where the institutional structure provides for few other signals of firm solvency, liquidity may be a particularly important signal of solvency, although other information would undoubtedly become available to banks in the course of a long-term relationship with their borrowers.[4]

On this, two points are particularly relevant for the discussion that follows. First, *it is the business of banks to generate private information about their borrowers,* a situation that puts both depositors and supervisors at an informational disadvantage vis-à-vis the banks. This is one important reason that depositors would have a hard time monitoring bank managers in the way that creditors of nonfinancial enterprises must do. A similar constraint applies to bank supervisors; the information possessed by supervisors about a bank's asset quality is a subset, and perhaps a small one, of the information available to bank managers.

Second, to the extent that borrower liquidity is an important signal of solvency, *the quality of the signal received by an individual bank depends very much on conditions in the loan market as a whole.* When credit is freely available, a firm can repay a loan to one bank with funds received from another, so liquidity may be a poor signal of loan quality during credit booms: good times are bad times for learning about the creditworthiness of borrowers. Lending booms tend also to be periods of buoyant economic activity and transitory high profitability, so that even shaky enterprises will be liquid and appear solvent, whether or not they have access to other sources of credit. In short, during lending booms banks may have trouble determining which of their loans are going bad. And if bank managers have a hard time determining which loans are experiencing difficulties, it should be clear that supervisors will be at least as much in the dark, and probably more so.

---

[3] Diamond (1984) presents the classic theoretical treatment of banks as financial intermediaries that specialize in the processing of information.

[4] Liquidity as a signal of borrower solvency is emphasized in the Latin American context by Rojas-Suárez and Weisbrod (1994).

Bank Solvency and Liquidity Interact

As discussed above, the essential illiquidity of banks means that a sudden need to contract lending of the banking system as a whole is likely to reduce the quality of bank assets, and if abrupt and extreme enough, to force borrowers into default. Banks may then be forced to take over and sell the assets of bankrupt enterprises at firesale prices, leading to a downward spiral in asset prices and a possible further deterioration in bank balance sheets. Thus, bank liquidity problems can immediately be translated into solvency problems: if there is a policy interest in ensuring that banks are solvent, there is also an interest in ensuring that they are liquid. At the same time, real or imaginary bank solvency problems are likely to create a flight by depositors, generating a liquidity shock that will, in turn, reduce the quality of the bank portfolios, possibly by enough to validate the initially exaggerated fears that motivated the bank run. This means that bank runs can occur as self-fulfilling prophecies of bank failure, driving even well-run banks into insolvency. The exit option for bank depositors is, therefore, a poor mechanism for exercising control over bank managers.

Banks Manage the Payments Mechanism

A fourth central feature of banks is that a fundamental class of their liabilities provides the vehicle through which the payments system operates. The payments system may furnish essential externalities for the economy as a whole, providing a policy interest in ensuring that it operates without disruption. The inability of one bank to honor its commitments may undermine the ability of other, generally healthy banks to honor theirs. This potential cascading of interruptions in the payments mechanism reduces the usefulness of all deposits as a means of payment.

Efficient functioning of the payments system also has major implications for the structure of bank liabilities. In particular, deposit claims on banks must be highly liquid. A substantial fraction of banks' liabilities will be owned by a huge number of very small creditors, who are ill-equipped to obtain reliable information about the quality of a bank's management or to coordinate a response to bad behavior. The only response available to such depositors is flight to another apparently safer bank or to cash. For reasons discussed above, such bank runs are a highly unreliable and inefficient way to discipline bank managers.

Bank Depositors Are Protected

As noted above, the fact that banks are in the business of generating private information about the quality of their assets means that monitoring their behavior is particularly difficult. Even if this were not the case, depositors are unprepared to perform the tasks required to control the incentive problems that face bank managers; and if depositors are exposed to the consequences of bank mismanagement, the banking system will be vulnerable to runs. To reduce the likelihood of such runs, and perhaps to advance a more fundamental political interest in protecting the interests of small depositors, implicit or explicit government-provided deposit insurance is a common feature of banking systems.[5] This insurance completely short-circuits the corporate governance of banks, for it eliminates any incentive for bank depositors to monitor managers of the banks in which they have left their money, opening the field for abusive behavior by banks at the ultimate expense of taxpayers.

Banks Are Regulated

For this reason, banks must be regulated. If the riskiness of banks' assets could be measured precisely, the most direct way to address the incentive problems that face banks would be to charge bank-specific deposit insurance premia that are precisely calibrated to the riskiness of a bank's investments. However, because information about portfolio quality is largely private to the bank, this is impractical, and indirect measures are required. In particular:

* Regulators should establish and enforce ground rules for bank portfolio choice, including rules about the permissible degree of loan concentration along various dimensions, restrictions on the types of instruments that banks may hold as investments, restrictions on international activities, and the like.
* Regulators should establish minimum standards for bank capitalization and liquidity, monitor banks, and enforce compliance with the standards.

---

[5] Diamond and Dybvig (1983) model deposit insurance as a response to the problem of bank runs. Dewatripont and Tirole (1994) start from the presumption that protection of small depositors is itself an objective of policy toward the banking system.

- Regulators should play the role of debtors in a private bankruptcy, and assert control over the assets of the bank in the event of bankruptcy.
- By limiting leverage and ensuring that shareholders have something to lose when risky loans go bad, minimum capital standards limit the magnitude of the incentive problem that faces bank managers. These standards are thus the first and arguably most important line of supervisory defense in the attempt to discourage excessively risky behavior by bankers.

Limits of Bank Regulation

From this brief discussion it is clear that bank supervision and regulation confront a problem that would be difficult to resolve even outside the political and economic hothouse in which decisions must actually be made. These difficulties place significant limits on bank supervision and regulation. We highlight a few of them now:

Prudential regulation is costly. Bank regulators deal with bankers' moral hazard problems by attempting to ensure that banks are more heavily capitalized and liquid than they would choose to be in an unregulated environment. Regulators could, in principle, eliminate risk in the banking system by forcing banks to greatly reduce their leverage and increase their holdings of safe liquid assets. But in so doing they would at the same time reduce the efficiency with which domestic savings are channeled into the productive, and inherently risky, investments required for economic growth. A balance needs to be struck between the need to contain bad incentives created by bank leverage and information problems, and the advantages of financial intermediation.

Supervision must be transparent. In an economic and political system based on individual property rights, bank supervisory determinations must be made in a transparent fashion that respects private ownership and business judgment, and that restricts the potential for arbitrary or discriminatory treatment of individual banks. This means that supervision must be based on observables, with limited scope for discretionary decisions based on undocumentable "gut feelings" or "instincts." This introduces a regulatory lag, since observable indicators of problems typically arrive well after the problems have started to emerge.

Table 2.1 Loan Delinquencies As Lagging Indicators of Banking Crisis

(Doubtful or defaulted loans as a percent of total)

	1975	1976	1977	1978	1979	1980	1981	1982	1983
Chile[1]	2.8	1.7	1.4	1.2	1.1	0.9	2.4	8.2	18.7
Colombia[2]	4.0	4.0	3.0	2.8	3.3	3.3	3.7	8.4	-

[1] Velasco (1988).
[2] Montenegro (1983).

This lag is illustrated in Table 2.1, which provides indicators of doubtful or defaulted loans in years leading up to the Chilean and Colombian banking crises (both of which began around 1982). In both countries these key indicators of portfolio quality were stable or even improving in the years leading up to the crisis, and only revealed problems in 1982, when the crisis materialized. In matters of bank regulation, it's not "what you see is what you get," it's what you *don't* see that gets you.

Due to the need for transparency, the burden of proof facing regulators must be higher than that facing private bank creditors. It is acceptable for large depositors to flee or demand a higher risk premium from banks on the basis of market rumors or gut feelings. But permitting regulators to act on the basis of essentially subjective indicators provides too much scope for abuse. Even if permitted to act on such a basis, regulators are likely to be reluctant to do so. Regulatory interventions may frighten the market and thus create a problem where one did not exist—like shouting "fire" in a crowded theater. To avoid criticism for having themselves created a crisis, regulators are likely to wait for concrete evidence of problems before taking observable action.[6]

Supervision is limited by regulators' information. It is the job of banks to generate private information about the value of their portfolio. In many circumstances, they will have an incentive to hide portfolio problems from supervisors, and in the all-important short run this can be done in a number of ways, including rolling over problem loans, gains trading, and

---

[6] Indeed, they may have incentives to delay action even after troubles are apparent. Kane (1989) discusses the incentive problems facing bank regulators.

so on. This places important limits on the ability of regulators to detect and prevent problems, particularly, as we shall argue below, during credit booms when problems are most likely to develop.

The need for transparency and the information disadvantage create serious problems for bank regulators, particularly during credit booms, as we discuss below. If bankers have a poor idea of asset-quality problems, the problem will be worse for regulators. Even when bankers know about problems, they will be able to disguise them, at least temporarily, from regulators. And there will probably be cases in which regulators suspect the existence of problems but are constrained from acting because the problems cannot be adequately documented.

Explaining Bank Crises: Shocks and Vulnerability

How do banks fail? There are many ways to die, but all involve certain physiological mechanisms, such as the cessation of heartbeat. Similarly, the mechanics of bank failure have a common outcome—the inability of banks to deliver funds that depositors demand. If the rate of growth of bank deposits is higher than the deposit interest rate, this will pose no problem: in this case, depositors are actually transferring financial resources to the banking system, and banks are able to remain liquid even if they roll over all their loans and make even more.[7]

However, when the rate of growth of bank deposits is lower than the deposit interest rate, banks must make a net transfer of funds to depositors. In order to do so, they must either extract a transfer of resources from their borrowers, or run down their stock of liquidity. Problems occur when the required transfer to depositors is so high—either because domestic interest rates are high or because deposit growth is low or negative—that banks cannot extract the required resources from their borrowers or their stock of liquidity.

In principle, banks can obtain the required transfer simply by calling in loans as they mature. In reality, banks are limited in their ability to do so because, whatever the nominal maturity of bank loans, nonfinancial firms would find a sudden curtailment of access to credit highly disruptive. If the credit crunch is not too large or long lasting, firms can make the required transfer by cutting back on investments that can be postponed, running down inventories, and so on. But if it is large or long

---

[7] This is akin to a Ponzi scheme, and can be only a temporary condition.

**Figure 2.1 Venezuela: Net Resource Transfer from Banks
to the Private Sector**
(Percent of GDP)

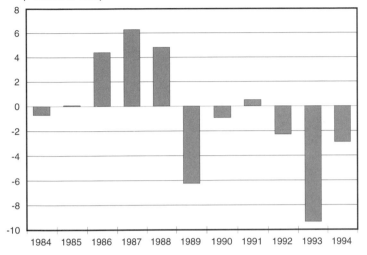

Note: 1994 data are for the first three quarters of the year. No attempt has been
made to estimate seasonal effects.
Source: Authors' calculations, based on IMF, *International Financial Statistics.*

lasting, a contraction of credit may imply a transfer that is simply unpayable, or that forces firms into default.

The destabilizing effect of large net resource transfers to depositors is evident in the recent Venezuelan crisis. In 1993, domestic interest rates rose to about 60 percent, while deposits grew only 17 percent, requiring a net resource transfer from banks to depositors of more than 9 percent of GDP. As Figure 2.1 indicates, this was very large by historical standards, large enough to drive the banking system into crisis.

Following this logic, we can identify two components of a banking crisis. The first is the magnitude of the net resource transfers required, which constitutes a shock, because under normal conditions net resource transfers should not pose important difficulties for banks. The second component is the threshold of resource transfers above which the system will crumble—this defines the vulnerability of the banking system. Banking crises are due to both shocks and vulnerability. We will deal with macroeconomic dimensions of these two components of bank crises in the following sections.

Figure 2.2 Terms of Trade and Banking Crises in Five Latin American Countries

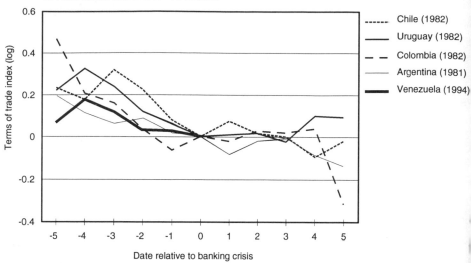

Figure 2.3 Real GDP and Banking Crises: Latin America

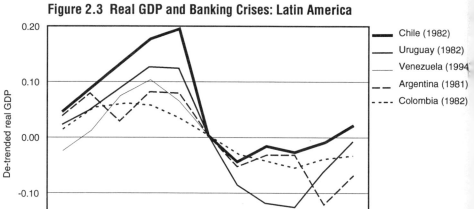

Macroeconomic Shocks and Bank Crisis

In virtually every major banking crisis, a macroeconomic shock of some sort was at least part of the story. Such shocks can take various forms and affect bank solvency in several ways. A major recession, a decline in the terms of trade, or some other adverse shock to national wealth reduces the profitability of bank borrowers; some are unable to service their bank debt, and what had been good loans turn out to be bad. Funding shocks may demand a sudden contraction of bank balance sheets, with adverse implications for the health of borrowers, and therefore of banks.

Macroeconomic Shocks to Asset Quality

There are many examples of adverse shocks to domestic income that, by reducing the debt servicing capacity of domestic bank borrowers, have adversely affected bank assets and contributed to bank crisis. The sharp decline in oil prices of the middle 1980s had a severe impact on banking systems in both Texas and Venezuela, as well as other oil-exporting regions. (That there was a crisis in Texas and not in Venezuela has much to do with the different monetary policy and exchange rate responses to the crisis, as will be discussed below.) As Figure 2.2 illustrates, adverse terms of trade shocks have been important factors in most Latin American crises, including those in Argentina, Chile, Colombia, and Uruguay.[8]

Substantial declines in the terms of trade also preceded banking crises in several industrial economies, including Norway, Finland (also adversely affected by the collapse of trade with the Soviet Union), and Spain—although not in Japan or Sweden.

In fact most banking crises are preceded by a generalized deterioration of the macroeconomic environment. This is illustrated in figures 2.3 and 2.4, which show the cyclical pattern typical of countries that have experienced banking crises. In general, a strong macroeconomic boom gives way to recession a year or two before the crisis, after which the recession deepens for several years.

This happens because systemic vulnerabilities develop during lending and macroeconomic booms that typically precede crises. These vulnerabilities lead to crisis after an adverse macroeconomic shock, which is usually associated with recession.

---

[8] Morris et al. (1990) and IMF (1993) also highlight the importance of terms of trade shocks for several of the banking crises that they analyze.

Figure 2.4 Real GDP and Banking Crises: Industrial Economies

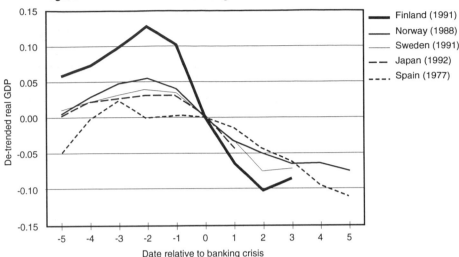

Adverse macroeconomic shocks may also directly affect bank balance sheets through induced effects on asset prices. A clear example of banks' exposure to asset prices is real estate: while banks typically do not speculate directly in the land or real estate markets, they do make loans to construction companies, whose ability to repay is threatened if the real estate market takes a dive. And bad real estate loans, associated with poor real estate markets, have in fact been an important feature in many bank crises.[9] If banks do hold marketable assets in their portfolio, they will be exposed to fluctuations in market prices.

This was a significant factor in the failures of several Argentine *bancos mayoristas* in early 1995. Those banks owned large quantities of Brady bonds, and the capital losses that those bonds suffered during the sell-off that followed the Mexican devaluation were fatal for the banks. Similarly, Japanese bank portfolios have been adversely affected by the collapse of land and equity prices in the 1990s. As banks become more involved in taking market positions through proprietary trading operations and the use of derivatives, their exposure to asset-price risk is likely to increase.

But more often, the effect on banks of asset-price shocks is indirect. For example, during the years leading up to the Chilean banking

---

[9] See IMF (1993).

crisis, banks were permitted to borrow in foreign currency but prohibited from taking the exchange risk, so that lending funded by international borrowing was required to be denominated in foreign currency.[10] This was supposed to transfer the currency risk from banks to the nonfinancial firms to which banks made loans, but after the unexpected devaluation many firms found themselves unable to repay their loans in full and on time. Thus, the exchange rate risk that faced nonfinancial firms was to a substantial extent borne by the banking system in the form of credit risk.

It is intuitively obvious that a decline in national income or wealth will lead to a reduction in the quality of bank portfolios. Less obvious is the fact that a large macroeconomic disturbance can harm banks' portfolios even when the country as a whole benefits from the shock, if the disturbance has large distributional effects. The reason is that bank loans extended to sectors adversely affected by the disturbance are likely to fall into arrears, while the increased income that accrues to sectors receiving a windfall from the shock is not captured by the banks, which mainly own debt rather than equity claims on firms. For example, the major macroeconomic reforms initiated in Venezuela in early 1989 included import liberalization and substantial realignments of relative prices, which led to insolvencies in some productive sectors, with adverse effects on the quality of commercial bank balance sheets.

In short, macroeconomic disturbances of almost any sort can adversely affect bank balance sheets, and if large enough, can threaten the solvency of large parts of the banking system. In addition to recession, other factors have seriously undermined the ability of bank debtors to service their debts. In the Chilean crisis of 1982-83, firms were undermined by a long period of exchange rate overvaluation and high interest rates, which had resulted from Chile's disinflation strategy. In Argentina, too, the 1980 financial panic was preceded by a period of highly unstable macroeconomic and financial policy, during which an increasingly overvalued peso put pressure on producers of tradeables, triggering a period of distress borrowing that put upward pressure on interest rates and downward pressure on the quality of banks' assets.[11] In Uruguay and Colombia, too, the crises of the early 1980s were precipitated by a prolonged period of currency overvaluation and a generalized economic downturn in the aftermath of adverse external shocks.

---

[10] Velasco (1988).
[11] Morris et al. (1990).

At the time of a macroeconomic shock, the policy regime in place will affect the probability that the shock is transformed into a banking crisis. A major example is the role of alternative exchange rate regimes. Consider an adverse external shock that reduces the capacity of domestic borrowers to service their debts to the banking system. If the shock is large and the banking system fragile, banks cannot write the debts down to realistic levels without themselves becoming insolvent, because they are unable at the same time to reduce the real value of their liabilities. But if nothing is done, depositors may begin to flee from the now precariously situated banks, thereby destabilizing both the banking system and the exchange rate regime.

Some kind of restructuring of bank assets and liabilities is clearly required; if the real value of assets has fallen, either bank creditors (in practice, depositors) must take a hit or taxpayers must pay for a recapitalization of the banking system. Under fixed exchange rates, depositors are protected: with the price level determined largely by the domestic exchange rate, the external shock will have no direct effect on the real value of bank liabilities, which will exceed bank assets until an explicit restructuring is arranged. Under flexible exchange rates, however, the adverse external shock will probably lead to a depreciation of the exchange rate, automatically writing down the real value of banking system assets to levels that can realistically be expected to be paid, and at the same time writing down the real value of bank liabilities so that banks are not thereby broken.[12]

Of course, depositors will demand higher deposit interest rates as compensation for the exchange rate risk, but this is arguably as it should be: better to put the aggregate risk on bank deposits, where it can be priced and allocated, than to off-load it to taxpayers, where it cannot be. The main point is that in a fragile financial system, external shocks are more likely to create a banking crisis under fixed than under floating exchange rates.

A case in point is how the mid 1980s collapse in oil prices affected the banking systems of Venezuela and Texas. In Texas, the collapse led to a crisis in the banking and the savings and loan industries, while in Venezuela a crisis did not result. Whatever weaknesses existed in the supervision of depository institutions in Texas, it seems unlikely that the absence of crisis in Venezuela was due to a supervisory framework supe-

---

[12] We implicitly assume here that the banking system is not dollarized. To the extent that it is dollarized, exchange rate depreciation will not affect the real value of bank assets or liabilities.

rior to that of Texas. Instead, a key reason for the absence of crisis in Venezuela was a maxi-devaluation following the oil shock. This devaluation effectively wrote down the real value of bank assets to levels that could—in the new, less prosperous circumstances—actually be paid, while simultaneously writing down the real value of deposits and other bank liabilities in the manner required to maintain bank solvency.

Macroeconomic Shocks to Bank Funding

Macroeconomic shocks can also affect the demand for deposits and other bank liabilities, and therefore the ability of banks to fund their lending portfolio. The two major funding sources for banks in Latin America are deposits and, in some countries and time periods, foreign borrowing. Both the demand for deposits and the availability of international capital are notoriously volatile in Latin America.[13] Deposit demand may contract because of an increase in expected depreciation, perhaps associated with an unsustainable balance of payments or real exchange rate. This was an important factor in the Swedish crisis of 1991, which was preceded in 1990 by a decline in deposits of roughly 5 percent of GDP. Expectations of inflation and devaluation may also be driven by worrisome fiscal developments, leading, again, to a decline in deposit demand and a rise in interest rates, as in Venezuela in 1993. A sudden fiscal expansion may also crowd out private sector borrowers, leading to a private sector credit crunch even if total bank credit does not decline.

Whatever the cause, a sharp decline in deposit demand or in the ability of domestic banks to borrow abroad will severely reduce the domestic banking system's liquidity. To restore their liquidity, banks will be forced to sell assets if possible, or more likely to reduce the size of their loan portfolio by failing to renew credits as they come due. But, as discussed above, such a sudden withdrawal of credit is likely to be extremely destabilizing for the nonfinancial private sector, and may lead to a severe business contraction, with highly adverse effects on the quality of bank loan portfolios.

Recent developments in Argentina provide a good example of the consequences of a severe liquidity shock. The Mexican devaluation of December 1994 led to a sharp increase in the perceived riskiness of

---

[13] Inter-American Development Bank (1995) documents the high volatility of both money demand and international capital flows to Latin America. They are roughly twice as volatile in Latin America as in the industrial economies.

Argentine assets, and in particular of the country's monetary liabilities. These fears were compounded by the failure of some small wholesale banks, which raised questions about the stability of the domestic banking system. These factors led to a sharp decline in domestic money demand; from the beginning of the Mexican crisis to the end of March 1995, Argentine bank deposits fell by nearly 8 billion pesos, a decline of nearly one-fifth.[14] At the same time Argentine commercial banks, like other Argentine borrowers, lost access to international financial markets, which were essentially paralyzed during the first half of 1995. The result was a sharp decline in commercial bank credit to the nonfinancial public, which contributed greatly to the deep recession in the country.

Macroeconomic policy played an important role in limiting the impact of the liquidity shock on the domestic banking system and the economy more generally. While severe, the contraction of credit to the nonfinancial sector was reduced substantially because Argentina's central bank was, within the limits of the convertibility law, able to provide some credit to the banking system during the crisis. More importantly, the central bank allowed the commercial banks to utilize their own reserves by relaxing the relatively high reserve requirements that existed before the crisis.[15] The relaxation of reserve requirements made roughly $3.4 billion of liquidity available to the banking system when it needed it most, greatly reducing the macroeconomic and financial impact of the liquidity shock. This highlights the importance of an active policy toward bank liquidity in responding to aggregate liquidity shocks.

The Argentine liquidity shock originated in an external shock that created concerns about the viability of domestic policy and financial institutions. Such a shock can also result from monetary policy choices. The ongoing Mexican stabilization is an illuminating example. During the first five months of 1995, Mexican bank deposits rose roughly 14 percent, representing a decline of roughly 12 percent in real terms.[16] At the same time, banks' net foreign liabilities fell by nearly a third in real terms, further contributing to a sharp reduction in their lending capacity.

---

[14] Banco Central de la República Argentina (1995). IMF data show smaller declines, although the story is otherwise consistent.

[15] Reserve requirements were 43 percent for demand deposits and 3 percent for time deposits of up to 60 days duration, resulting in an average reserve requirement of 17 percent, or $7.7 billion. (All dollar amounts are in U.S. currency.) During the course of the crisis, the reserve requirements were reduced in stages to 30 percent for demand deposits and 1 percent for time deposits.

[16] All data are from IMF, *International Financial Statistics (IFS)*. Deposits include money market instruments. We have no data on bank lending rates, which we conservatively estimate at 10 percentage points over the Treasury bill rate reported in *IFS*.

Unlike in Argentina, bank reserves could provide no buffer, because at the beginning of the crisis, reserves were only about 2.5 percent of deposits. As a result, domestic credit became very tight: bank lending to the private sector grew by only about 17 percent in nominal terms, and fell by roughly 10 percent in real terms.

While bank credit has been growing slowly, Mexican banks were forced by financial market conditions to charge high interest rates to their borrowers. The net result was a sharp swing in the net resource transfer between the banking system and the nonfinancial private sector. Having received large net transfers during the several years leading up to the crisis, the private sector had to make large transfers to the banks in its aftermath. These transfers were small in the first three months of 1996, as credit growth roughly matched domestic interest rates, but they rose dramatically in April and May, when credit growth slowed and domestic interest rates remained high. In those months, we estimate, the nonbank private sector was asked to transfer financial resources to the banks in the amount of more than NP25 billion per month, or 300 billion per year, representing some 15 to 20 percent of GDP.

Of course, transfers so large cannot long be sustained, which explains the need for the various schemes to reschedule and restructure domestic private debt that are sponsored and supported by the government. In the absence of such schemes, bank borrowers' inability to make the transfers banks need to pay their depositors would generate bank insolvencies, runs, and a breakdown of the financial system. The magnitude of the crisis to be dealt with through these programs is greatly influenced by macroeconomic strategy, in particular, by the very tight credit policies that were dictated by an apparent desire by the Mexican authorities to secure a sharp appreciation of the exchange rates. That policy was motivated, in turn, by a strong and understandable desire to control the inflationary effects of the financial crisis.

Without questioning this strategy or the policy objectives that underlie it, we merely point out some of its implications for the domestic banking system. This strategy has meant very high domestic interest rates and slow credit growth. The result has been an enormous net resource transfer from borrowers to banks, which has clearly dealt a severe blow to the real economy, and which would almost certainly have been unpayable in the absence of officially sponsored debt workout programs. What was the alternative? Had the authorities aimed at a less ambitious target for the price level, perhaps by engaging in unsterilized purchases of foreign exchange when the peso started to strengthen in April and May, bank credit would not have been so tight, interest rates would not have been so high, and the problems facing bank debtors—and therefore banks—would not have been so large.[17]

Macroeconomic Sources of Financial Vulnerability: The Role of Credit Booms

We have considered situations in which a banking system and an economy can be taken by surprise by some macroeconomic shock that undermines the viability of financial institutions and creates a crisis. But macroeconomic surprises do not completely explain banking crises. Why are some banking systems weak enough to be submerged by macroeconomic shocks, and others strong enough to survive them? As we have emphasized, crises result from the interaction of shocks and vulnerability; here we explore macroeconomic determinants of bank vulnerability.

What exactly do we mean by vulnerability? A bank is vulnerable when relatively small shocks to income, asset quality, or liquidity make the bank either insolvent or so illiquid that its ability to honor short-term financial commitments is brought into doubt. Vulnerability exists when the bank's buffer stocks of capital and liquidity are small in relation to the riskiness of its assets and its funding sources. A decision to engage in riskier lending or investment activities will thus increase vulnerability unless there is a commensurate increase in the bank's capital base. An increasing proportion of doubtful or bad loans will also increase vulnerability by reducing the capital available to cover further losses. Again, such loan losses are often temporarily invisible to both bankers and supervisors, in which case the latent vulnerability will not be apparent until an adverse shock forces bad loans to the surface—but it is nevertheless present.

Many features of the institutional and regulatory environment can contribute to the banking system's vulnerability. Here we focus on the role of macroeconomic forces, and in particular on the lending booms which, we will argue, can foster financial vulnerability by contributing to an endogenous decline in the quality of banks' assets.

Why the focus on lending booms? First, because the empirical link between such booms and financial crisis is very strong. Figure 2.5 illustrates that nearly every financial crisis in the countries in question was preceded by a period of rapid growth in banking system credit, measured

---

[17] See Gavin and Hausmann (1995) for a more detailed discussion of the tradeoffs involved.

Figure 2.5 Bank Credit to Private Sector in Eleven Countries
(Percent of GDP)

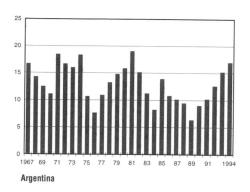

Argentina

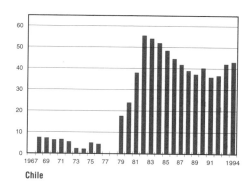

Chile

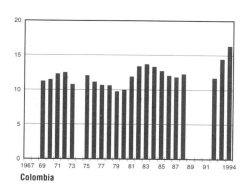

Colombia

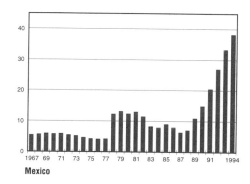

Mexico

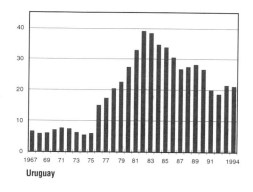

Uruguay

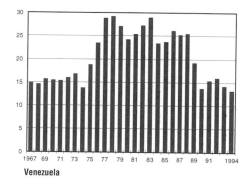

Venezuela

(Continues)

Figure 2.5 (Cont.)

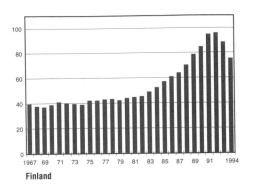

Finland

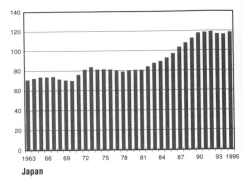

Japan

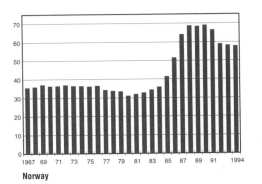

Norway

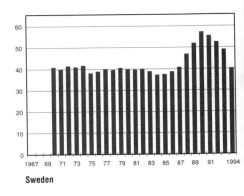

Sweden

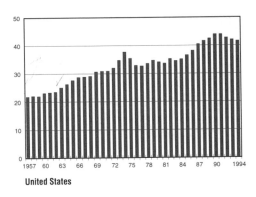

United States

as a proportion of domestic GDP. This was the case in Argentina (1981), Chile (1981-82), Colombia (1982-83), Mexico (1995), Uruguay (1982), Norway (1987), Finland (1991-92), Japan (1992[18]), and Sweden (1991).[19]

In recent discussions of banking crises,[20] various explanations have been offered for why lending booms may precede crisis. We review some of those explanations below, followed by an alternative explanation that we find more convincing. Briefly, we consider the following theories:

- *"Rope for their own hanging"— liberalization, bad banking, and crisis.* Argument: Liberalization often permits bankers to engage in businesses from which they were previously restricted. Bankers are likely to make big mistakes simply because they are unskilled.
- *Competition, bank franchise value, and attitudes toward risk.* Argument: Bank liberalization is typically associated with an increase in competitive pressures, which puts downward pressure on the expected future profitability of being in the banking business. By reducing the value of the equity that would be lost in a bankruptcy, this exacerbates the underlying incentive problems (discussed above) that encourage bank managers to take excessive risks in their lending.
- *"One bad apple spoils the bunch"— destructive competition in the market for deposits.* Argument: Perverse incentives may be created when deposit interest rates are deregulated. Competition in the market for deposits may force prudent borrowers to adopt the risky strategies of less prudent borrowers.
- *"Good times are bad times for learning"— lending booms, information, and collapse.* Argument: Lack of information, rather than lack of incentive, is the link between lending booms and financial vulnerability. When credit is abundant and the economy booming, banks have a difficult time sorting good risks from bad. Bad loans therefore tend to accumulate during lending booms, and result in crisis when the boom is interrupted by an adverse macroeconomic shock.

---

[18] It is difficult to date the onset of the Japanese crisis, but its dimensions were at least approximately apparent in the early 1990s. By 1992, it was apparent to informed observers that Japanese banks had serious problems with asset quality, although the magnitude of the problems is only now becoming clear.

[19] Our data show a lending boom in the United States in 1985-1990. While no banking crisis resulted, it was a close call. In 1990 the U.S. deposit insurance fund was nearly wiped out by a large number of bank failures, leading to speculation that a crisis was imminent (such as presidential candidate Ross Perot's prediction of a "January surprise" announcement of a crisis after the presidential elections). In fact, the banking system was rescued by several years of monetary and macroeconomic conditions highly conducive to bank profitability.

[20] For example, see IMF (1993).

Advocates of the "rope for their own hanging" theory frequently argue that bankers in recently liberalized financial systems are likely to make excessively risky loans and incur large loan losses simply because they are unpracticed in the new lines of business in which they are operating. This argument is particularly common in the cases of recently privatized banks, as in Mexico in the late 1980s, but it applies in principle to any market in which the regulatory environment has recently been relaxed in ways that permit bankers to take risks from which they were previously sheltered by legal restrictions. The lending boom, and the accompanying decline in banks' portfolio quality, are viewed as resulting from the youthful exuberance of an adolescent industry—like the teenage years, a dangerous, but one can hope, a temporary period.

We have two main problems with this argument. First, it seems to rely not only upon a lack of skills, but also on a degree of irrationality in the actions of private bankers. Recently privatized banks, which were primarily in the business of taking deposits and buying government paper, may have relatively unrefined skills in commercial risk assessment. But rational bank managers would take this lack of skill into account in their lending decisions. Understanding the need to hone skills and develop institutional expertise, unpracticed and unskilled bankers would presumably expand their balance sheet cautiously, and not engage in the sort of lending boom that generally precedes a financial crisis. Second, the regulatory and business environment that faces bankers is in almost continual change, as new technology, ideas, and policies change the opportunities and constraints facing bankers. Moreover, this theory of banking crises does not explain why other market developments and regulatory reforms did not lead to lending booms or banking crisis.

The theory of "competition, franchise value, and risktaking" emphasizes that financial system liberalization is often accompanied by an increase in competition in the banking sector.[21] In some cases, the increase in competition was a cause of the liberalization; as institutions grew in unregulated sectors at the expense of highly regulated banks, regulators responded by relaxing restrictions on banks. The competition was also a direct consequence of the reforms themselves, which in many cases eliminated a de facto cartelization of the industry, allowing other institutions to compete with banks, and banks to compete with other banks,

---

[21] A prominent exponent of this view is IMF (1993). That report argues that the "...common thread running through many banking crises ... is the recognition that the competitive pressures unleashed by financial liberalization do not merely increase efficiency: they also carry risks, as banks and other financial institutions alter their behavior to ward off institutional downsizing" (IMF, 1993, pp. 2-3).

in ways that had not previously been permitted. The increased competition lowered the franchise value of a bank; that is, the expected stream of future profits from banking. This effectively reduced the equity at stake in domestic banks—not, perhaps, by standard accounting or regulatory definitions, but in the economically meaningful sense of the value that shareholders would lose in the event that a bad roll of the dice led to bankruptcy. The increased competition in effect raised the incentive for bankers to adopt excessively risky investment strategies.

This theory has the advantage of focusing on well-understood incentive problems that face rational bank managers. It may seem logical, but we question its basis in fact. Although deregulation generates increased competition, it also provides opportunities for bankers to enter profitable new activities.[22] The impact of liberalization on bank profitability is, therefore, not obviously negative. The empirical question can be settled by looking at bank equity prices: if liberalization actually reduces the franchise value of banks, the reduction should be reflected in banks' stock market valuation. In fact, bank stocks have not been particularly depressed during many of the lending booms that preceded banking crises in Latin America and the industrial economies, whether or not they followed a major liberalization—casting doubt on the franchise value hypothesis.[23]

The "one bad apple spoils the bunch" theory focuses on a different aspect of financial liberalization, the deregulation of deposit interest rates. When deposit interest rates are freed, banks are linked to one another through the competition for deposits. Unfortunately, this may not be a competition in which the fittest survive, but rather one in which bad behavior drives out the good. Suppose there exists a "bad" bank, whose managers are more prone to make risky investments—perhaps because the bank is insufficiently capitalized, its managers are particularly risk-loving, or for some other reason. This bank will be willing to pay more for deposits than safe banks, and will bid aggressively for deposits and in

---

[22] Bankers tend to favor bank liberalization, which suggests that any adverse effects on profitability are probably not too large.

[23] IMF (1993) shows that bank stocks lagged behind broad indexes of equity prices in most of the countries that they examined. But the economically relevant question is what happened to the stock prices themselves, not relative to a broad market index. Equity markets boomed during the period of the analysis, and it appears that bank stock prices increased as well, although more slowly than did the markets as a whole. As a related aside: at the time of this writing, concern was expressed in several policy circles about aggressive and apparently risky lending behavior by industrial country commercial banks in the syndicated loan market. This has taken place in an environment of relatively high bank prices and strong bank capitalization, at least in the United States. Interestingly, some commentary attributes aggressive competition to the *high* degree of bank capitalization (outside Japan, of course). (See *The Economist*, Sept. 23, 1995.)

the interbank market (if it exists) as well. Because of deposit insurance, depositors will be happy to move their deposits from the safe to the riskier banks. This presents the "good" banks with the choice of either downsizing dramatically or matching the interest rates offered by the "bad" banks, a strategy that may not work unless the good banks adopt the aggressive and risky lending strategy adopted by the bad banks. Whether the good banks choose to downsize or emulate the bad ones, the outcome is the same: the portfolio of banks adopting risky lending practices will grow at the expense of more conservative banks, and the banking system as a whole will therefore become more fragile.

This is an interesting theory about how financial vulnerability can be generated and transmitted from one institution to others. It raises important questions about the appropriate regulatory response to, for example, aggressive bidding for deposits by individual banks. But it has little to do with the macroeconomic factors that are the subject of this paper, and in particular does not explain the aggregate lending booms that precede crises.

The preceding explanations for the observed link between lending booms and financial collapse place responsibility for both credit booms and deteriorating bank portfolios on financial liberalization. The "good times are bad times for learning" theory, however, suggests that macroeconomic developments largely unrelated to developments in the banking industry cause the lending boom. The credit boom then creates information and incentive problems for banks that lead to a deterioration of portfolio quality and an increase in financial vulnerability.

In fact, when the banking system as a whole is expanding rapidly, it is very difficult for bankers to obtain information about the creditworthiness of borrowers. There are several reasons for this. Lending booms tend to take place during periods of macroeconomic expansion, when borrowers are transitorily very profitable and therefore liquid. In addition, the speed with which loan portfolios grow during a lending boom may itself worsen the information problems that confront bankers. First, in order to expand a loan portfolio very rapidly, bankers typically need not only to increase the size of their exposure to their existing clientele, but also to find new borrowers. But, almost by definition, new customers are those about whom bankers have relatively little information, so that as the lending boom proceeds, the riskiness of the portfolio will rise and loans to uncreditworthy enterprises are likely to increase. A second reason why "good times are bad times for learning" about creditworthiness is that when credit is plentiful, borrowers can easily pass liquidity tests for solvency by obtaining credit from another lender, rendering the test much less useful than in times of scarce credit. This not only predicts that credit booms will be associated with deteriorating loan portfolios, but also suggests the presence of an information externality in the credit market: because bankers do not account for the adverse impact of the loans they grant on other bankers' information, they will be excessively willing to grant loans. That is more reason to worry that, in the absence of official intervention, credit booms will be excessively rapid.

In short, these information problems imply that the rapid expansion of bank balance sheets during a lending boom is likely, over time, to generate a deterioration of those balance sheets. However, the deterioration is unlikely to be visible to either bankers or regulators until after the lending boom slows and borrowers' ability to generate financial resources for repayment is put to the test. But while the information problems explain why lending booms may be dangerous, they do not explain why booms occur. What might generate the booms?

Here we can make a conceptual distinction between demand-driven and supply-driven lending booms. In demand-driven booms, the shock is to the demand for domestic credit. For example, an actual or perceived productivity shock can raise investment demand and expectations of future income, which may raise demand for credit to finance consumption spending. In supply-driven lending booms, the initial shock is to the supply of loanable funds at banks' disposal—due to either increased deposit demand or a surge of international capital flows to the domestic banking system.

Mexico during 1990 to 1994 appears to be a good example of a lending boom driven by the supply of loanable funds at the disposal of the domestic banking system. Due in large part to consolidation of the inflation stabilization that began in the mid 1980s, bank deposits rose from about 20 percent of GDP in 1989 to 30 percent in 1994. At the same time, government demand for bank credit was declining and the ability of banks to borrow abroad was increased. The increase in real deposit demand provided banks with resources to lend, and in fact lending to the private sector exploded, from about 10 percent of GDP in 1990 to nearly 40 percent in 1994. In retrospect, this rapid rate of growth in lending seems at least partly responsible for the loan quality problems that were becoming apparent in many Mexican banks even before the crisis began in December 1994.

Does this mean it was a bad idea to permit Mexican banks to lend to the private sector? Of course not; one of the most important reasons for securing an inflation stabilization is to reap the benefits provided by normal patterns of financial intermediation. However, if the information problems discussed in this section are taken seriously, a case can be made for policy initiatives designed to slow the rate at which bank credit rises to its new steady state. This and other policy conclusions are taken up in the next section.

Conclusions and Policy Implications

What does a macroeconomic perspective on banking crises add to the policy discussion? We offer three main points for discussion. First, the macroeconomic roots of many banking crises suggest a need for appropriate regulatory and supervisory structures for macroeconomically volatile regions such as Latin America. Second, the fragility of banking systems can greatly complicate domestic monetary and exchange rate policy. Third, the influence of lending booms in the generation of banking crises raises the question whether policymakers should intervene to prevent such booms, and if so, how. We argue that authorities should attempt to slow down lending booms; that prudential regulation focusing on the capitalization of individual banks is likely to be least effective when it is most required; and that monetary policy instruments may be better suited to the task of slowing lending booms.

Macroeconomic Volatility and the Structure of Prudential Regulation

What are the implications of Latin America's highly volatile macroeconomic environment for the structure of bank regulation and supervision in the region? With respect to mandated capital asset ratios, a bank's capital can be thought of as a buffer stock that permits it to weather shocks to asset quality without becoming insolvent. The larger and more frequent the shocks, the larger the buffer stock of capital required to keep the probability of bankruptcy to acceptable levels. Latin America is much more volatile than the industrial economies: during the past quarter century or so, the volatility of Latin American GDP and terms of trade have been twice that of the industrial economies, and the real exchange rate has been nearly three times as volatile.[24] All these factors, and oth-

---

[24] Volatility is measured here by the standard deviation of percentage changes. See Inter-American Development Bank (1995) for an extended discussion of causes, consequences, and policy responses to volatility in Latin America, pp. 53-62.

ers, impart greater volatility to the earnings and net worth of Latin American banks than is found in those of industrial economies. The question then arises: are the BIS standards for capital adequacy appropriate for the region? Or should Latin American banks be more highly capitalized than banks in industrial countries? Are there better ways than the Basle standards to reflect the specific macroeconomic risks that face Latin American banks?

Bank liquidity is the second important buffer stock held by banks. A stock of liquid assets helps the banking system withstand a sudden drop in deposit demand or international credit without an abrupt and potentially very costly contraction of lending. However, holding liquid assets is costly for banks, because they earn less interest than loans and other nonliquid investments.[25] It is costly to society as well, in the sense that the long-term investments foregone when banks hold high levels of liquidity are the investments required for growth and development. So a tradeoff must be struck between the dangers of illiquidity and the benefits of effective financial intermediation, just as bankers must strike a private balance between the costs and benefits of holding liquid assets. The question is: will bankers have an incentive to hold sufficient levels of liquid assets?

There are reasons for concern that banks will choose socially suboptimal levels of liquidity if left to their own devices. First, the presumption in many countries, that the central bank will act as lender of last resort to banks that need liquidity, weakens banks' incentives to remain sufficiently liquid. Also, the financial disruption associated with an aggregate liquidity shock may be felt not only by illiquid banks, but also by other banks and indeed the entire economy, and these external consequences will not be borne in mind when individual banks decide how much liquidity to hold. And more generally, because bank losses are borne in part by the deposit insurance fund, banks have incentives to engage in excessively risky behavior, and illiquidity is one manifestation of such behavior. Prudential regulation reduces but does not eliminate this distortion, so there may be a policy interest in requiring banks to be more liquid than they would choose to be if unconstrained.

Of course, high liquidity requirements are not much help if banks have no access to the liquidity when it is needed. The point, therefore, is

---

[25] Often liquidity requirements take the form of unremunerated reserve assets, which generate a tax on financial intermediation. Nothing demands that liquidity requirements be associated with such a tax, and our discussion will assume that officially mandated liquidity is held in safe and liquid but interest-bearing assets.

to maintain liquidity requirements high enough in normal times so that they can be lowered in the event of an aggregate liquidity shock, to prevent the adverse consequences of an excessively rapid contraction of bank credit. The recent Argentine experience illustrates the advantages of such a policy.

So far we have taken the risky environment in which Latin American banks operate pretty much as given, emphasizing some implications of the fact that this environment forces banks in the region to confront more volatility than do banks in many other regions. But the riskiness of Latin American banks and banking systems may be reduced through regulatory initiatives. In particular, internationalization of domestic banking systems may substantially reduce macroeconomic risks faced by the system. Permitting domestically owned banks to diversify internationally will render them less vulnerable to large economy-specific shocks. Similarly, since foreign banks are less concentrated in local investments, a shock to the domestic economy will have a smaller effect on their capital base, and foreign banks may also have better access to foreign liquidity. For these reasons, we expect foreign banks to provide a stabilizing influence in the domestic banking system.

Financial Fragility and Macroeconomic Policy

Just as macroeconomic considerations may influence the design of bank regulatory regimes, the fragility of domestic banking systems has important implications for the conduct of macroeconomic policy. We first discuss the implications of financial fragility for the choice of exchange rate regime, then turn to constraints on macroeconomic policy that may be imposed by fragile banking systems.

When choosing an exchange rate regime, the first question to address is the sustainability of the alternatives. While there may be disagreement about the insulating properties of alternative exchange rate regimes, there is no room for doubt about the destabilizing consequences of being forced to abandon a regime that has failed to withstand a serious shock.[26] And there is good reason to believe that fragile financial systems are a major stumbling block in the attempt to maintain a fixed exchange rate regime.

---

[26] Inter-American Development Bank (1995) documents the destabilizing consequences of frequent changes in the exchange rate regime.

To see this, consider the adjustment to an adverse external shock under fixed exchange rates, from the perspective of the financial system. Balance of payments deficits resulting from the shock will lead to a decline in the domestic money supply and an increase in domestic interest rates. The higher interest rates will make it more difficult for domestic borrowers to service their debts to the banking system, and the contraction in bank credit that goes along with the decline in money supply will put further pressure on borrowers and, therefore, banks. On top of all this, the adverse external shock may itself have caused a decline in the quality of bank assets.

The mechanisms of adjustment under flexible exchange rates differ in important ways. Under flexible rates, the external shock will lead to exchange rate depreciation and a rise in the domestic price level. As emphasized above, this will reduce the real value of bank loans to levels that can actually be paid, while at the same time reducing the real value of bank liabilities in the manner required to maintain bank solvency.

This suggests that adjustment under *flexible* exchange rates will be substantially less traumatic for fragile domestic banking systems; under fixed rates, however, adjustment to a large shock may place unbearable stresses on the banking system. If forced to choose between the banking system and the exchange rate regime, policymakers will always save the banks. To do so they must either raise conventional taxes or ease monetary conditions, thus abandoning the fixed exchange rate regime and effectively paying for the bailout with inflation taxes.

This problem can also be viewed as an issue in optimal tax policy. Under fixed exchange rates, bank depositors are largely protected against macroeconomic shocks that impinge on the banking system, and taxpayers assume responsibility when shocks are large enough to require a bailout. Under flexible exchange rates, a substantial part of the costs of bank crises are borne by depositors when the underlying macroeconomic shock generates an exchange rate depreciation, thus lowering the real value of bank deposits.

From this perspective, the question becomes whether to finance the cost of restoring bank balance sheets damaged by macroeconomic shocks solely through ordinary tax revenue, or if instead depositors should finance part of the cost by paying a state-contingent inflation tax. No answer is obviously right for all countries under all circumstances; volatile inflation creates economic distortions, but then again, so do other forms of taxation. There are some reasons, however, to believe that depositors should be liable. On pure public finance grounds, Calvo and

Guidotti (1993) have shown that the inflation tax should be highly responsive to shocks, when authorities are able to make credible commitments. Although this will introduce an element of uncertainty about the real value of bank deposits, it may be preferable to place such uncertainty on bank deposits, where it can be priced and allocated in a market setting, rather than on individuals' ordinary tax liabilities, which are not marketable.

We add two caveats to this discussion. First, when the domestic financial system is highly dollarized, exchange rate depreciation has a correspondingly smaller effect on the real value of financial assets and liabilities. Second, in a dollarized economy where the exchange rate has been *credibly* fixed, the structure of assets and liabilities will reflect the expectation of exchange rate stability, which will cause an accumulation of dollar-denominated debt in both the nontradeable and household sectors. This will make an exchange rate adjustment particularly devastating for bank solvency, since there will be significant exchange rate risk hidden in the form of credit risk, as in the Chilean crisis of 1982.

Fragile financial systems complicate the management of macroeconomic policy in other dimensions as well. Consider, for example, choosing the speed of disinflation. A rapid disinflation may involve very high interest rates and low monetary growth, particularly if it is less credible than slower disinflation would have been. This will lead to strongly negatively net resource transfers, which could deal a fatal blow to the domestic banking system.

As another example, consider the monetary response to a fiscal shock that increases public sector demand for credit, thus crowding out private borrowers and raising domestic interest rates. If the banking system is strong, the central bank can offset the potential inflationary implications by maintaining a tight monetary policy. But if the banking system is vulnerable, the high interest rates, by damaging the banks, may create the need for a costly bailout, causing higher expected inflation. Thus, when the banking system is weak, tight money may only postpone, rather than reduce, inflation. And it may not even do that, if those who anticipate higher inflation flee the domestic currency.

Managing Lending Booms

We have emphasized the apparent role of lending booms in creating financial vulnerability. This means that macroeconomic policy should not be indifferent to the speed with which banks expand their portfolios.

Central banks should monitor the rate of credit growth, and take action when it appears to be growing too rapidly.

During such booms, prudential regulation based largely on enforcement of capital adequacy standards is likely to be ineffective in preventing the booms. The reason is that during a boom, loan problems are not visible, bank income appears high, and bank capital appears to be growing at a rate sufficient to support the rapidly growing loan portfolio. However, banks are incurring greater risks when they lend to new borrowers, borrowers whose cash flow is only temporarily high, and borrowers whose ability to pay depends on the availability of credit from other banks.

Since supervision cannot be expected to adequately limit the expansion of bank assets, an active monetary policy may be required. For example, when the credit boom is driven by a surge in deposit demand, it may be appropriate to adjust bank reserve or liquidity requirements as needed to ensure that banks expand their loan portfolio gradually, rather than abruptly. This would involve temporarily high liquidity requirements that would gradually be lowered, or more generally, a policy of "leaning against the wind" of credit growth.

Michael Gavin is Lead Research Economist, Office of the Chief Economist, Inter-American Development Bank. Ricardo Hausmann is Chief Economist, Inter-American Development Bank.

References

Banco Central de la República Argentina. 1995. "Managing a Liquidity Shock: Regulating the Financial System in Argentina, December 1994 to July 1995." mimeo. *Gerencia de Estudios Económicos,* Buenos Aires.

Brock, Philip, ed. 1992. *If Texas Were Chile: A Primer on Banking Reform.* San Francisco: Institute for Contemporary Studies Press.

Calvo, Guillermo. 1994. "Financial Vulnerability and Capital Flows." mimeo. Department of Economics, University of Maryland.

Calvo, Guillermo, and Enrique Mendoza. 1995. "Reflections on Mexico's Balance-of-Payments Crisis: A Chronicle of a Death Foretold." mimeo. Department of Economics, University of Maryland.

Calvo, Guillermo, and Pablo Guidotti. 1993. "On the Flexibility of Monetary Policy: The Case of the Optimal Inflation Tax." *Review of Economic Studies* (July) (Oxford).

Dewatripont, Mathias, and Jean Tirole. 1994. *The Prudential Regulation of Banks.* Cambridge: MIT Press.

Diamond, Douglas W. 1984. "Financial Intermediation and Delegated Monitoring." *Review of Economic Studies* (July) (Oxford).

Diamond, Douglas W., and Philip H. Dybvig. 1983. "Bank Runs, Deposit Insurance, and Liquidity." *Journal of Political Economy* (June) (Chicago).

Economist. 1995. "Syndicated Lending: Chemical Reaction" (September).

Gavin, Michael, and Ricardo Hausmann. 1995. "Will the Mexican Stabilization Program Allow the Banks to Survive?" mimeo. Inter-American Development Bank, Washington, D.C.

Goldfajn, Ilan, and Rodrigo Valdés. 1995. "Balance of Payments Crises and Capital Flows: The Role of Liquidity." mimeo. Massachusetts Institute of Technology, Cambridge, MA.

IDB (Inter-American Development Bank). 1995. "Overcoming Volatility in Latin America," in *Report on Economic and Social Progress in Latin America 1995.* Baltimore, MD: Johns Hopkins University Press.

IMF (International Monetary Fund). 1993. *International Capital Markets, Part II: Systemic Issues in International Finance*. Washington, DC: IMF.

IMF. *International Financial Statistics*. (various issues). Washington, D.C.

Kane, Edward J. 1989. "How Incentive-Incompatible Deposit-Insurance Fails." National Bureau of Economic Research Working Paper No. 2836. Washington, D.C.

Mayer, Colin, and Xavier Vives, eds. 1993. *Capital Markets and Financial Intermediation*. Cambridge University Press.

Montenegro, Armando. 1983. *"La crisis del sector financiero colombiano."* In *Ensayos sobre política económica* (December). Banco de la República (Colombia).

Morris, Felipe, with Mark Dorfman, José Pedro Ortíz, and María Claudia Franco. 1990. "Latin America's Banking Systems in the 1980s: A Cross-Country Comparison." World Bank Discussion Paper No. 81. Washington, D.C.

Rigobón, Roberto. 1995. "Notes on Financial Crisis." mimeo. Office of the Chief Economist, IDB, Washington, D.C.

Rojas-Suárez, Liliana, and Steven R. Weisbrod. 1994. "Financial Market Fragilities in Latin America: From Banking Crisis Resolution to Current Policy Challenges." mimeo. Office of the Chief Economist, IDB, Washington, D.C.

Roldós, Jorge E. 1991. *"La crisis bancaria Uruguaya de los '80."* Working Paper. Centro de Estudios de la Realidad Económica y Social, Uruguay.

Stiglitz, Joseph E. and Andrew Weiss. 1981. "Credit Rationing in Markets with Imperfect Information." *American Economic Review* (June).

Velasco, Andrés. 1988. "Liberalization, Crisis, and Intervention: The Chilean Financial System, 1975-1985." mimeo. IMF, Washington, D.C.

Commentary to Part II

Guillermo A. Calvo

The paper by Gavin and Hausmann addresses some of the key macroeconomic issues related to banking crises. However, it places relatively little weight on the role of expectations, herd behavior, and self-fulfilling prophecies. My comment will attempt to bring these issues into balance, as well as elaborate on some of the fascinating issues raised in the paper.

There are two types of financial crises: those caused by a change in the economic fundamentals, and those caused by herd behavior, in which some market participants do what the others do simply because the others are doing it. Herd behavior is particularly worrisome because participants will have no reason to regret their actions and will therefore be encouraged to continue behaving in that fashion. Because recent financial crises in Latin America have been unduly deep, given the changes in fundamentals, they appear to contain critical elements of herd behavior.

Changes in fundamentals have preceded many crises. In fact, it is difficult to find examples of crises in which fundamentals have played no role. However, herd behavior seems to be a key factor in amplifying these crises. For example, a rise in international interest rates, which in the absence of herd behavior would result in no more than a modest decline in bank deposits, may lead instead to massive withdrawals if individuals come to expect massive withdrawals. Under such circumstances, depositors who do *not* take their money out of banks may end up suffering a sizable capital loss. Clearly, herd behavior is at the root of this example, because individual behavior is predicated not only on what is happening in the banking system but also on how some participants expect others to act.

Under these circumstances, history matters, and it matters a lot. For example, the recent rise in international interest rates left Austria—which has a fixed exchange rate against the Deutsche mark—relatively unscathed, while it wreaked havoc in Mexico. Thus, it is fair to conjecture that the Mexican debacle may have included an important component of herd behavior.

The paper argues that banking crises are largely a result of a previous sizable expansion of bank credit, which induces a surge of nonperforming loans. This is an intriguing idea, and may well be right. However, I believe that both the abruptness and the considerable depth of recent banking crises hinge on the existence of some kind of herd behavior, which is not necessarily irrational.

Consequently, I would advise regulators to give special consideration to policies such as high reserve requirements, which help to stem herd behavior at the root. The authors recommend high reserve requirements to slow the growth of credit and thus prevent the emergence of bad loans. But such a policy would also stem herd behavior by giving the central bank an additional instrument to offset the credit contraction effects of a sudden decline in the stock of bank deposits. This perspective also suggests that higher reserve requirements be set for short-term rather than for long-term deposits. Then if there were a decline in the stock of bank deposits (and long-term deposits were sufficiently well staggered), banks would have more time to react and roll back credit lines without causing undue disruption in productive, credit-dependent sectors.

The analysis of bank crises in terms of herd behavior also suggests that special attention be paid to what makes the demand for bank deposits unstable. For example, I believe that the instability of deposit demand in Mexico was associated with a consumption boom rather than an investment and output boom. The demand for money can be shown to be better correlated with expenditure than with output or income. Thus, an unsustainable level of expenditure brings about an unsustainable expansion of monetary aggregates. This was arguably what happened in Mexico: when monetary aggregates started to fall at the beginning of 1994, the central bank was forced to increase domestic credit in order to prevent a banking crisis. The increase in domestic credit entailed a substantial loss of international reserves, making the central bank highly vulnerable to the endgame speculative attack on the *tesobonos* (dollar-indexed, short-term public debt). In contrast, if output had boomed because of higher capital accumulation, for example, it would have helped sustain a *permanently* higher level of expenditure, and thus a permanently higher demand for money. In that case, the decline in the demand for money during 1994 would have been less pronounced, resulting in a smaller loss of international reserves. An interesting implication of this analysis is that the more a current account deficit takes the form of a consumption boom, the higher will be the country's optimal reserve requirements.

The authors argue that a floating exchange rate regime may be preferable to one of fixed exchange rates. Their principal piece of evidence is the difference in the way Texas and Venezuela were impacted by a collapse in oil prices. The authors suggest that exchange rate flexibility in Venezuela was key in preventing in that country the kind of massive bank failures that took place in Texas. This is an interesting observation, because it links the banking system to the traditional debate over flexible versus fixed exchange rates.

For example, the conventional wisdom is that fixed rates are preferable to flexible rates if the main source of instability is a change in the demand for money. The basic reason is that under fixed exchange rates, the stock of money becomes demand determined, and therefore a situation of excessive or deficient liquidity should never occur. Bringing banks into the picture may radically change this conclusion. Money, as usually defined, includes bank deposits. As a general rule, a change in the stock of bank deposits calls for a change in the stock of credit in the same direction (credit, after all, is on the other side of the balance sheet). Thus, although fixed exchange rates allow the supply of money to automatically adjust to the demand for money, a sharp fall in demand (especially for bank deposits) may imply a sharp contraction of bank credit and massive bankruptcies. In contrast, a regime of floating exchange rates allows the system to respond to a contraction in the demand for money with a devaluation. The resulting rise in domestic prices *increases* the demand for *nominal* money balances and thereby reduces the need to roll back *nominal* credit, lowering the chances of generating massive amounts of nonperforming loans. And, most important, it lowers the probability of disrupting the productive side of the economy.

However, there are other ways to prevent bank credit contraction, which can be implemented within a regime of fixed exchange rates. For example, the amount of reserves that banks must hold against deposits could be lowered. Argentina undertook such a policy with great success during the 1994-95 tequila episode.

The authors also point out that a devaluation causes a redistribution of wealth from depositors to borrowers. Clearly, this wealth transfer may help to prevent a *negative* real shock (e.g., a deterioration of the terms of trade) from unleashing a surge of bad loans. However, the effectiveness of a devaluation as a wealth redistribution device is questionable when the banking system is highly dollarized, as in Argentina, Bolivia, Peru, and Uruguay, or when it is highly indexed, as it is in Chile and soon will be in Mexico.

In practice, it is hard to find cases of *pure* floating exchange rates. Most actually involve some kind of exchange market intervention with a low degree of transparency: what is called a "dirty float." The main drawback of a dirty float regime is that it opens the door to discretionary monetary policy, which has a poor track record in many Latin American countries. I would, therefore, be very cautious about advising exchange rate flexibility as a means of preventing banking crises, especially when there are feasible alternatives.

Guillermo A. Calvo is Director, Center for International Economics and Distinguished University Professor, University of Maryland.

Morris Goldstein

Michael Gavin and Ricardo Hausmann are to be congratulated for a very good paper on the macroeconomic roots of banking crises. The analysis is insightful, and the conclusions and recommendations, which are on the whole soundly based, are influenced—as they should be—by a wealth of country experience. My comment will amplify on several of their themes and raise questions about a few others.

First, the authors are certainly right to suggest that banking crises do not arise in a macroeconomic vacuum, and that a satisfactory explanation of these crises has to go beyond the difficulties of individual financial institutions. In the context of emerging Latin American markets, the authors stress that declines in the terms of trade and the onset of major recessions are among the most important macroeconomic shocks to banking systems. They also emphasize the value of lending booms as a leading indicator of banking crises.

To take a wider view, there is by now considerable evidence that the incidence of financial crises is higher after increases in interest rates, large declines in equity prices, the onset of recession, and unanticipated declines in inflation rates, as well as during times of unusually great uncertainty.[1] Moreover, a popular explanation of why such factors should matter for financial crises runs very much along the same lines as those put forward to explain banking crises; it is an argument based on asymmetry of information. For example, when interest rates are high, prob-

---

[1] See Frederick Mishkin (1994), "Preventing Financial Crises: An Historical Perspective," NBER Working Paper No. 4636. See also Robert Eisenbeis, "Systemic Risk: Bank Deposits and Credit," in G. Kaufman, ed. (1995), *Research in Financial Services*, JAI Press.

lems of adverse selection and credit risk will be greater, because it is precisely those borrowers with high-risk investment projects who will be willing to pay the highest interest rates. Likewise, because a sharp decline in the stock market leads to a large decline in the market value of firms, the problems of moral hazard and adverse selection in financial markets become worse: with lower net worth, firms have less of their own money at stake when taking risks, and less of a cushion against future losses. Similar arguments have been offered to explain why unanticipated declines in inflation and increased uncertainty make financial crisis more likely. In short, not only banking crises but financial crises more generally have some important macroeconomic roots, and Gavin and Hausmann are on the right track in emphasizing the role of information and incentive problems in such crises.

My second point works somewhat in the opposite direction: I am much less convinced of the authors' argument that "good times are bad times for learning" for banks. The question is, compared to what? It is true that when credit is plentiful, borrowers can easily pass liquidity tests, and that borrowers will be temporarily highly profitable during macroeconomic expansions. But it is also true that during times of crisis—and even during some bad times preceding crises—informational and incentive problems can be even worse. In the aftermath of a disturbance, lenders might temporarily have great difficulty sorting out which borrowers are affected and which are not, because they might not yet understand the nature and extent of interdependence among the borrowers. As suggested above, the decline in net worth that comes about during bad times—after an equity market crash, for example—can also exacerbate moral hazard problems. Borrowers whose lowered net worth puts them in deep financial trouble may be more likely to take desperate, double-or-nothing risks—to "gamble for resurrection." In short, information and incentive problems will appear during both good times and bad. I would therefore have preferred a more balanced treatment of this issue than the authors have given us.

A related issue is how financial markets respond to a worsening of information. Some researchers (e.g., Frederick Mishkin) have suggested that the dominant response will be a widening of the yield spread on bonds issued by low- versus high-quality borrowers. Some regard such a widening as the best indicator of a true financial crisis, and in fact we often observe this behavior (typically characterized as a "flight to quality") during crises. If good economic times are particularly bad times for learning, why don't rational lenders offer some response to their learning difficulties, instead of just lending more to all comers? If neither the interest differential nor the volume of lending responds to increased uncertainty during good times, what does? Some discussion of interest rate spreads—both across borrowers and over the cycle—would therefore be a useful addition to the paper. If lending booms regularly precede banking crises, it would also be useful to hear the authors' views on *why* banks do not learn over time from these episodes of overlending.

Third, the authors quite rightly draw attention to the role that declines in real estate and equity prices play in banking difficulties. Part of the reason why these present such a problem is that the same deflationary shock that reduces a borrower's ability to repay—say, because the contraction of the real economy leads to increased bankruptcies and job losses—simultaneously reduces the value of the collateral underlying the loan. In principle, lenders should ask for collateral that has a value relatively independent of shocks to the borrower's ability to pay. That is not a very restrictive condition at the level of the individual borrower, but it becomes more restrictive at the level of the economy as a whole. It supplies further justification for considering the macroeconomic roots of banking problems.

Fourth, a natural response to high risk and volatility is diversification. Two aspects of diversification are relevant in the context of banking crises in emerging market economies. The first relates to the role of the international interest rate cycle in driving net private capital flows to emerging markets. Thanks in good measure to the empirical work of Guillermo Calvo, we know that changes in interest rates in major creditor countries explain probably better than anything else the time pattern of net private capital flows to these markets.[2] These capital flows, in turn, typically are intermediated by the banking system and can contribute significantly to the large swings in bank lending documented in the paper. Given that the international interest rate cycle is beyond the control of emerging market economies, how can they protect against it? Aside from the use of market-based hedging instruments, one way is for banks to limit the share of their loans that goes to the most interest rate sensitive sectors, such as real estate and construction.

The second approach, to which the authors allude, is to permit foreign lenders to take up a larger share of the risk. In this regard, it is sometimes argued that increasing reserve requirements in an effort to

---

[2] See Guillermo Calvo et al. (1993), "Capital Flows and Real Exchange Rate Appreciation in Latin America: The Role of External Factors," IMF Staff Papers 40:1.

sterilize large capital inflows is unwise, because it penalizes domestic banks relative to foreign ones and therefore drives some business abroad. But if the demand for credit comes mainly from high-risk sectors, it may be good strategy to allow foreign banks to grab a greater share of these risks. Then, if some of these high-risk projects go sour, it will be foreign monetary authorities, and not the home authorities, who are called on to provide emergency assistance. Sometimes it pays not to win all the business.

Fifth, the authors argue that because Latin American banks face more volatile conditions than do their industrial country counterparts, they probably should hold more capital in relation to their total assets than suggested by the international capital standards set by the Bank for International Settlements. I agree with that view, but what happens when bank capital falls below the regulatory standard? This issue featured prominently in the design of recent banking legislation in the United States. The FDIC Improvement Act of 1991 introduced a series of threshold capital-asset ratios for banks which, when crossed, should trigger prompt and progressively harsher mandatory sanctions on the troubled institutions, to turn them around before they reach insolvency or, failing that, to close them before the market value of their capital turns negative. Some analysts argue that these multiple capital zone tripwires, and the graduated regulatory responses mandated by the structured early intervention requirement, make enforcement more credible than under a single capital asset-ratio requirement.[3] This raises the old "rules versus discretion" debate in another guise, but it is highly relevant to the question of whether the problem of "gambling for resurrection"—and, ultimately, of banking crises—is made more severe by the absence of structured early intervention and a firm closure rule. The more discretion bank regulators have to procrastinate, the higher the likely cost to the public of eventually resolving the problem.

Sixth, the authors argue that in a fragile financial system, external shocks are more likely to create a banking crisis under fixed than under floating exchange rates. I agree with that conclusion but would add that commitment to a fixed exchange rate—including, of course, through a currency board arrangement—can severely constrain the scope of the central bank to act as lender of last resort. Thus, if a country with a fixed exchange rate regime has a banking system likely to need official assis-

---

[3] See George Benston and George Kaufman (1994), "Is the Banking and Payments System Fragile?" Working Paper 1994/28, Federal Reserve Bank of Chicago.

tance in the medium term, the government should be prepared to line up outside financial assistance to enable it to assist the domestic banking system without creating a conflict for domestic monetary policy. The recent experiences of Argentina and Mexico are consistent with that proposition.

Finally, the authors argue explicitly that fragility in the financial system does and should place limits on the tightness of monetary policy, and in particular, on the aggressive use of high interest rates in defense of fixed exchange rates. This is something that central bankers are typically loath to acknowledge, lest it weaken the credibility of their anti-inflationary or exchange rate commitments. Yet there is now plenty of evidence—bolstered most recently by the ERM (exchange rate mechanism) crises of 1992–93 and the Mexican economic crisis of 1994–95—that financial fragility *does* influence the stance of monetary policy. On this score, I commend the authors for telling it like it is.

Morris Goldstein is the Dennis Weatherstone Senior Fellow, Institute for International Economics, Washington, D.C.

Roberto Zahler

My comments on the paper by Gavin and Hausmann center on the links between macroeconomic instability and financial crises, and the implications of this interaction for the framing of economic policy. I will also touch indirectly on another issue very important to understanding how such crises develop and how they can be averted: the structure of financial regulation and supervision.

The main subject of the article is the interconnection between macroeconomic fluctuations and the health of the banking industry. The authors look at the significance of this interaction for purposes of designing financial policies that are consonant with the macroeconomic environment in which a country's banks operate, and macroeconomic policies that are concordant with the strength of the banking system.

The first part of the article looks at certain special features of the banking sector that explain why it warrants particularly close official scrutiny. Among the examples cited are banks' heavily leveraged financing structure and the mismatch of assets and liabilities in terms of liquidity and currency denomination. The resulting misalignment leaves the sector vulnerable to crisis situations, which are then amplified by macroeconomic fluctuations. The authors next examine the central role played by the financial system, and particularly a country's banks, in the workings of a modern market economy, especially by providing an expeditious payments system and channeling credit flows. The paper then refers to the atomized nature of the depositor base, which is typical of banks; to implicit and explicit government-provided deposit insurance; and to the problems of asymmetric information that are inherent in banking operations. As a consequence of these characteristics of the banking industry, the private sector alone cannot be expected to properly monitor the quality of financial assets and their economic correspondence to bank liabilities. Moreover, it is well known that this set of conditions can adversely influence the actions of banks, giving them, for instance, incentives to engage in excessively risky behavior; such incentives may be even more powerful when banks are undercapitalized.

In this context, sharp macroeconomic fluctuations tend to magnify the financial system's intrinsic vulnerability, and such vulnerability is usually not symmetrical in the phases of the cycle. In a contraction phase banks tend to absorb losses, but they do not capture additional profits in expansionary phases. Among the types of macroeconomic shocks mentioned by the authors are abrupt deterioration in the terms of trade, and adverse sectoral shocks that can impair bank asset values when borrowers' ability to service their debt is undermined or the collateral they have posted loses value. Likewise, a sudden decline in public demand for deposits, or a curtailment of access to external credit, can spark a liquidity crisis within the banking system, which can develop into a solvency crisis when there are stumbling blocks for bank borrowers seeking access to long-term financing.

Such circumstances do not necessarily unleash a financial crisis, but if a country's banking system is fragile to begin with, even minor macroeconomic missteps can throw the entire financial system into disarray. Accordingly, financial, regulatory, and supervisory arrangements that will reinforce a solvent, adequately capitalized banking system are fundamental—though not sufficient in themselves—to ensure stability. Macroeconomic policies should also be designed to dampen sharp economic fluctuations, so as to prevent widespread accelerated credit growth, for example. As the authors indicate, such phenomena are often at the root of the vulnerability that can ultimately lead to a banking crisis.

I will now comment on some of the policy implications discussed by the authors. With respect to financial policy, the paper suggests that capital and liquidity requirements should be related to the frequency and size of macroeconomic shocks. The authors raise a valid question as to whether capital and liquidity requirements that are adequate for advanced economies, such as those embodied in the Basle standards, are sufficient for the economies of Latin America.

Since the Latin American economies are far more volatile than their industrialized counterparts, greater precautions must be taken to prevent formal or de facto deposit insurance from becoming a source of financial instability and government bailouts. Also, requirements such as the Basle rules can be improved upon. Credit risk criteria need to be accompanied by other criteria encompassing risks associated with exchange rates, interest rates, and loan concentration. In other words, in establishing capital requirements, overall portfolio risk should be considered, rather than focusing exclusively on the risk attaching to individual assets. To remedy problems on this front, the regulatory authorities should set standards for portfolio diversification, such as ceilings on maturity and currency mismatches.

The authors also support the two-way internationalization of domestic banking systems as a means of achieving greater diversification in the source and use of funding, and thereby reducing the likelihood of a crisis. Generally speaking, I agree with this second proposition, but this must be accompanied by adequate regulation and supervision to guard against the additional risks introduced by the internationalization of banking. Otherwise such an approach could work against the ultimate aim of greater financial solidity. For instance, the ability of regulators and private agents to monitor and supervise international banking transactions is constrained by higher information costs, differing accounting practices, and different laws and regulations in different countries. And less effective private and public supervision of banks leaves a nation's banking system more vulnerable. In sum, the globalization of the banking industry should be underpinned by international agreements on financial matters so that compatible and mutually consistent financial rules and capitalization and liquidity requirements can be developed, along with uniform accounting practices to expedite information flows.

Another related point is the possible triangulation of risks and their effects. Banks from countries with low sovereign risk can serve as intermediaries for operations in higher-risk economies. Although this approach offers attractive opportunities for financial arbitrage, it should not be deployed at the cost of implicit or explicit government-provided insurance for banking system liabilities.

In the area of macroeconomic policy, the authors posit that a weak banking system is not compatible with a fixed exchange rate regime. If a country's banks are already fragile, they maintain, the automatic monetary adjustment mechanisms under fixed exchange rates can trigger a financial crisis if the economy has to face external financing problems. In the short run, such automatic adjustment does indeed produce a liquidity crunch that can drive interest rates up dramatically. In the long run, a disinflation will follow, which will, in turn, allow for the local currency to depreciate in real terms; the real value of bank liabilities thus rises without a corresponding increase in the creditworthiness of borrowers. In contrast, with flexible exchange rates, the authors suggest, exchange rate depreciation can afford automatic relief to the banking system as the real value of bank liabilities is written down.

From my personal standpoint, particularly in the light of Chile's experience in the early 1980s, this seems to be a reasonable statement. However, a flexible exchange rate system will not be problem free either, if a country's banks are weak. For instance, if the monetary authorities seek to neutralize inflationary pressures resulting from an increase in domestic aggregate demand by boosting domestic interest rates, the banks will be subjected to stresses similar to those mentioned above. If the banking system is already weak, those tensions could trigger a financial crisis. In contrast, if the exchange rate is fixed, the rise in domestic interest rates will be constrained by the level of external interest rates. An increase in domestic demand, by putting upward pressure on domestic interest rates, would produce a compensatory capital inflow that would increase domestic liquidity, offset the upward pressure on domestic interest rates, and validate the increased inflationary pressures. The key problem is that a weak banking system severely curtails the flexibility of monetary and foreign exchange policies to pursue other aims such as inflation control, and this occurs regardless of how such policies are implemented in practice.

The second conclusion in connection with macroeconomic policy has to do with the need for policy action to dampen the effects of the economic cycle. Specifically, it is suggested that an active monetary policy may be required to adequately limit the growth of credit in the economy, because too-rapid expansion can ultimately throw the entire banking system into crisis. On this point, it should be emphasized that an effective regulatory and supervisory system is not sufficient in itself to stave off a widespread banking crisis. Supervision is fundamentally microeconomic in scope. It is geared to monitoring the solvency of each individual financial institution, and takes for granted that the rest of the system is functioning normally. Given the close interdependency of banks, however, a broader perspective should be taken in order to assess risks at work within the global system. For example, widespread and accelerated credit growth can generate an asset price bubble, which in turn will enhance the value of collateral offered by prospective borrowers, thereby generating further credit growth, and so on. Individual banks may appear to be perfectly viable as long as the credit expansion continues, but the system itself may be left highly exposed, so that a relatively small setback could unleash a systemic financial crisis.

Accordingly, effective supervisory mechanisms at the microeconomic level should be accompanied by macroeconomic policies that will dampen such expansive cycles, which can bring about an economy-wide banking crisis. Economic policies should give priority to macroeconomic stability, seeking to prevent significant fluctuations in the rate of GDP growth and unsustainable current account deficits. In particular, massive inflows of foreign capital can lead to very rapid growth of domestic credit, setting the stage for a future financial crisis. Such policies, likewise, should strive to avoid imbalances in key macroeconomic prices—exchange rates, wages, interest rates, and asset prices— since the adjustment process is costly and inevitably generates heavy stresses within the financial system.

Roberto Zahler is former President, Central Bank of Chile.

Sebastian Edwards

The Mexican crisis has left no doubt that the issues of bank supervision and banking crises are fundamental for developing economies. Yet banking crises were once considered a *micro*economic issue, the province of financial specialists. For years economists made little connection between macroeconomic developments and the strength or weakness of financial and banking systems. I remember that ten years ago, at a conference organized by the National Bureau of Economic Research and the World Bank, Guillermo Calvo presented an important paper analyzing the role of banks in the macroeconomic performance of developing economies. Many at the conference expressed doubts about whether this was the right way to proceed. Today we recognize Calvo, in this as in many other areas, as a pioneer; and banking and bank supervision are essential elements in macroeconomic policy.

The first topic I will consider is *credit booms* and what to do about them. There is little doubt that credit booms are central to banking problems. The road to a bank crisis starts with market euphoria and the expansion of credit. Banks begin to grow at unprecedented rates, only to see that expansion eventually unravel. The traditional way of dealing with such booms is to make sure that, during this euphoric phase, banks do not become too reckless—that they take into account the risks of a rapid expansion of credit. In managing the banking system we rely on such things as supervision, reserve requirements, and liquidity analysis. These are important, but they fall more within the realm of micro than of macroeconomics.

At the same time, however, most credit booms in developing countries are accompanied by large and unsustainable current account deficits, which brings us into the macroeconomic domain. For example, between 1992 and 1994 Mexico ran current account deficits that were unsustainable from every possible perspective. Now, according to Herbert Stein's law, if something is unsustainable, it will stop. And stop it did in the Mexican case. The question was never *whether* it would stop, but only when and how. The challenge was then to avoid a crash—to make the inevitable adjustment as smooth as possible. And the airplane in that episode made rather a jarring landing and skidded off the runway for a time, but now seems to be safely taxiing toward the terminal.

For many developing countries, the future challenge will be how to deal with a current account deficit that has grown to accommodate a sharp upturn in popular expectations—an increase in the country's perceived wealth. The question is, should authorities try to spread such an increase in the deficit over time? For example, instead of allowing the deficit to rise to 10 percent of GDP for several years before collapsing to 2 to 3 percent, should they try to keep it at a more sustainable level of about 4 to 5 percent of GDP?

This relates to the sequencing of financial reforms, and in particular, the speed with which capital controls are relaxed. If a country suddenly relaxes controls, without putting up impediments to inflows, capital will move in quickly, generating large current account deficits, as expectations about the country change. The problem arises, of course, when expectations reverse course and the deficit has to be reduced.

As the IMF, the World Bank, and others have pointed out, the issue of when and how fast to reduce capital controls is still unresolved. There is some merit in proceeding cautiously, gradually reducing controls first for long-term capital and only later for short-term capital, to ensure that the adjustment is smooth and the economy's vulnerability is kept to a minimum. But one can go overboard in recommending gradualism, and turn it into an argument for maintaining capital controls indefinitely. These are very different: whereas gradualism is the right policy, perpetuation of controls is the wrong one. How does one reduce a too-large capital account without capital controls, in a way that ensures a soft landing? The answer has to do with the exchange rate regime, to be discussed later.

My second topic is *international reserves policy*. Management of international reserves was an active area of economic research until about ten years ago, but since then the topic seems to have expired from inattention. The traditional literature emphasized the role of trade flows in determining the optimal level of a country's reserves. Analysts would typically relate the optimal level of international reserves to variability of export earnings and the degree of openness of the economy. Even today, when multilateral institutions assess the adequacy of a country's reserves, they usually focus on the number of months of imports that the reserves will cover.

Meanwhile, in a world of vastly increased capital mobility, increased financial integration, and greater financial sophistication, the question of optimal reserves now has less to do with trade flows than with the need to avoid financial crises. Perhaps the right way to analyze reserves is to relate them to government or banking sector liabilities instead of trade, or even to the stock of high-powered money: M1 or maybe M2. The truth is that we do not how to do this analysis yet. Much careful work is needed in this area, so that we can learn how to deal with these issues and establish the right kind of macroeconomic policies. The international reserves policy of a central bank is a powerful macroeconomic policy tool. Considering the scarcity of macroeconomic tools in Latin America relative to the number of objectives, learning how to use that tool to best advantage would be an important step forward.

My third topic is the choice of *exchange rate regimes*. Here, unlike with reserves policy, mainstream thinking has evolved very rapidly. At first the discussion was couched in geographic terms—how to determine the optimal currency area. We then began to relate exchange rate systems to the types of economic shocks to which an economy is prone, going on to distinguish between internal and external, monetary and real shocks. Which exchange rate regime was recommended—fixed, crawling peg, managed floating, pure float—would then depend on the particular vulnerabilities of the economy in question. This line of thinking gave way eventually to another kind of analysis that emphasized credibility and consistency over time. In this context the enthusiasm for fixed exchange rates reappeared in the late 1980s—it was argued they would strengthen governments' credibility.

The Mexican crisis has again shaken our confidence in the way we approach exchange rate regimes. I think Guillermo Ortiz hit the nail on the head by saying that one lesson learned from Mexico's crisis was to use an exchange rate anchor only in the early phase of stabilization, and switch later to flexible rates and greater reliance on conventional monetary and fiscal policy [p. 217]. The key question then becomes when to make the switch. At what point in a stabilization program should the authorities abandon the fixed exchange rate regime in favor of a more flexible monetary and fiscal policy? The answer is still unknown, but we are working on it, and the question may become normative.

A related question, perhaps more suited to a historian than a policymaker, is why governments find it so hard to exit from a fixed exchange rate regime. The same policymakers who write and argue forcefully that fixed rates are only a temporary device, find it curiously difficult to abandon the fixed rate regime when the time comes. In recent memory probably only Israel has made the move at about the right time, and according to my colleague Michael Bruno, even there internal political problems delayed it for a year.

The answer has much to do with the banking system, I believe. Some fear that departing from a fixed exchange rate regime will produce a sharp one-time drop in the value of the domestic currency—and that can happen even when the switch is executed in a graceful, dignified manner in calm financial seas, to say nothing of the middle of a crisis. A sharp fall in the currency usually implies a sharp increase in interest rates, which is bad news for the banking system. If the banking sector is weak and a crisis results, the costs of switching to a flexible exchange rate regime are high and are incurred immediately, whereas the benefits are deferred. If policymakers and politicians aim for short-term solutions, preferring front-loaded benefits and back-loaded costs, this could explain why they are reluctant to take the plunge from a fixed to a flexible exchange rate regime. Ortiz's proposal, to adopt a fixed rate initially and later switch to a flexible regime, may be technically sound but politically infeasible. Under such political and economic circumstances, it is worth analyzing whether a fixed exchange rate even in the early phase is a good idea.

Finally, a brief remark about *fiscal policy.* One lesson of recent episodes is that during a credit boom in conditions of high capital mobility and a well-developed but relatively young banking system, fiscal policy must be extremely careful. The fiscal authorities should focus not only on whether the budget is in surplus or deficit, but also on maintaining, and especially not weakening, the fiscal stance. A strong fiscal policy stance, of course, contributes to overall saving, and as Calvo points out, lower levels of expenditures reduce the need to expand monetary aggregates, thus reducing the likelihood of a currency collapse.

Eduardo Aninat, Chile's Minister of Finance, makes the point that, although assets are difficult to evaluate in a rapidly growing developing economy, the "emotional" pricing of assets must be avoided [p. 232]. Indeed, the euphoria that characterizes credit booms can carry asset values to irrational heights. Regulators and policymakers alone, however, cannot control the market's emotions. The authorities can and must make available the necessary information—to provide markets with a reality check—but the private sector has to analyze that information and take responsibility for its own actions. If both sides act responsibly, our countries will be in much better shape, and we stand a chance of avoiding the kinds of crises that have blocked our region's progress in the past.

Sebastian Edwards is Professor of Economics at UCLA.

Part III

The Roots of Banking Crises: Microeconomic Issues and Supervision and Regulation

Aristóbulo de Juan

Commentary

David Folkerts-Landau
Carlos Santistevan
Angel Rojo
Fernando de Santibañez

The Roots of Banking Crises: Microeconomic Issues and Supervision and Regulation

Aristóbulo de Juan

Some macroeconomists believe that the causes of banking crises are always macro in nature and that only the real economy matters. To them, the financial sector is just a byproduct of the real economy. This view is shared by many bankers, who never consider that they are to be blamed for poor management. It is also shared by some politicians, who find it easier not to take any remedial action in the financial sector or just to take bail-out action across the board, rather than implementing unpopular restructuring measures on a case-by-case basis.

According to that school of thought, if the economy is prosperous, the good health of the banking sector is taken for granted. On the other hand, if the economy has serious problems, you still don't have to worry about the banking sector, because there is nothing useful you can do about it.

Yet international experience shows that even in the midst of economic recession, good banks can operate satisfactorily. On the other hand, in prosperous economies, there are banks that go under. What is the key element in this apparent contradiction? *Management.* Good management can weather the storm of macroeconomic trouble and poor management can lead a bank to insolvency in a booming economy. For example, in Spain in the late 1970s and early 1980s, in the midst of an economic slump and a simultaneous deep and widespread banking crisis, some well-managed banks adjusted their policies to those conditions and became stronger than before, actually very strong. On the other hand, in Spain during the late 1980s and early 1990s, in a satisfactory economic context followed by a moderate slump, a large bank, Banesto, failed—due to poor management practices, not systemic problems.

The same issues pertained in the recent financial crises in Mexico and Argentina. Were those crises due only to macroeconomic factors: namely, the December crisis of the Mexican peso and its implications for both Mexico and Argentina? Or did a number of banks in both countries have a poor quality portfolio, and were some already in serious trouble because of poor management practices?

During the Spanish banking crisis of the 1980s, I was head of the Inspection Services at the Central Bank of Spain. In a context of depression, many banking failures were diagnosed and taken to the Board for a decision on how to address the problem. When Board members systematically inquired about the reason for the failure, the answer was always poor managerial practices.

Likewise, in the United States, a 1988 survey on bank failure published by the Office of the Comptroller of the Currency evaluated the factors contributing to the failure of national banks, based on an analysis of the behavior of banks that had failed between 1979 and 1987. The survey concluded that the major cause of decline for problem banks was poor asset quality, which eventually eroded their capital; and the common factor responsible for poor asset quality was the banks' management practices, not the economic environment. To quote the survey: "Banks are able to remain healthy throughout the fluctuations by establishing and maintaining strong internal policies, system and controls. Problem and failed banks are almost never simply the result of depressed economic conditions."

Establishing the proportion of banking crises triggered by the economic environment and the proportion by poor management would be very difficult. It could be done only by analyzing each country and each bank. In systemic crises, macroeconomic factors outweigh micro ones, and microeconomic causes are more relevant in isolated bank failures. In any case, systemic crises include a number of deeper crises of individual banks due to poor management, which are often neglected. Thus it is clear that both systemic and individual bank crises have macroeconomic and microeconomic causes.

While some analysts claim that any kind of regulation can enhance the incentives for risky management, the author believes that, as a rule, *poor prudential regulation and loose supervision* are among the main causes of bank failure, because they lay the groundwork for poor management, that is, lack of proper control and remedial action.

Management Issues

This paper concerns the causes of banking crises related to poor management and to regulation and supervision. If the poor management practices described here were matched with the suggested guidelines for prudential regulation and supervision, it would be clear that the management flaws could be prevented or limited. In the absence of such a regulatory and supervisory framework, however, bank management can get out of control and cause serious damage to the financial sector and the economy. While poor management exists in a variety of circumstances, there are two typical situations.

When new bankers take control of a bank, by setting it up or by buying a controlling interest, policies and practices may prove inadequate. The funds used to take over the bank may even be guaranteed or ultimately financed by the bank itself. Examples of deterioration due to new bankers can be found in most Central and Eastern European countries, where new bank licensing has been too liberal. New investors took over numerous Spanish banks in the 1970s, and the same happened in Mexico after the privatization of nationalized banks in 1991.

When bankers remain at the helm of existing banks, but fail to adapt to rapidly evolving markets. That was the case with some large banks in Spain during the 1990s. Bankers can also drive a bank to ruin by failing to show problems in the bank's books. Normally, if problems "do not exist" in their accounting, or in the public perception, bankers will fail to correct them. In almost every country, there are banks with serious portfolio problems trying to avoid disclosure and imposition of corrective action by the supervisory authority.

The typical features of poor management are overextension, rapid growth, poor lending policies, poor internal controls, and poor planning. Any of these, singly or in combination, can lead to current losses, capital erosion, and insolvency.

Overextension

Overextension—doing too much—can occur in various ways. A bank can be overextended by *lending in excess,* in comparison with its equity capital or deposit base. In the former case, the bank is relatively decapitalized and its cushion for losses (i.e., capital) may be insufficient if the loan portfolio deteriorates. This happened to many American banks as a result of their massive lending to developing countries in the 1980s. When a bank lends too much in comparison with its deposit base, it will have to tap the interbank market for resources, sometimes to an extent that may affect its balance and stability, due to the volatility of those resources and the reduction of spreads. For example, Continental Illinois Bank became illiquid in 1984 when creditor banks discontinued lending to it and then proved to be insolvent themselves.

Overextension can occur *geographically*, when a bank decides to establish itself in foreign countries without having a precise goal or proper control over its activities. This is sometimes due to the wish to follow a fashion: "If everyone else goes international, why shouldn't I?" In one case, a bank launched an aggressive international policy, but its key international managers could hardly speak a foreign language and paid few visits to their foreign operations.

Overextension can result from *uncontrolled diversification* of products. Because of the international application of strict rules on capital adequacy, most banks try to diversify their products in order to make profits through commissions. This is a correct policy. But a number of banks overdiversify, in the hope that their new source of income may outweigh income from their loan portfolio. If banks are not skilled in managing those new products or their control systems are not sufficiently reliable or sophisticated, this is very risky. The examples of derivatives in general and Barings in particular come to mind.

Rapid Growth

Quick or overly aggressive growth can also lead to insolvency. To attract prime customers and gain social preeminence are frequent motivations for quick growth. But aiming for growth at the risk of decreasing stability or profitability is dangerous. First, to make your resources grow quickly, you have to pay very high interest rates, to the detriment of your spreads, and at the risk of financial overextension. Second, in order to grow quickly, you look for lending opportunities as a matter of life or death and selection criteria tend to be loosened, which causes deterioration of the loan portfolio. This syndrome can be seen at Continental Illinois in 1984, and at Banesto in Spain from the time a new management team took over in 1988 until the government intervened in 1993.

Poor Lending Practices

Poor lending practices are another key cause of bank failure. A good banker will invest the resources he takes from the market in such a manner that they give a satisfactory yield and are recovered. It should always be remembered that those resources are other people's money, not the banker's, and ultimately must be reimbursed. Forgetting this leads banks to illiquidity and insolvency. That is why *poor lending practices are at the heart of banking crises.* Poor lending practices include loan concentration, connected lending, term mismatching, interest rate risk, currency risk, and poor recovery.

Loan concentration. Concentrating excessive resources on a few borrowers in certain sectors of the economy or geographical areas goes against the principle of risk diversification, which is essential for sound banking. In such cases, the failure of just a few borrowers, or a crisis in a given sector, can lead the creditor bank to insolvency. Loan concentration is risky when the banker bases it on an erroneous assessment of the borrower's quality, and particularly so when the borrower is connected to the bank or to the banker, as described below. But loan concentration may also be involuntary, as when a considerable portion of the bank's lending, originally of good quality, becomes frozen at a later stage and the bank is forced to continue lending to the bad borrowers in the hope of an ultimate solution—as happened in the 1980s with U.S. banks' loans to the real estate and energy sectors.

Connected lending. Often associated with loan concentration, connected lending also carries other risks described below. Connected lending may involve lending to the bank's or the banker's participated companies.

Lending to the bank's participated companies is typical of both universal banks and development banks, when their charter allows them to hold equity participation in nonfinancial companies. This was the situation with most of the banks that failed during the banking crisis in Spain in the 1980s. In principle, this practice is not wrong if the bank operates on an arm's length basis, as if the borrower were an ordinary third party. The problem is that these kinds of operations often involve the following imperfections: (i) the conditions and the volume of such facilities are looser than appropriate; (ii) the availability of such facilities leads to less than first quality management in the participated company, since the company's liquidity is assured; (iii) information flows from the borrower to the creditor bank suffer, since the banks' interests are normally represented by top managers who are, in this case, an obstacle to good information; and (iv) when these loans go wrong, they are seldom classified as bad loans, provisioned for, and recovered. This kind of lending is particularly risky in state-owned banks, when short-term and long-term social objectives are not differentiated or when there is political pressure for banks to keep lending to insolvent borrowers or not to recover previous loans extended to them. The risk involved in connected lending is becoming more general, since most developing countries seem to be in favor of universal banking. One of the few successful development bankers in Colombia, when asked the secret to his success, answered: "We do not lend to our participated companies at all." In this case the banker's prudent behavior would make corrective action unnecessary.

Lending to the banker's participated companies could be a borderline or clearly fraudulent practice. After all, it means using a bank's resources to benefit bankers. The probability of default might even be part of the banker's calculations when making the loan. A typical example is the failure of the Rumasa Group in Spain in 1983: over 60 percent of the lending capacity of the Group's twenty banks was concentrated in industrial and service companies belonging to the banks' holding company, and in the holding company itself.

Term mismatching. Another source of banking trouble is term mismatching, because of the *liquidity risk* involved. Term mismatching can result from a predetermined bank policy or from the freezing of originally sound short-term loans that become longer term because of default and rescheduling. Although term transformation is essential to banking, it should have limits. Mismatching is more likely to lead to liquidity problems caused by the *volatility of resources,* as opposed to the slower rotation of assets. Recent cases of serious illiquidity in Mexican and Argentine banks illustrate this (although illiquidity due to slower rotation of assets is often related to insolvency). In any case, even less dramatic illiquidity leads to an increase in the cost of resources needed for survival, and therefore reduces profits. When the interbank market and bank deregulation were introduced in Spain in 1977, some banks lacked the skills to handle terms and embarked on a growth policy based on the transformation of funds from that market—sometimes overnight funds—into disproportionately longer terms. Such policies led them to near illiquidity and to a rigorous adjustment to make the loan portfolio rotate and reduce the size of the banks.

Interest rate risk. While it causes fewer failures than loan losses, interest rate risk can seriously reduce profitability, which is becoming more worrisome. Interest rates can fluctuate sharply (particularly in times of deregulation), with remuneration on deposits increasing sharply overall, when most or all of the lending portfolio is based on fixed rates. The American savings and loan crisis in the 1980s, when loan portfolios were concentrated in fixed-term housing loans, is a clear example. Another risky situation arises when market interest rates fluctuate and banks holding sizable portfolios of government securities see their market value diminish significantly. Although interest rate risk has not often caused failures in Latin America, the crisis of the *ajustabonos* in Mexico in 1992 and 1993 is a good illustration of its impact.

Currency risk. One type of currency risk is the case of foreign currency lending, where the borrower may run out of the required currencies and default permanently or for a long time. Loans to developing countries by American and European banks in the 1980s are a case in point. Also, in times of devaluation, borrowers of foreign currency may find themselves unable to return the loan if their business does not produce foreign currency or if an extremely high exchange rate prevents them from exchanging domestic currency. Another type of risk exists when a bank borrows foreign currency and converts it into domestic currency, in order to lend at a much higher interest rate. This is profitable short term, but the exchange rate risk is serious: the borrower may repay in domestic currency, but if there is a devaluation, it will cost the bank much more in terms of domestic currency to repay its foreign currency borrowings. This was a common practice in Turkey in the mid 1980s.

Poor recovery. In developing countries, including those of Latin America, recovery rates are a widespread problem. When both borrowers and their banks have problems, they may reach a tacit agreement to avoid formal bankruptcy: nobody pays and nobody recovers. Poor recovery may also be closely related to connected lending and fraudulent practices, when connected lending is made on the banker's assumption that no recovery action will ever be taken. Additionally, the legislation and court practices on loan foreclosure and bankruptcy are obsolete in many countries, making recovery by legal channels lengthy and difficult. Is recovery poor in Latin America because bankruptcy laws are inadequate or because of lax management practices? Even without statistical evidence, it appears that lax management practices are more to blame, not only at the recovery stage, but particularly at the time of lending. Actually, as a result of poor lending policies, even the largest borrowers often have little repayment capacity, no matter how effective foreclosure or bankruptcy procedures might be. Moreover, recovery is sometimes complicated by tacit complicity between the borrower and the bank. A good example is the Chilean banking crisis of the mid 1980s, where despite an effective restructuring and recovery mechanism, loans were recovered at no more than 20 percent of their book value because of poor lending practices.

Poor Internal Controls

Poor internal controls have always been a cause of bank failures. Now that products such as derivatives require more sophisticated skills and technology, the absence of internal controls is even more serious. Here again, Barings is a typical example. Poor controls may exist in the areas of loan decisionmaking or follow-up systems; internal audit mechanisms; or management information systems, where information is not timely or sufficient for good analysis.

Poor Planning

Planning can help bankers adapt to changes in strategy, products, technology, or personnel. While planning does not always help corporations achieve their objectives, it can prevent them from going in the wrong direction. Lack of planning may lead to a slow decline and demise. Before that occurs, banks in decline are often acquired by new owners or merged with a stronger bank.

If regulation is good enough to set limits on the above practices, and if supervisory mechanisms are good enough to verify compliance with regulations and timely remedial action, such problems can be avoided or corrected at an early stage. Banking failures will be less frequent and deep if, under these assumptions, the necessary recapitalization takes place when the banks' equity capital is slightly eroded, and poor management is changed in all necessary areas. However, *regulations are not always effective, bankers do not always take remedial action, and supervision is not always perceptive or forceful enough.* As a result, problems increase, while bankers hide behind cosmetic practices.

Concealing Problems in Banks

Cosmetic practices are a way to hide problems from the public and the supervisor in order to buy time. Banks can hide problems through imaginative accounting in many ways. Bankers might even develop a special technique to systematically deceive the supervisor. The most typical technique is to *avoid provisions for bad loans and to recognize income when interest on a past due loan is refinanced* by the creditor bank.

In other words, when a loan—particularly a large loan—becomes questionable or bad because of the borrower's lack of repayment capacity, the bank rolls the loan over so it does not become past due. Alternatively, the borrower may be given a new loan to repay the previous loan. The rolled-over loan does not become past due in the books and the new loan is not in arrears, but the actual debt is. In both cases, the volume of rolled-over or new loans enables the bank to nominally repay interest accumulated until that moment. In reality, the money comes from paper operations, with no money movement. When questionable loans are converted into evergreens, they are almost never classified as doubtful or bad; they are classified as current. Supervisors should therefore focus their attention on the "good" loan portfolio rather than on the bad one.

Another typical way to avoid provisioning and to recognize income that has not been earned is to collaterize bad assets with poor quality collateral. Bad loans are sometimes be transferred to subsidiaries, either national or international, which finance them with fresh credit received from the original creditor bank.

These manipulations are based on an approach that can be called an *upside-down income statement.* Instead of reaching certain results in the income statement by adding income and subtracting expenditure, the banker in difficulty has a certain objective in mind. To that end, he manipulates the components of the income statement, particularly interest income and provisions, to reach the desired goal. The goal is achieved only on paper—not in reality.

Cosmetic practices aggravate banking problems, because the problems tend to get worse with the passage of time. Even if other losses are stemmed, refinancing the existing stock of losses increases those losses. Moreover, the lack of disclosure, to the public and even inside the bank, makes it more difficult to take adjustment measures that would appear to be unjustified. *Cosmetic accounting is, therefore, one of the roots of deeper banking crises.* Cosmetic accounting practices are universal, ranging from the Scandinavian countries, as shown during their recent financial crisis, to Latin America, to mention two very different regulatory environments.

While engaging in cosmetic practices, the banker in difficulty is often unwilling to solve problems with appropriate restructuring actions, and will probably *resort to high-risk policies and practices* in the hope of recovering by way of a lucky strike. In this way, the bank will further concentrate its lending on its worst borrowers, lend or speculate in high-risk areas, pay high interest rates to obtain liquidity, or even purchase its own shares on the market to prevent them from declining in price. These actions, which belong to a second, deeper stage of bank insolvency, are among the roots of dramatic financial crises. Each type of action is discussed below.

- When a bank further *concentrates its lending on the worst borrowers*, i.e., on larger borrowers with repayment problems, it rolls over those loans, refinances and capitalizes the interest on the loans, and, worse, extends further credit to those debtors. Otherwise, if the borrower defaults, it will become publicly known and so will the bank's difficulties. This is something many bankers try to avoid by any means. When this situation is widespread and affects a considerable number of banks, the implications for the economy are very serious, because concentrating loans on the largest bad borrowers crowds out financing to the better segments of the economy.

- The bank will also try to *speculate.* This may be done by lending to high-risk borrowers to obtain a high yield. But this yield will probably show up only on the contracts, not in terms of real interest payment. Because borrowers that accept very high interest rates are usually the ones that end up in default, high interest rates lead to a perverse selection process. Speculation may also mean financing or investment operations in the real estate or securities market, particularly in times of inflation, when the bank hopes to later disinvest either the borrower or the bank with a sizable capital gain. But things seldom happen like that: anti-inflationary policies bring about stagnation and a slump in those markets; and the bank, rather than recovering from past losses, will probably see its assets freeze and incur new losses. When American banks experienced serious portfolio problems in the 1980s because of real estate difficulties, they decided to shift to oil rigs, which also proved to be very risky.

- At this stage, the bank has serious liquidity problems and goes out for resources—deposits or interbank funds—at whatever cost. It might even need cash to pay for operational costs. When a bank pays *high interest rates on resources,* it hopes to maintain a good spread by passing these high rates on to the lending portfolio. The dangerous implications of such a policy were described above.

- Also at this stage, the market has probably perceived that the bank has some problems, and common shareholders sell their shares.

Sometimes some of the insiders, who are better informed about the bank's situation, also sell some of their stock. To avoid the price of shares dropping and feeding the process of deterioration, *the bank will purchase its own shares* in the market, directly or through subsidiaries or paper companies financed by the bank. In addition to distorting the market to the detriment of minority shareholders, the bank thereby incurs further losses and further erodes its own equity capital.

The end of the process will be *illiquidity,* which leads inefficient supervisors to discover that the bank has hidden its insolvency behind fake accounting. By this time, the insolvency has become much deeper and more costly to remedy. Except when there is systemic illiquidity derived from macro circumstances, lasting illiquidity in individual banks always means they are insolvent and have hidden it for a long period. In the mid 1980s, Argentina suffered a very serious banking crisis that affected mostly new banks and banks run by new bankers. Some two to three hundred banks experienced interventions and/or were liquidated. Practically all were insolvent, but intervention was triggered by illiquidity. Only through illiquidity was the insolvency discovered.

Finally, *fraudulent practices* are also at the root of banking crises. Cosmetic accounting, particularly in an industry based on public confidence, may constitute fraud. Other than that, the most common fraudulent practice is the banker's self-lending, which is extended in such a way that the loans are never repaid to the bank. Lending through paper companies and with no collaterization are the most common modalities. Receiving commissions for the bank's investment or disinvestment operations, or purchasing bank assets at a low price, are also common ways that a banker commits fraud.

Regulation and Supervision

Of these main micro roots of banking crisis, the most significant, according to international experience, are *bad lending practices, poor internal controls, cosmetic accounting, and fraud.*

Can these problems be limited by more stringent regulation and supervision, or should the emphasis be switched to market discipline? In other words, as an alternative to tougher controls, should regulation and supervision be loosened and banks be allowed to fail, to force them to apply sound policies and internal controls under market pressure? In the author's opinion, market discipline is important, but one should have no illusions about it. One reason is that for market discipline to operate, disclosure is very important. But disclosure, even in sophisticated countries, leaves much to be desired, and the unsophisticated majority of depositors and investors—even, at times, analysts or creditor banks—can hardly tell a good bank from a bad bank. Two examples are Continental Illinois Bank, in 1984, which was able to keep borrowing huge amounts of interbank money until the eve of failure; and Banesto, in Spain, where a well-known international investment bank designed and supported a huge but insufficient capital issue in 1993, based on the bank's good prospects, just a year before its failure. Another reason is that, with the exception of Barings, which was not a commercial bank, large banks are never closed by government, no matter what the implications for moral hazard. Moreover, in many countries, medium-sized and even small banks are not closed either. Therefore, the two key assumptions that would justify emphasizing market discipline and loosening government control, i.e., disclosure and bank closure, are questionable. Market discipline is always a good companion to bank supervision, but is a poor replacement for it.

In this regard, four other questions are worth considering:

- Do high minimum levels of capital adequacy create incentives for an adventurous search for off-balance sheet products involving higher risks? In the author's view, they do create incentives for product diversification, which is often risky because of lack of proper controls. But loosening controls is a departure from sound banking, not a natural implication of diversification.

- Do geographic limitations on the operations of individual banks lead to loan concentration in given economic segments, and to the disproportionate use of interbank funding to ensure asset growth? The answer to both questions is yes, but the problem hardly applies in Latin America.

- Does specialized banking—where commercial banks cannot operate in investment and other areas—lead to riskier lending? Not necessarily, as shown by the existence of many good banks in the context of the U.S. regulatory framework. In any case, Latin America's commercial banks can generally operate in noncommercial areas through universal banking status or through subsidiaries.

- Do deposit protection and bank restructuring mechanisms foster moral hazard and make failure more frequent? In the author's opinion, they are the lesser evil compared with what would happen if those mechanisms did not exist. This is discussed further below.

Prudential regulation is part of the overall concept of bank supervision. It is a necessary supplement to market deregulation and provides both bankers and supervisors with the *rules of the game* to achieve sound banking. If bankers follow the regulations, which are inspired by traditional banking orthodoxy, the supervisor will hardly have to step in. But if bankers depart from the rules of the game, the supervisor will have to impose remedial action for the good of both the financial system and the real sector. The most important laws and regulations are described below.

Proper rules for access to banking are essential for a sound banking system. New entrants can be founders of new banks or investors that buy control in an existing bank. Opening the door to new entrants is very important for sound competition. But in order to strengthen a banking system, regulators must apply stringent tests to applicants. The key tests are as follows:

- The initial capital of new banks—and of existing banks at the time they are acquired—should be high, to provide a good cushion for losses from the outset and ensure solvency.
- The origin of the capital to set up a new bank or acquire control of an existing bank should be clear and should not have any relationship with the bank itself.
- The new bankers should be fit and proper investors and/or professionals with a clean, competent record in previous business activities.
- The government should be satisfied with the new bankers' business plan, which should make contributing to the economy one of the bank's objectives.

When these rules for access to banking are not in place, the market becomes crowded with undesirable bankers who disrupt competition, tend to concentrate the banks' lending in the financing of their own businesses, and frequently end up failing. This was the case in Argentina in the early 1980s and is now the case in most Central and Eastern European countries, where fewer than 10 percent of the newly created banks are sound. The problem is that the failure of banks run by new bankers is not always addressed through proper exit measures, i.e., closure or rehabilitation with change of ownership and management. Instead, they remain in the market as "zombie banks," a serious source of many kinds of distortion. Therefore, if a country has a liberal entry policy, proper symmetry should be established with *tough exit policies*.

Some argue that criticism of liberal access policies is often used to keep out competition and protect the old monopolies, but the situation described above is a reality when policies are too liberal. Additionally, some argue that initial capital requirements should not be so high as to exclude many potential entrants, which could operate as small local banks and serve local interests. If banks have lower initial capital, however, their range of activities should be limited. For instance, they could be kept out of the payments system and their geographic spread could be limited until they increase their capital. Also, finance companies with no deposit-taking functions could have more liberal access rules. In any case, controls on the origin of capital and the fit and proper test for bankers should be strict.

In general, in times of systemic crisis, it is advisable to slow the entry of new bankers. Nevertheless, well-known foreign institutions are normally sound and should be given reasonably liberal treatment for entry purposes. They can prove very useful in solving individual banking crises by acquiring the problem institutions, provided they are properly recapitalized by the government.

All banks—commercial as well as development or universal banks, private as well as state-owned ones—should be subject to *uniform capital adequacy requirements.* Ensuring a given level of cushion for losses and competition on equal footing is very important. Most countries have adopted the Basle Committee standards, whereby all banks should have a minimum equity capital of 8 percent compared with their risk-weighed assets. The problem is that many countries, particularly in Latin America, do not have stringent rules on loan classification and provisions, or stringent supervision procedures to ensure compliance with those rules. As a result, many banks claim a capital adequacy of 8 percent or above while a high percentage of their assets are impaired and not recorded as such in their books. These banks might in reality be insolvent.

Good accounting systems should also be in place. Accounting is not a mere technicality. Rather, it is a procedure to properly show the condition of a business and identify problems so they can be promptly corrected. Good accounting rules also should apply to financial conglomerates, since problem banks tend to allocate their problems to their subsidiaries, particularly to foreign subsidiaries or off-shore operations, in order to hide them from the supervisor.

Good accounting systems should also include stringent rules for *proper asset classification and valuation,* whereby they are adjusted to their market value by way of adequate provisions for loan losses. This can be achieved by classifying assets according to their performance; i.e., if they are past due, they should be classified as different categories of bad loans, according to the length of time past due. Because it is easy for a bank to roll over former loans and/or extend new loans to avoid formal arrears and capitalize interest that is really refinancing, a good system requires two sets of criteria for loan classification: one based on formal default, which often does not capture the worst loans, and one based on the repayment capacity or riskiness of the borrower, whether formally in arrears or otherwise. Additionally, every category of classified loan should have a mandatory provision commensurate with the loan quality that applies to the whole of the outstanding balance of loans and to guarantees extended to the same borrower or group of borrowers. Of course, interest on doubtful loans should only be recognized on a cash basis, not if it is refinanced by the bank.

This paper has stated that *loan concentration and connected lending* are among the most frequent causes of bank failure. Good banking regulation should limit both practices. Limits on loan concentration should refer to the total volume of business, not just with every single borrower but with every group of borrowers, because borrowers in difficulty tend to develop groups through associates, relatives, or paper companies to circumvent the limits applied to them individually. These limits are normally set as a proportion of the bank's equity. Limits on connected lending may range from establishing a certain proportion of the bank's equity for loans to connected parties, to prohibiting connected lending altogether, as is the case in Colombia.

Effective recovery and bankruptcy procedures should also be part of a proper regulatory framework. In many countries, including most in Latin American, foreclosing on a loan to recover money lent is a cumbersome and lengthy procedure, because of both the procedural rules governing this action and the inefficiency of the courts.

The supervisor should have clear *enforcement powers* to take remedial action when the banker does not comply with the regulations or has serious difficulties. Corrective action is the primary responsibility of the banker, but the supervisor should have the authority to impose fines, remove and/or replace board members and managers, prohibit bankers from continuing to perform banking activities, cancel licenses, prohibit dividend payments, recapitalize, and initiate restructuring procedures.

Deposit insurance mechanisms to protect small depositors when a bank is closed are also advisable. Over a certain limit, however, depositors should be exposed to some risk.

There is an ongoing debate about whether deposit insurance is counterproductive for a sound banking system, to the extent that it may foster moral hazard and lead bankers to risky practices and depositors not to discriminate between good and bad banks. In the author's opinion, there may be moral hazard in depositors placing their money in banks offering high remuneration without fear of losing it because of deposit protection. As for the banker, deposit insurance will not prevent an insolvent bank from being closed and bankers from losing their money-making instrument and their social influence, or even from going to jail, if they engage in irregular practices. Therefore, the banker should be very careful, with or without deposit insurance. In any case, the absence of explicit deposit insurance leads to two alternative courses of action towards insolvent banks, both of which are worse than the protection of small depositors: (a) the insolvent banks are closed and all of the deposits are paid off; or (b) the insolvent banks are not addressed for fear of systemic implications, and remain in the market as marginal institutions.

In fact, the European Union has now established deposit insurance as a standard feature of the banking systems of all its member countries, and the health of those systems does not seem to have deteriorated as a result.

Some countries have *bank restructuring agencies* as an instrument to restructure insolvent banks through capital injections or by purchasing and liquidating bad assets. Such agencies are funded by the government (as in Mexico), international funds (Argentina), the banking sector (United States), or a combination of government and banking sector funds (Spain). In some countries (United States and Spain), these institutions are simultaneously deposit insurance agencies, and they receive funding for both deposit insurance and bank restructuring.

There is some debate about whether restructuring rather than closing insolvent banks fosters moral hazard and worsens the health of banking systems. In the author's opinion, if the insolvent banks are large or insolvency is widespread, the systemic dangers of closure will pose a serious risk. The two other alternatives are bank restructuring or taking no action. Bank restructuring might involve a certain element of moral hazard, but it is less dangerous than no action at all. In any case, the moral hazard might not be significant if financial restructuring is accompanied by a change of ownership and management.

Two examples can be mentioned. When the *Fondo de Garantía de Depósitos*, a deposit insurance and restructuring mechanism, was set up in Spain in 1980, the banking industry became much more disciplined than before, since bankers became aware that the government now had a strong instrument to expel bad bankers from the system. Before 1980, the government was much more hesitant to address insolvent banks because of the lack of institutional and financial mechanisms. Also, in the United States, in the mid 1980s, there was great pressure on the government not to take action on the savings and loan associations. The growing insolvency of these associations was not the result of deposit protection and restructuring schemes, but of the fact that they had remained idle for a long time for lack of funds and/or the political will to take remedial action.

Tools of Banking Supervision

Banking supervision is used to verify that regulations are followed and that the banking system is healthy. Supervision allows for proper information disclosure and early remedial action. Of course, the supervision of both compliance and quality is primarily the responsibility of each banker, through proper internal controls. But, in case bankers fail to fulfill this function properly, the supervisor's function is essential to identify and correct insolvency problems, and, if necessary, to set the legal grounds for action. The main elements of banking supervision are disclosure, off-site surveillance, inspection, and external auditing.

Disclosure

Proper disclosure by banks is essential for market discipline, for remedial action by the bank's managers, and for government control. Therefore, proper information should be disclosed to the public as well as to the supervisory authority. If there is no proper disclosure, depositors and investors will not be able to tell a good bank from a bad bank and improve market discipline, managers will not have adequate justification for stringent remedial action, and governments will not be able to detect problems until illiquidity has appeared.

The most common location of the supervisory function is the central bank or a special superintendency independent from the central bank. When located within the central bank, supervision may have priorities other than monetary problems, but it will still ensure better oversight of those problems. Location of the supervisory function within a superintendency ensures independence and proper prioritization, but could pose coordination problems. International experience does not show clearly which is better; it might vary from country to country. In either case, supervision should be high enough in the government structure to ensure proper coordination with monetary policy. Supervisors should be paid well enough to be independent, and the supervisory institution should have mechanisms to deal with insolvent banks.

Surveillance

Off-site surveillance by the government is based on analysis of information received from banks. Reporting requirements should therefore be uniform for all banks. They should allow for an overall computerized analysis of the growth of each bank, of the banking system as a whole, and of peer groups of financial institutions. Such analyses would lead to the establishment of warning systems, which could be supplemented with discussions with bankers and external auditors. As a result of off-site surveillance, banks can be rated according to indicators in key areas such as capital assets, management, earnings, and liquidity. These ratings would feed back to the inspection and enforcement areas of supervision for the necessary action.

In many contexts, including in Latin American countries, *on-site supervision, i.e., inspection, is essential* because of the lack of reliability of the banks' own reports on returns when they are in trouble. Inspection should focus on quality rather than compliance. Of course, these problems can be interrelated, but early action on problems of quality proves much more effective than administrative action on compliance. Actually, early detection of quality problems allows for gradual and less expensive remedies, and also for establishing grounds for legal action when necessary.

Inspection should cover many areas, but should pay particular attention to the *loan portfolio*, which should be examined through direct access to files containing borrowers' financial statements and the record of their relationship with the bank. *Inspection is the key instrument* for discovering bad management practices, capital erosion, and decreasing profitability—particularly if the regulatory framework includes proper rules for loan classification, provisioning for loan losses, and income recognition. When the Spanish banking crisis of the late 1970s and early 1980s began, there were no such rules, and central bank inspectors lacked the skills to examine loan portfolios. As a result, insolvent banks were identified only when they became illiquid. During the crisis, proper regulations were put in place and inspectors learned how to evaluate the quality of loan portfolios. As a result, the last banking failures in the crisis and those isolated cases that occurred more recently—including Banesto— were identified before illiquidity appeared. After the regulations were adopted, many other banks did not reach failure because capital erosion was identified at an earlier stage and remedied through ordinary corrective action imposed by the supervisor.

There is a practical way to discover evergreen practices, the main technique used by bankers to conceal insolvency. A loan should be classified as doubtful or bad whenever the repayment capacity of the borrower is weak, even if the loan is not in arrears. The following are signs of weak repayment capacity:

- The financial statements of the borrower show negative net worth and/or negative cashflow.
- The loan has a history of consecutive rollovers, and the volume of each new loan is equal to or above the principal plus interest of the previous loan.
- The principal or interest of previous loans is not paid in cash, but through refinancing facilities extended by the same creditor bank.

In any of these cases, the loan should be classified as doubtful or bad, provisions should be imposed on the bank up to the amount of the expected default, interest recognition should be discontinued, and, most important, the bank should not be allowed to extend new facilities to those borrowers.

External audits are extremely useful for supplementing bank supervision. Such audits were originally a control instrument for use by shareholders and the market. But their annual periodicity and the existing constraints on a number of supervisory institutions are gradually leading to close coordination between auditors and supervisors. Annual external audits should be mandatory. Supervisors should also order targeted audits of specific areas. Also, the legislation should authorize the auditors to coordinate their work with the supervisors and make it mandatory for them to promptly inform the supervisors whenever they identify serious problems in a bank or when proper information is not supplied to them by the bank's management. An essential part of the auditors' work should be the direct examination of the loan portfolio. If the government is not able to perform simultaneous annual inspections of the most significant banks or is not satisfied with the quality of the external audits, external auditors could be used—and paid—by the supervisory authority, as if they were government inspectors, to establish a proper diagnosis of a banking system.

The following key instruments of bank regulation and supervision can prevent or remedy banking crises:

- stringent entry rules and inspection;
- rules on capital adequacy combined with rules on loan classification, provisioning, and income recognition, based on the repayment capacity of the borrower;
- limits to loan concentration and connected lending; and
- strong enforcement powers for the supervisory authority, including exit and the triggering of bank restructuring mechanisms.

In Latin American countries, as in many others, banking regulation and supervision generally have positive results. If regulation and supervision contain the elements described here, most of the causes of failure derived from management would be either prevented, limited, or remedied at an early stage, and at lower cost to both the government and the banking system. Needless to say, regulation and supervision do not work miracles; there will always be some banking failures. After all, even good laws and good police do not eliminate crime. What matters is that crime diminishes and that the criminals are not always the same.

Aristóbulo de Juan is President of Aristóbulo de Juan y Asociados in Spain.

Commentary to Part III

David Folkerts-Landau

The paper by Aristóbulo de Juan reflects his long experience, first as head of Inspection Services during the Spanish banking crisis in the 1980s, and later as a consultant on bank restructuring to the World Bank and other institutions. In my comment I will draw on experience gained from our financial sector surveillance activities at the International Monetary Fund, to discuss four recurring themes in the paper.

First, there are many theories of banking and bank failures—adverse selection among borrowers, asymmetric information, rational bank runs, and managerial incentive incompatibility, to name a few—as well as the impact of macroeconomic disturbance. Most of these theories add something to our understanding of banks and bank failures, but the explanation of why banking crises occur with such regularity is probably to be found elsewhere.

The banking industry is unlike other industries—for example, the steel industry—for several reasons. The main one is that banks are subject to intense moral hazard. They invest other people's money, not as agents, but as principals. When the returns are good, they prosper. But when the recovery value of their loan portfolio makes them insolvent, they can usually count on getting bailed out. Another reason is the subjective nature of credit risk assessment, which means that banks have many opportunities to lend to friendly parties, that they can acquiesce in government pressure to lend to particular enterprises, and that they can enter into high-risk gambles—double-or-nothing plays—all to improve the characteristics of their own payoff matrix. They can do all of this because in most countries the accounting, regulatory, supervisory, and legal infrastructure is neither sufficiently well defined nor sufficiently forceful in its implementation to detect and stop these practices early on. Still another reason is that financial markets do not punish banks. Implicit guarantees and the absence of reliable information on the quality of their portfolios tend to muddy the waters. Depositors fail to demand risk premia, as do investors in bank commercial paper.

Bankers are not bad people; they are not the used car salesmen of finance. Nevertheless, they can be expected to react rationally to the incentives they face. For example, suppose the fifty-five-year-old chief executive of a large bank in a prominent Latin American country chooses to expand his bank's loan portfolio aggressively during a period of strong asset price appreciation. If the asset price boom is sustained long enough, he profits handsomely. If instead the bubble bursts, he retires with his full pension and a golden handshake and moves on to greener pastures. Hence, overlending to real estate and stock market speculation need not always be an insider's game; it might merely reflect managerial gambles, or what the author of the paper calls bad management. In contrast, it takes much longer to run a steel firm into the ground: there is much less scope for gambling, investment decisions or labor policies that result in deteriorating performance cannot be hidden and are more quickly and accurately reflected in market prices, and exit from the industry is less traumatic. Not so with banks: bad loans can lie dormant through the better part of a business cycle, and even then the capitalization of interest can hide the deterioration of balance sheets for a long time.

The second theme in the paper is that many banking crises are preventable. The available evidence clearly indicates that it is possible to design and implement an accounting, regulatory, supervisory, and legal infrastructure that can prevent most—although not all—banking crises. An example is Hong Kong, where throughout much of the 1980s the banking system was riddled with unsound practices such as lending to interconnected entities, lending in excess of large-exposure rules, and leveraged lending for speculative purposes. A determined effort over the past eight years has created an effective, clean system. And there are other examples. Indeed, the lack of an effective supervisory and regulatory infrastructure, with credible enforcement, has been the chief cause of banking crises during the past fifteen years, not some information-theoretic feature peculiar to the banking system.

What are the most basic ingredients of an effective supervisory and regulatory infrastructure? In our work on capital markets surveillance at the IMF we apply the following rules:

- *Licensing requirements* should make it difficult, but not impossible, to enter the industry.
- *Capital requirements* should be well above the requirements set by the Bank for International Settlements. In emerging market economies, subject as they are to the vagaries of international capital markets, the ratios should probably be closer to double that number.
- Explicit and tightly written *large-exposure rules* should be accompanied by a central credit registry to establish the total exposure of borrowers.
- There should be frequent *on-site inspection* to verify compliance.

• Tough *loan classification procedures and provisioning rules*, combined with early corrective actions (interest more than sixty days overdue should be reserved against dollar for dollar), are essential: banking crises start on the asset side, not on the deposit side.

These are all the rules that a country needs to avoid most banking crises. Yet we all know that rules alone are not sufficient. The proof of the pudding is in the implementation. And that leads to my discussion of the paper's third major theme. It is in the area of implementation that the failures of banking supervision and regulation have been most glaring. Very few developing countries are prepared to implement bank regulation and practice bank supervision free of political pressure. Indeed, few *industrial* countries let supervisors perform their tasks free from political pressure. It has proved difficult for governments to resist directing credit, and even harder for governments to act resolutely to resolve banking crises, which means closing institutions and allocating losses. This is important, because some banking crises cannot be avoided. Banks hold asset and liability contracts that are fixed in nominal value. Hence a sudden depreciation in asset values will invariably trigger a crisis. Similarly, instances of individual bank failure—Continental Illinois in the 1970s, Barings more recently—cannot be avoided. However, in these cases a quick, nonpolitical resolution will limit the damage.

The fourth and final theme is that banking crises and their resolution are political events; therefore the establishment of a sound and efficient banking system is not just a technical economic or financial problem but a political problem. The political challenge is to establish a credible independent supervisor with regulatory powers, cease-and-desist powers, on-site inspection ability, licensing powers, and the ability to remove managers who are not fit and proper. Such powers are best located inside an independent central bank. A good deal of supervisory intervention is in the nature of moral suasion, and this works better when the disciplining powers of the central bank provide the muscle.

Inefficient financial systems and banking crises are too costly to be dealt with in a politically expedient manner. During the past fifteen years we have traveled a long way toward the consensus that the primary objective of monetary policy should be price stability, unfettered by political considerations. To create supervisory and regulatory policies free of political pressures is just as worthy a goal.

David Folkerts-Landau is Chief of the Capital Markets and Financial Studies Division, International Monetary Fund.

Carlos Santistevan

Aristóbulo de Juan's paper provides a comprehensive review of the main microeconomic factors that, by themselves or in combination with macroeconomic problems, can lead to systemic banking problems and crises. He advocates more rather than less supervision and regulation. Of the many issues that his paper covers, this comment will discuss primarily the regulation and supervision of banks and the managerial factors that can lead to failures or crises.

On banking supervision and regulation, I have three points. First, I belong to the traditional school of banking that believes that governments give banks a franchise to perform a public service. Banks are entrusted with clients' funds, which they manage not as agents but as principals. Those clients come from different kinds of businesses and social strata and differ in their sophistication and economic power. Their capacity to assess information and to determine the solidity and soundness of banks varies accordingly. At the same time, banking plays an important role in supporting and facilitating economic growth, and its stability is an important factor in the stability of an economy. For these reasons, I believe that banks should be regulated and supervised.

Second, by regulation I do not mean financial repression, but rather the need to regulate banks in a liberalized financial environment. In my experience, in order to prevent banking crises to the extent possible, be they individual or systemic, it is imperative that certain parameters be established within which banks can operate and that serve as benchmarks for supervision. Regulation should focus on capital, ownership, quality of management, and business plans.

Capital is the expression of shareholders' commitment to a bank, and a bank's maintenance of a certain capital ratio is the way in which it controls undue expansion and exercises discipline in selecting its level of risk. If shareholders want a bank to take in more risky business, they have to put in more capital—assuming, of course, that the bank is already at the optimum capital ratio that is appropriate for it. In this regard, the capital ratios set by the Bank for International Settlements are conceptually the right ones for banks in the industrial world. Ratios of the BIS type are also appropriate for Latin America because they give different weights to different risks, but the levels for Latin American banks probably should be higher, to include some risks that are not now included.

Ownership—the quality of shareholders—is another important criterion for banking regulation. Who should be a bank shareholder? Who should be allowed to open a bank, or to buy an existing bank? In Europe, the supervisors decide who is qualified to be a bank shareholder. This is a very good practice and is suitable for Latin America. Before they will declare a potential shareholder fit and proper, the supervisors must be satisfied that the would-be shareholder not only is solvent for the amount of money that will be invested, but also has a good reputation and a good track record. Since bankers are entrusted with clients' funds, authorities should be assured to the extent possible that shareholders deserve that trust.

Quality of management is also very important. As Enrique Iglesias has pointed out, bankers need to be not only professionally competent, but also ethically fit. One can never be completely sure, but checking the business record and reputation of potential shareholders should help minimize the number of banks owned and managed by people who do not meet ethical standards. To this end, authorities must always know the identities of a bank's shareholders, and it is therefore very important to have tough exit rules. In the case of bank holding companies, the authorities must know the identities of the ultimate owners and ensure that these owners can divest their holdings only after the authorities have approved. If banks are owned by banks in other countries, it should be clear who will be ultimately responsible for supervision—the supervisory authority in the home country of the parent bank, or the authority in the host country.

Adequate business plans are also essential. It is not enough to set a required minimum amount of capital and conditions to ensure adequate ownership. The authorities must also be satisfied, at the time the bank is licensed and throughout its subsequent development and operation, that banks have plans to ensure adequate diversification of funding, lending portfolios, and sources of income. Such plans are also necessary to ensure that banks understand the risks involved in off-balance-sheet transactions. Authorities also need to be assured that there is an adequate balance between lending and trading—in other words, between income from interest payments and income from fees.

My third point is that supervision should ensure that banks function within the established parameters. To do this, supervisors have to go beyond ensuring simple compliance; they also need to emphasize the quality of banking activities. Supervision should involve in situ inspections that not only verify the accuracy of returns and other information submitted by banks, but also assess management quality and practices. Only through the latter will supervisors be able to determine whether the quality of assets is represented accurately. The assessment should test whether the bank's management knows its clients and periodically evaluates and records their repayment capabilities; whether it is rigorous in classifying loans; and whether it has established adequate loan loss provisions. The role of internal auditors in this regard can be very important; auditors can help supervisors to more effectively judge a bank's management capabilities and quality of assets.

Effective supervision also involves imposing remedial actions. Authorities should have the power to require that banks increase their loan loss provisions for loans of deteriorating quality, and should be in a position to require additional capital from shareholders when needed.

If remedial actions do not work, the authorities should act promptly to resolve the problems they discover—whether through intervention, closing, or merger—at the lowest possible fiscal cost. The cost of resolving banking crises should fall on shareholders and management, because government bailouts will only encourage other banks to take undue risks. Deposit insurance should exist for small shareholders and should be limited in amount; if handled in this manner, it should not provide an incentive for undue risk taking.

Whether depositors should have an implicit government guarantee is a political issue, particularly in the case of banks considered too big to fail. There may be some cases where banks are saved by governments, but in those cases, shareholders and management should lose their stakes and small depositors should be protected.

In summary, regulation should establish a framework for bank operations that is consistent with the banks' role of using client funds. Supervision should be prudent and judgmental and should be aimed at preventing problems. To do that, it should not only focus on compliance but also judge the quality of assets and of management, as well as the capacity of banks to deal with risks to which banks are routinely exposed. Finally, supervisors should have the tools to implement corrective measures and the political independence necessary to act.

If regulation and supervision are conducted properly, the risk of banking problems, particularly those resulting from microeconomic causes, can be significantly reduced. In the debate over whether to rely more on supervision or on market discipline, I favor adequate supervision to protect depositors—and protect the system—because not all interested parties can exercise effective market discipline. Unless parties are in close contact, are equally sophisticated, and have equal access to information, it is unlikely that they will be able to determine the quality of assets or the full extent of risk that a bank has incurred, let alone decide when and how to get out of a troubled bank. Nor do the markets have sufficient or transparent enough information to learn about bank problems early enough to exercise the necessary discipline.

Another important microeconomic issue that relates to possible bank failure is the quality of the loan portfolio. Solvency problems are more likely to come from the asset side. Banks have to pay interest on the deposits they take in, as well as eventually return the principal. Funds for these payments have to come from the servicing and repayment of loans. It is therefore crucial that banks have a performing portfolio; otherwise they will become illiquid.

Performance, in my opinion, is affected by loan concentration, which has several dimensions. Some banks concentrate their lending in related companies. If I were a supervisor, I would look very carefully at such practices, because several banks in Latin America and elsewhere have failed because of such lending. The problem with making loans to related companies is that it compromises the judgment of professional bankers, whose lending decisions may then be based not on the best interests of the bank, but on the interests of the economic group of which the bank is a part.

If a bank is concentrated in loans to related companies, then loans that never mature but are perpetually renewed and rolled over—so-called evergreens—are going to appear sooner or later. There will be a tendency to continue lending to make these loans appear current, in order to avoid the decisions necessary for requiring interest payment or for reclassifying the loans according to the borrower's capacity to pay. Of course, evergreens also exist in banks that do not make loans to related companies, but related companies are an additional incentive for bankers to roll over bad loans.

Loan concentration also occurs by type of industry or economic activity, as well as by geographical location or maturity. Here, too, concentration can have a direct impact on the soundness of a bank, because it can lead to illiquidity and losses if macroeconomic or other disturbances affect the industries or countries in question. They can also lead to interest rate mismatches if the loans are concentrated in terms of maturity.

Concentration of the loan portfolio is not the only problem; concentration of funding sources can also make a bank vulnerable. Banks should try to manage their liabilities to avoid concentration in either volatile funding or expensive liabilities. As already noted, however, most banking crises originate with problems in the loan portfolio, and concentration is one of the issues that creates vulnerability. Therefore, banking supervision should focus on assessing the true value and condition of loan portfolios.

Carlos Santistevan is Senior Deputy Finance Manager and Treasurer, Inter-American Development Bank.

Angel Rojo

Bank supervision and the management of banking crises are complex, multifaceted, and constantly changing issues. Bank examiners are inevitably greatly influenced by their own experience within a particular system and tend to make unwarranted generalizations based on that experience. However, apart from the special case of a bank's sudden collapse due to reckless trading in derivatives, one can identify several premises that are generally true of all well-designed regulatory and supervisory systems.

The first is that problems in a banking system take a long time to evolve and even longer to detect. Second, once a problem has been detected, bankers often resist recognizing it as serious. Third, restoring a bank to health is a lengthy process as well. Fourth, when problems do arise in one or more banks, prevailing economic conditions and a lack of confidence on the part of the public and markets can bring matters quickly to a head, depriving bank supervisors of the time needed to avoid a system-threatening collapse.

Thus particular kinds of systems, instruments, and mechanisms are needed to avoid bank crises, or to prevent crises that have occurred from spreading to other banks. This raises the question of the objectives and limitations of supervisory systems. On one extreme are those who regard banking, in theory at least, as no different from any other economic activity and therefore requiring no special oversight. A bank that is foundering should be allowed to fail, just as would any other business elsewhere in the economy.

At the other extreme, basing their arguments less on theory, are those who believe in security at all costs. Their justifications for intervention run the gamut, from protecting small shareholders and depositors to preventing the potentially disastrous repercussions of a single bank's failure on the financial system and the economy. They argue that bank portfolios should be maintained at very low levels of risk, even if that means foregoing in large measure the services we expect from a bank today. They also advocate a strict supervisory authority, prepared to intervene whenever necessary.

Differences in actual banking supervision among countries are much more nuanced. Such differences do exist, but countries generally seek a balance between the safeguards that supervision can provide and the costs that it entails. These two issues—benefits and costs—can be treated separately.

The final rationale for bank supervision is to reduce the vulnerability of credit institutions to that ultimate depositor defense mechanism, the run on the bank. When depositors begin to make massive withdrawals from a bank whose solvency has come into question, their lack of confidence can quickly spread to other banks, jeopardizing the system as a whole. Other factors enter into play besides the volatility of bank deposits. First, the fact that banks engage in term conversion—playing the yield curve by paying low interest rates on short-term deposits while charging higher rates on their longer-term loans—subjects them to liquidity threats. A second factor is the interdependence of banks through their participation in interbank markets. A third is that banks perform vital auxiliary functions for the rest of the economy, particularly in connection with the payments system. From these considerations it is easy to understand supervisors' interest in keeping banks solvent and preventing any individual failure from spreading into a systemwide crisis.

The costs of supervision are less widely advertised. First, supervision carries costs for the government, which it may or may not pass on to the institutions supervised. Second, supervision imposes a cost on those same institutions in the form of minimum capital requirements and funding ratios, the obligation to provide information to the supervisors, and so on. Of course, bank managers would voluntarily incur some of these costs in any case, but the information and degree of leverage that bank managers would seek on their own may not coincide with those that the supervisors prefer. A third potential cost is that of excess supervision stifling individual initiative, imperiling the entire system by making it less efficient and eroding internal and external competitiveness. These potential social costs are not easily quantifiable, but they can outweigh the other, more obvious costs.

The optimum level of supervision can be determined only after considering both the objectives to be pursued and the costs to be incurred. Although it is not easy to demonstrate empirically, it appears that beyond a certain point, even modest additions to supervisory objectives can bring about an exponential growth in costs and can lead to a qualitative change in the supervisor's responsibility.

Moreover, in determining the optimum level of supervision, the strictly economic considerations just enumerated are not the only ones to be taken into account. Beyond internal and external cost constraints, one must consider the limitations placed on supervision, under whatever rule of law, by the legal philosophy governing the sector and the system as a whole. The supervisory authority cannot and must not interfere with the jurisdiction of each institution, as determined by the law and by reason. Nor should it wish to: the supervisory authority should endeavor to divest itself of those duties that it can discharge only poorly and at great cost. In short, the aim of supervision—to safeguard the stability of the financial system—should be seen not in absolute terms but rather as an effort to seek a delicate balance that avoids economic imperfections and respects the existing legal framework.

Such a balance entails a limited supervisory mandate that does not extend to preventing crises in inefficient or poorly managed institutions. Isolated crises should be allowed to occur—they are the price of ensuring that supervision does not suppress the efficient operation of the financial system. The optimal level of supervision thus does not preclude an occasional crisis, but supervision must, when such a crisis occurs, prevent it from spreading through the system. Recent developments in financial markets have heightened the risk of such contagion, with potentially serious repercussions for the payments system and the economy as a whole. To eliminate that risk, a safety net must be provided in the form of deposit guarantee funds. In Spain, to prevent contagion at minimum cost, these guarantee funds are free to choose the lowest-cost solution to bank problems, whether that be restoring the bank to health through restructuring, or liquidating it and paying off the insured depositors.

If it is agreed that bank supervision should be subject to limitations imposed by the legal framework and should be justifiable by a social cost-benefit analysis, we may still wonder whether there is room to improve bank regulation and supervision so that it can check the downward path of a distressed bank before it is too late. To be sure, the regulatory system must employ a set of financial coefficients and ratios to determine solvency, asset concentration, and the like, based on proven prudential criteria. Risk concentration coefficients are very important, especially in countries whose banking systems are closely intertwined with major industrial interests that can sustain serious damage in recessions. Solvency ratios are also quite important, but they provide insufficient information when management is poor, and they can deteriorate rapidly when difficulties arise. The answer is not, however, to stiffen requirements to create a margin of safety against poor management by a few institutions. To do so would jeopardize the competitiveness of the better managed banks in what is an increasingly open global financial environment.

Monitoring institutions through the use of coefficients and ratios is important, but it is not enough in itself. To quickly detect and intervene in cases of poor management—the key to managing banking crises—frequent on-site inspections, although costly, are indispensable. One cannot perform such inspections of every institution every year; the cost would be prohibitive. But annual inspections are essential for those institutions that, by virtue of their size or other characteristics, could place the whole system in jeopardy if they should fail.

The chief problem in dealing with cases of poor management is how to get rid of the managers. Spanish law allows the supervisory authority to intervene in or temporarily take over the management of an institution only in extreme cases. That is as it should be, because excessive official discretion is bad for both the examiners and the examined. In the end, the task of monitoring management and removing it when warranted properly belongs to the bank itself—that is, to its directors and shareholders. To ensure that such monitoring occurs and is done properly, decisionmakers must have the requisite information, generated by strong internal controls. The supervisor should also periodically report to the board of directors on observations, new requirements, and other information. Boards must be aware that they have an inescapable responsibility to monitor and oversee the bank's management, and that to do so requires adequate information. On the other hand, to ensure that monitoring works properly, excessive safeguards must be avoided.

In short, optimum supervision must remain within limits dictated by the principle that the benefits of supervision should outweigh the costs. Limited supervision of this kind is not incompatible with the occasional isolated bank failure—this makes for a healthy system—but it does call for reliable safety nets to minimize the risk of contagion. Monitoring of compliance through a set of prudential coefficients is important, but monitoring must be accompanied by close scrutiny in the form of frequent on-site inspections. Finally, since poor management is generally the principal cause of bank crises, the top decisionmakers in each bank must be clearly held responsible for ensuring that the necessary internal controls are in place. They must also have sufficient information to oversee the actions of managers and to replace them, if need be, while there is still time to salvage the situation.

Angel Rojo is Governor of the Bank of Spain.

Fernando de Santibañez

The paper by Aristóbulo de Juan offers an excellent analysis of the factors that lead to problems within a bank, and recommends ways to detect such problems and reduce their potential damage to the economy, through effective regulation and supervision. He provides a clear justification for banking supervision in the context of a market economy.

The paper also offers guidance on how to respond to banking crises, how to supervise banks, and how to design and regulate a financial system—all of which involve very different approaches than in any other industry. Banking is unique because bank failures have great potential to spill over into the rest of the financial system and thus to affect the economy as a whole.

At least two factors make the banking industry different from other industries, both of which are significant in time of crisis. The first is the callable nature of a major part of banks' liabilities (i.e., their deposits). The second is the difficulty that depositors have in evaluating the soundness of individual banks and the banking industry.

One of the principal products of any bank is confidence. Confidence, or reputation, is an abstract, nontangible good, which is related to information about the bank's financial situation. Customers cannot evaluate this information as easily as they can information about, say, the quality of a car. Because of the complexities involved in evaluating banks, there is a need for efficient regulation and supervision as well as for schemes to protect small depositors, for whom even processing the necessary information is too costly.

At least two types of shocks to the system can give rise to a banking crisis. In the first type, problems in one or more institutions, due to deficient management, are identified late by the supervising agency. This mechanism is perfectly analyzed in Mr. de Juan's paper. I would add only that the legal system within which the agency is embedded must leave it enough discretion to perform efficiently.

The second type of shock originates with problems arising from capital flows due to adverse macroeconomic situations. Not all banks will be affected in the same way by such an external shock, but after an initial period an external shock can be transmitted to an increasing number of banks. Whether this happens depends on two variables: the structure of the bank's liabilities, and the structure and quality of its assets.

For example, in Argentina during the most recent crisis, the weakest entities were those that had liabilities concentrated in a few investors and also had significant mismatching of maturities of their assets and liabilities. This can pose a particularly difficult problem when the financial system does not include a lender of last resort that can rediscount the assets. Furthermore, supervision can be less effective in preventing a crisis generated by an external shock than one caused by an internal problem. Whether the crisis is generated by an external or an internal shock, a country's legal institutions can affect both the performance of the supervisory authority and efforts to reform the financial system.

Another remarkable feature of the most recent crisis in Argentina was the presence of nondeclared offshore operations, which the supervising authorities failed to detect. Many of these operations held more assets than did the parent institution, and the revelation of this fact caused investors to have doubts about other institutions in the system. This underlines the importance of the supervising agency punishing such behavior, which produces negative externalities throughout the banking system.

What are the best mechanisms for limiting the effects of an initial shock on the rest of the economy? The answer will depend on perceptions about the strength of the financial system, which in turn will depend on its history. The weaker countries or systems will be those that have disappointed their investors in the past, while safer systems will be those that have been better supervised.

Systems that offer more reliable information will also be less vulnerable to shocks. Information is important, but because it is not costless, it is not available to everybody. Therefore depositor protection schemes are necessary.

To keep the initial shock from spreading, access to sources of funding to rediscount assets is essential, especially in emerging market economies where capital markets are still limited in size. Otherwise, banks will face falling prices and further losses as they try to sell their liquid assets, thus feeding fears and producing a capital outflow.

In addition to the microeconomic issues of supervision and regulation, banking systems everywhere are affected by the problems arising from globalization of markets and the increasing volume of international capital flows. In countries such as those in Latin America, where positive structural reforms are in progress, these developments make the tasks confronting bankers increasingly risky—and more challenging.

Fernando de Santibañes is Chairman of the Board of Banco de Crédito Argentino.

Part IV

The Do's and Don'ts of Banking Crisis Management

Liliana Rojas-Suárez and Steven R. Weisbrod

Commentary

Roque Fernández
E. Gerald Corrigan
Stefan Ingves

The Do's and Don'ts
of Banking Crisis Management

Liliana Rojas-Suárez and Steven R. Weisbrod

> "What were the real reasons for doing the ...
> bailouts? Simply put, we were afraid not to."
> *Irvine H. Sprague, former manager of FDIC*

Rescuing a banking system suffering from widespread bank failures surely ranks high among regulators' worst nightmares. At the outset, policymakers face uncertainties as to the magnitude of the problem and the resources available to cope with it. In addition, regulators often do not have a firm grasp of the tools at their disposal to deal with failures, such as markets to sell insolvent banks. These uncertainties are magnified for policymakers in developing countries. First, accounting and legal standards are less exacting, making it difficult to assess the scale of banking problems. Second, both resources and tools for dealing with banking crises in developing countries are much more limited than in industrial countries.

    This paper focuses on the design of successful bank restructuring programs in Latin America—a region where banking crises have been frequent in the past two decades. In each episode, Latin American policymakers operated under the severe constraints imposed on developing countries, which become particularly binding during periods of financial problems. Nevertheless, a review of these experiences demonstrates that a well-conceived bank restructuring program can succeed under even the most adverse conditions.

The paper is organized as follows. The following section establishes a framework for carrying out a successful restructuring program, which includes defining objectives and the principles for executing these objectives. Regulators face differing constraints in industrial and developing countries, which affect the application of principles to achieve a successful restructuring program. The next section uses the framework to evaluate two bank restructuring efforts in Latin America in the early and mid 1980s that had very different outcomes—Argentina, which emerged from its crisis with a much weakened banking system, and Chile, which used its restructuring program to strengthen its banking system. The kinds of constraints faced by regulators, and their willingness to adhere to basic principles of effective crisis management, explain the sharply contrasting outcomes. We then consider the management of the current banking crises in Argentina and Mexico, based on the framework as well as the lessons of the 1980s. Finally, we present concluding remarks.

Principles and Constraints in Managing Banking Crises

When a large portion of a country's banking system is threatened with insolvency, funds set aside to resolve isolated bank failures, such as deposit insurance funds and emergency central bank credit, are usually inadequate for the task. Thus, in systemic crises, if the integrity of the banking system is to be maintained, public funds must often be used to resolve bank failures. Particular reasons for using public money to rescue banks vary across countries; in many but by no means all countries, the purpose is to shield small depositors from the consequences of bank failure. However, since the Great Depression in the United States, there has been almost universal agreement that, because banks play a crucial role in the payments system, public funds must be used to resolve individual bank problems to ensure that a banking system survives the crisis.

Whether or not the regulatory system has an explicit deposit insurance program, maintaining the integrity of the banking system inevitably requires protecting some bank liability holders from the consequences of bank failure. Hence, the commitment of public funds for restructuring implies a transfer of resources from the public sector to the banking system. The objective of public policy is to ensure that the transfer is limited to those parties who must be protected from bankruptcy to preserve the integrity of the banking system.

Three Basic Principles

To execute a bank restructuring program that fulfills the above objectives, policymakers must follow three basic principles. *Principle one is to ensure that parties that have benefited from risktaking bear a large portion of the cost of restructuring the banking system.* For example, bank stockholders should be first to lose their investment, along with large holders of long-term liabilities such as subordinated debt.[1] Also, delinquent borrowers must not be given favorable treatment at public expense. By forcing private parties to bear part of the loss, this not only limits current restructuring costs but it also creates incentives to restrain risktaking in the future, which strengthens the banking system in the long term.

Principle two is that prompt action should be taken *to prevent problem institutions from expanding credit to high-risk borrowers or from capitalizing unpaid interest on delinquent loans into new credit.* Such action reduces the moral hazard risk that arises when institutions with low and declining net worth continue to operate under the protection of public policies designed to maintain the integrity of the banking system. This principle implies that when possible, insolvent institutions should be removed from the hands of current owners, through either closure or sale.

Because executing the first two principles requires adequate funding to pay off some liability holders of institutions with negative net worth, the third principle for successful restructuring is that a society muster the political will *to make bank restructuring a priority in allocating public funds, while avoiding sharp increases in inflation.*

To execute a successful rescue program, policymakers must faithfully adhere to all three principles. However, the ability of regulators to carry out these principles is affected by the economic environment in which they must operate. Even if a society has mustered the will to fund a bank rescue, it may face a severe resource constraint; for example, an economy may not be able to access debt markets for funds. In this case, to finance bank restructuring, it may be necessary to reduce fiscal expenditures in other areas to avoid inflation. As the funding constraint becomes tighter, the task of assigning priorities is more difficult.

A second constraint affecting implementation of the principles is the availability of markets for financial institutions or for their assets. Such markets can be useful for minimizing public expenditure because

---

[1] Some large liability holders of money market instruments must inevitably be subsidized to some extent, because the money markets must continue to function to support the payments mechanism.

they permit private investors to recognize the franchise value of a failed bank's customer base and its distribution system. Revenues from the sale of these valuable assets can offset public absorption of credit losses.

If markets are large and funding is relatively abundant, regulators can choose from a wide variety of methods to resolve banking problems. Their choices fall into three broad categories: private sector merger or sale; takeover and management by the regulatory authorities; and, as a last resort, bailout of an existing institution, with ownership left largely in place.

• Under the first option, irrecoverable loans are charged off,[2] which may require a write-down of bank capital if loan loss reserves are inadequate, often to the point where the value of liabilities exceeds the value of assets. When the institution is sold or merged, the price a buyer is willing to pay may not result in an adequately capitalized institution. Hence, public money is often used to pay off the excess liabilities or to extend credit to the private sector to finance acquisitions. Under this option, when private investors are unwilling to pay a positive price for the customer base and the distribution system of the failed bank, the regulator closes the institution and sells its financial assets to help pay off depositors.

• The second option, takeover by the authorities, is used when impaired institutions cannot be sold (either because the market is underdeveloped or because the crisis has made banking properties unattractive) and regulators have sufficient knowhow to operate them. If delinquent loans are to be charged off and capital written down, this option usually requires more public funds than the first option, because regulators do not receive an up-front payment for the franchise value of customers and the distribution network. However, if regulators have experience in managing failed banks, they may eventually be able to recoup the franchise value through earnings on their investment. The government can postpone some of the cost by permitting seized institutions to operate temporarily at capital levels that would be inadequate for privately owned banks. This policy has risks, however, since governments, like private owners, may take excessive risks with inadequately capitalized institutions. Moreover, the success of this alternative lies in ensuring that banks are returned to private ownership as soon as market conditions permit.

---

[2] A loan charge-off is the process of removing an irrecoverable loan from the asset side of the balance sheet. The loan loss reserve account is the corresponding liability account that is reduced. (Often loan loss reserves are a contra asset item.) If loan loss reserves are inadequate, the charge-off forces a reduction in the capital account.

• The third option, a bailout, must be used when funds that can be committed quickly are scarce, markets are undeveloped or illiquid at the time of the crisis, and regulators do not have the knowhow to manage banks. This method of resolution is the most complicated, because it leaves insolvent institutions in the hands of their present owners, who are given public funds to maintain the viability of their institutions.

Differences in Constraints between Developed and Developing Countries

Regulators in developing countries face more extreme constraints in terms of resources, markets, and knowhow than their counterparts in developed countries. Even if fiscal policy was very conservative before the onset of a banking crisis, policymakers face a daunting task in obtaining adequate funds for a restructuring program.

In contrast to industrial countries, developing countries rarely possess a domestic long-term bond market, although many have access to international bond markets. When international markets perceive that a crisis is imminent, however, access to long-term bond markets dries up. For example, during the financial crisis precipitated by the devaluation of the Mexican peso in December 1994, Brady bond spreads over comparable U.S. Treasury securities increased from one to 4 percentage points for Mexico and from 2 to 4.5 percentage points for Argentina between December 1994 and the end of February 1995.

This would seem to leave the issuance of short-term debt as a more common funding option in developing countries. However, the risk in the short-term market is that the government must cover not only interest payments but also principal payments if the debt cannot be rolled over. Thus, the slightest hint of deterioration in the government's capacity to service its debt may shut the government out of the market, which, in turn, increases the pressure for inflationary finance.

The market for bank assets is also much more limited in developing countries. Although skilled professionals could be imported, a particular legal and market infrastructure is necessary for secondary markets to develop. This point is illustrated by recent attempts by U.S. real estate investors to purchase properties in default in Mexico.[3]

---

[3] Press reports have described the difficulty that U.S. real estate investors have faced in attempting to purchase properties in the Mexican market. For example, many of the properties used as collateral for loans in default have not been legally foreclosed; hence, they cannot be transferred to new owners.

Regulatory knowhow is sometimes in short supply in developing markets as well. Even in markets with skilled professionals in bank supervision, if bank regulators do not have political independence, they may be unable to sell banking properties through arm's length transactions. This problem also arises in the developed world, as suggested by the scandals connected to the U.S. savings and loan restructuring, but there other constraints are less severe.

Due to these constraints, bank supervisors in developing countries are much more likely to take the bailout option than are supervisors in industrial countries. Nonetheless, even under the most severe constraints, restructurings will achieve better results if policymakers attempt to enforce the three general principles outlined above. The capacity of the authorities to adapt principles to local conditions often determines whether a bank restructuring effort will be successful.

Application of Principles under Ideal Conditions

The U.S. savings and loan rescue and restructuring plan exemplifies how access to funding and the availability of markets permits bank supervisors to apply principles to good effect. However, unless policy objectives are clearly defined and the political will can be mustered to commit funds, relatively lenient constraints do not lead to good policy.

The U.S. savings and loan crisis had its origins in two fundamental changes in U.S. financial markets. The first was the broadening of potential investors for mortgage-backed securities, and the second was a rapid increase in nominal interest rates as a result of inflation. The first event reduced the economic value of institutions dedicated solely to directing funds to the residential housing market. The second increased the spread between open market interest rates and the interest rate ceilings on savings and loan deposits, making it difficult for these institutions to raise funds through the deposit market.

As a result of these fundamental market changes, many institutions lost their net worth during the late 1970s and early 1980s. The magnitude of the problem exceeded the resources of the insurance fund available to insulate small depositors from the impact of bank failures. Missing was principle three: the political will to provide additional public funds to cover the loss. Hence, regulators attempted to solve the problem by manipulating accounting rules and pumping emergency funding into institutions in trouble.

Even without funding, regulators could have controlled the expansion of savings and loans with zero market net worth had they established supervisory guidelines for asset growth relative to an institution's capital base. However, the political power of the real estate industry, combined with regulatory lethargy, prevented any application of the principles of sound crisis management. Because principles two and three were not followed, the owners of these institutions, having nothing to lose, took additional risks in hopes of recovering their investment.

By the late 1980s, it became obvious that the programs in place only magnified the cost of restructuring. Then authorities obtained sufficient public funds to operate in accordance with sound restructuring principles. For example, they were able to seize and sell failed institutions. Bidders assessed the value of the bank's assets as well as the franchise value of its distribution network. If bids were too low, regulators paid off depositors from sale of assets and government funds and closed the institution.

The policy accomplished two objectives of principle one: it forced stockholders of failed institutions to take losses, and borrowers in default to lose their collateral. (Large liability holders did not suffer losses, because they had left during the prolonged period of political indecision.) Then sufficient funds to close failed institutions could be raised without generating inflationary fears, and there was a market for the seized assets.

The importance of clearly defining the objectives of restructuring and making funds available to carry it out promptly is illustrated by Japan's recent banking problems.[4] Large segments of the Japanese banking system are suffering from an overhang of nonperforming loans from the asset inflation of the 1980s. The potential supply of funds available to bank supervisors is evidenced by Japan's large current account surpluses.

A public policy debate is now taking place over the use of public money to restructure the system. If public funds are used, the policy question is how these funds ought to be applied to rescue failed institutions. For example, several large cooperative banks have recently failed. Banks in this segment of the industry had made exceptionally risky investments because their traditional market had disappeared.[5] No public consensus has yet emerged as to what ought to be done with the cooperative banks.

---

[4] For a discussion of the banking problems in Japan, see Goldstein and Folkerts-Landau (1993).

[5] That market comprised small traditional businesses that were shrinking as a percentage of GDP, since the market was not attracting young entrants with a need for capital.

Because objectives and funding needs are not yet fully determined, initial steps focused on maintaining the viability of existing institutions. For example, decreases in the central bank discount rate are reducing banks' cost of funds, making it easier to hold nonperforming loans.

Even after the objectives and level of funding are decided upon, Japan faces a constraint not present in the United States: the lack of a deep market for impaired institutions or for nonperforming loans. Rather than being able to sell collateral held against defaulted loans in private markets, banks have written down loans through sales to an agency wholly owned by the banks, the Cooperative Credit Purchasing Corporation (CCPC). Each bank, however, must supply funds to the CCPC equal to the amount of loans sold to it; hence, the only gain to the banks is a tax write-off equal to the difference between the book value of the loan and the price at which it is transferred to the CCPC. The transfer prices are determined by appraisers rather than by market transactions.

Efforts have also been made to sell bonds backed by distressed properties in the Euromarket. However, a major obstacle to encouraging new borrowers to enter the market is that financial institutions resist placing distressed properties on the market for fear of depressing prices further. Hence, foreigners are reluctant to buy in a thinly traded market.

The experiences of bank supervisors in the Nordic countries illustrate how, even without a thick market for financial institutions or seized collateral, a bank restructuring can be successful with adequate funding and a transfer of ownership of closed institutions to the government. In Sweden, once noninflationary funding was made available to deal with the crisis (principle three), problems were handled promptly. Institutions with zero or negative net worth were closed (principle one), and stockholders lost their investment (principle two). In addition, it appears that the seized institutions have returned to financial health and are outperforming banks that were not closed.[6]

Constraints in Developing Economies

During bank rescue efforts in Latin American countries, regulators have often resorted to inflation and interest rate controls to resolve bad debt problems. These solutions were used because countries entered banking crises with large fiscal deficits and with no political will to reduce them,

---

[6] For a detailed analysis of the evolution of the banking crisis in the Nordic countries, see Burkhard and Pazarbasioglu (1996).

in violation of principle three. Argentina in the early 1980s and Mexico and Peru in the mid 1980s are prominent examples. Depositors took severe losses due to inflation, and in each country it took more than five years for investors to recover confidence in the financial system.

However, other examples in Latin America demonstrate that even under tight constraints, regulators can sometimes fashion a policy sufficiently close to the principles to be successful. The most noted example is Chile in the early and mid 1980s. While funds to close failing banks were limited and markets were not available to sell large impaired institutions, regulators fashioned a recapitalization and loan rescheduling program that minimized incentives to capitalize unpaid interest or expand balance sheets by taking increased risk. This case will be dealt with in detail below.

Colombia also designed a program to rescue its banks in the mid 1980s without inflation. Colombia's tight fiscal policy enabled it to use export earnings to resolve nonperforming banks. A bank insurance fund was used to recapitalize impaired institutions, which were transferred to government ownership. By forcing stockholders of impaired banks to lose their investment, Colombian authorities strictly enforced the first principle for good crisis management.

Thus the experiences of both industrial and developing countries in bank restructuring programs indicate that the three principles of crisis management are the most important determinants of success. However, in developing countries, the constraints imposed on regulators carrying out these tasks are more severe. In the next section we consider in some detail how regulators in Latin America deal with the constraints they face.

Lessons from Bank Restructuring in the 1980s: Argentina and Chile

Banking crises followed the 1980s debt crisis in a number of Latin American countries. As case studies in crisis resolution, the experiences of Argentina and Chile stand out for their contrasting results. Argentina's crisis ended in hyperinflation and substantial disintermediation, as evidenced by a sharp decline in bank deposits to GDP, whereas Chile's crisis ended with a strengthened banking and financial system. Did outcomes differ because of initial constraints, or because of regulators' tenacity in applying the three principles even under severe constraints?

Constraints and Designs

Chile experienced a severe banking crisis beginning in 1982, and after an inadequate attempt to deal with the crisis, by 1984 had put into place a bank restructuring program that is heralded for its singular success.[7] Nevertheless, Chile's basic program was not unique: the program originally proposed in Argentina in 1981 contained many of the same elements, as a brief description of each program indicates.[8] Indeed, the design of both programs was fully consistent with principles one and two. The implementation rather than the design of each program accounted for the different outcomes. In carrying out their programs, Chile followed principle three closely, whereas Argentina did not.

By late 1981 in Argentina and by 1984 in Chile, regulators in both countries recognized that they had to prevent banks from capitalizing interest on loans to borrowers that were in default. They also realized that they had to force stockholders of risky institutions to bear part of the costs of cleaning up the system.

The programs the regulators designed included mandatory restructuring of approximately half the loans of the banking system. Each program tied the principal of restructured loans to an index that reflected the rate of inflation and required the payment of a predetermined real interest rate. Both programs permitted banks to place loans with the central bank in return for a long-term bond. Under the Argentine program, banks were permitted to discount restructured loans with the central bank, and they were required to purchase a government bond with the proceeds. In the Chilean program, the banks were required to purchase a central bank security with the funds received from the transfer of restructured loans to the balance sheet of the central bank. In both countries, banks were required to buy back loans sold to the central bank at the price at which they were sold, plus, in most cases, accumulated interest, by a specified date.

With the exception of a few small banks in Chile, the programs did not include the sale of banks with depleted capital to new owners, nor did they include a government takeover of failed institutions. The programs in both countries, therefore, can be classified as bailouts of exist-

---

[7] Chile's restructuring effort actually began in 1982, but, after proving inadequate for the task, it was revised in 1984. The remainder of the subsection discusses only the revised program, since it illustrates how regulators can successfully overcome funding constraints to execute a successful program.
[8] For a detailed description of events leading up to the Chilean crisis, see Velasco (1991). The case of Argentina is discussed in Baliño (1991).

Table 4.1 Fiscal Deficit and Long-Term Debt
(Percentage of GDP)

	Fiscal Deficit		Long-Term Debt	
	Argentina	Chile	Argentina	Chile
1979	-2.6	4.8	20.5	37.7
1980	-2.6	5.4	22.0	35.4
1981	-6.0	2.6	29.6	40.7
1982	-4.8	-1.0	34.2	62.6
1983	-7.9	-2.6	36.5	82.0
1984	-3.4	-3.0	33.4	99.5
1985	-5.5	-2.3	50.2	122.6
1986	-2.0	-0.9	44.8	114.9
1987	-2.9	0.4	49.2	95.1
1988	-1.9	-0.2	40.7	72.4
1989	-0.4	1.8	76.4	52.8
1990		0.8	36.0	51.9
1991		1.5	26.9	46.0
1992		2.2	21.9	38.6
1993		1.9	24.5	38.0

Sources: IMF, *International Financial Statistics;* World Bank, *World Debt Tables.*

ing banks since they contemplated that existing banks would, in effect, be recapitalized. As discussed in the previous section, regulators choose bailouts when they face severe funding constraints and inadequate markets for bank assets, and lack knowhow to manage seized financial institutions. In managing their crisis in the early 1980s, both Chilean and Argentine authorities were faced with all three of these problems, but the funding constraint was probably the most onerous obstacle to establishing a good restructuring program.

In Chile, the accumulation of foreign debt in the late 1970s and 1980s hampered the authorities' ability to tap noninflationary sources of funds to deal with banking problems. In spite of its strong fiscal position, Chile had limited capacity to tap domestic savings to fund bank restructuring, because much of its savings was needed to service the high ratio of foreign debt to GDP (Table 4.1). The funding constraint became more onerous with the onset of the debt crisis in 1982, which effectively shut

Latin American countries out of private international debt markets. Thus, in the absence of markets for bank assets, Chile was forced to seek funds from multilateral agencies to restructure its banking system.

In sharp contrast, the funding constraint faced by Argentine regulators arose from that country's large fiscal deficit relative to GDP rather than from its international debt burden, which was substantially less than Chile's as a percent of GDP (Table 4.1). Allocating tax money to resolve banking problems was given a low priority, since these funds were used to finance government spending on other projects.

As discussed below, differences in the nature of each country's constraint had a crucial impact on how each program was implemented. Since neither country's bank regulators could unilaterally determine domestic priorities, they faced a common problem: a shortage of noninflationary funds to shut down insolvent institutions and pay off liability holders. Hence, it was no surprise that authorities in both countries followed a strategy of recapitalizing existing institutions by extending loan maturities and easing payment schedules. However, a restructuring program will succeed only if authorities convince bank liability holders that the banking system can be returned to solvency and that the value of their investment will be maintained in real terms. The Chilean authorities eventually succeeded in making this case, whereas the Argentine authorities did not.

Implementing Strategies

Why did the outcome of Argentina's restructuring program differ so sharply from that of Chile, in spite of the similarity of their original designs? The analysis indicates that, in implementing its program, Argentina departed from principle three: its authorities did not place a high priority on funding the restructuring program with real resources; instead, banking problems were solved through inflation. In contrast, Chile rejected the policy option of inflation, the major reason for its program's success.[9]

Clearly, the difference in constraints played a key role in the outcomes. Inflation could not have eliminated the bad loan problem in Chile, because a large portion of bank liabilities were to foreigners and denominated in foreign currency. While Argentina's bad loans were denominated largely in domestic currency, Chile's funding constraint was more

---

[9] Of course, Chile could have defaulted on its foreign debt as some borrowers did, but policymakers believed that the consequences of this action would have been too severe to make it a viable option.

**Figure 4.1 Central Bank Credit to Banking Systems
in Argentina and Chile, 1981-87**
(Percentage of bank loans)

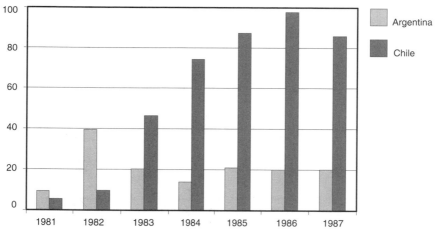

Sources: Superintendencia de Bancos e Instituciones Financieras (Chile),
various issues; IMF, *International Financial Statistics.*

external, and that imposed an element of market discipline on the implementation of the program.

To meet foreign commitments, Chile had to manage its banking system bank to solvency. This policy had the added benefit of restoring domestic investor confidence in the banking system by the late 1980s, almost five years before such confidence returned in Argentina. How each program was actually implemented is discussed in the remainder of this section.

As indicated above, regulators in both countries attempted to recapitalize banks by extending loan maturities, which implies a slower pace of principal repayment than was originally contemplated, and consequently, an increase in the funding commitment of banks. Hence, even with strong funding constraints, regulators had to find a source of funding for their programs. In both cases, resources for bank restructuring programs were channeled through the central bank to the banks. Hence, the magnitude of the funds required to restructure loans can be estimated by considering the extent to which gross central bank loans to each banking system, as a percentage of total loans made by banks, increased as the restructuring effort progressed. As Figure 4.1 indicates, in

Figure 4.2 Banks' Net Position with Central Bank, 1981-87
(Percentage of Central Bank credit to banks)

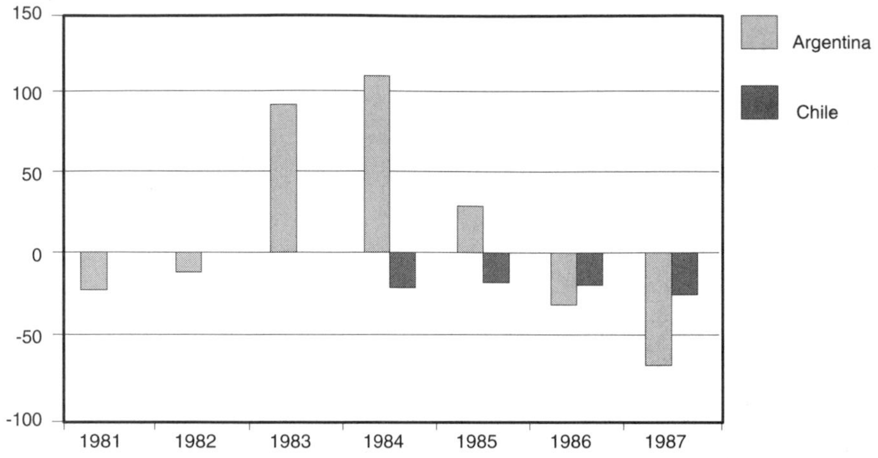

Sources: Superintendencia de Bancos e Instituciones Financieras (Chile), various issues;
IMF, International Financial Statistics.

1982 Argentina's central bank supplied gross loans to the banking system equal to 39 percent of banks' loan portfolios, compared to about 9
percent in 1981. By contrast, Chile's gross central bank loans in 1985
equaled 87 percent of total loans, compared to about 6 percent in 1981.[10]

Regulators faced initial constraints in each market that made it
difficult to fund the restructuring effort; hence, each central bank borrowed a large portion of the funds necessary to bail out insolvent banks
from solvent banks in its own system. Of course, in order for solvent
banks to lend funds to the central bank, they had to reduce credit to their
own borrowers.

As Figure 4.2 shows, the net credit position of Argentina's banks
with the central bank (as a percentage of central bank credit to banks)
equaled -22 percent in 1981 and increased to just over -12 percent in
1982.[11] This implies that 88 percent of central bank credit to banks in
1982 was funded by the banks themselves. For Chile, the data begin in
1983 because prior to that date, detailed asset breakdowns are not avail-

---

[10] In the case of Chile, loans include loans sold to or placed with the central bank. Gross borrowings
from the central bank include these items as well, since banks were required to buy them back.
[11] A negative net position signifies that banks are net borrowers.

able. In Chile in 1984, at the inception of the second restructuring program, banks' net position with the central bank was -21 percent, declining to -25 percent by 1987, implying that 75 percent of central bank credit to banks was funded by banks.

In Argentina, central bank loans to impaired banks were funded with reserve requirements on bank deposits, whereas in Chile, they were funded by central bank bonds purchased by solvent banks. Thus, in both cases, the central bank absorbed the credit risk of lending to impaired banks by acting as intermediary between banks lending funds and banks borrowing funds.

Events changed dramatically in Argentina in 1983. In contrast to the two years prior, by 1983 the banks became net lenders to the central bank, as their net position increased to positive 90 percent. The central bank used loans from the banks to fund the fiscal deficit, while central bank loans to the public sector increased from 11 percent of GDP in 1982 to 27 percent of GDP in 1983.[12]

Since the central bank was no longer lending to the banks, it found another method for dealing with problem loans. This method was to impose interest rate ceilings on bank loans during a period when inflation reached almost 500 percent a year. As a result of these policies, the real value of loans was inflated away, falling from 51 percent of GDP in 1982 to 39 percent in 1984. Real interest rates on deposits were also negative, falling to about -50 percent by 1984.

In short, in Argentina, in violation of principle three, there was no political commitment to control the fiscal deficit: in real terms, no funds could be committed to the bank bailout. Principles one and two were also violated, since the negative real interest rate on loans provided a subsidy to borrowers and heavily penalized depositors, who bore little responsibility for the crisis. Stockholders, on the other hand, emerged from the crisis with much of their wealth preserved in real terms. The ratio of deposits to GDP declined from 22 percent of GDP in 1981 to 14 percent of GDP in 1985 (see Figure 4.3a), as depositors fled the banking system.[13]

In contrast to Argentina, Chile gradually worked its way out of bad loans. It was not until 1992 that the banks became net lenders to the

---

[12] The ratio declined in 1986 and 1987, which were years of fiscal tightening. However, fiscal policy became highly expansionary again in 1988.

[13] A short period of relatively low inflation (100 percent a year) occurred in 1986 and 1987, and bank deposits as a percent of GDP recovered to their pre-crisis level (see Figure 4.3a). However, in 1988 and 1989, the government again used the banks to fund a growing fiscal deficit, and the inflation rate rose to 3,000 percent. Deposits as a percent of GDP fell precipitously to 8 percent.

Figure 4.3a Ratio of Deposits to GDP in Argentina, 1980-92
(Percent)

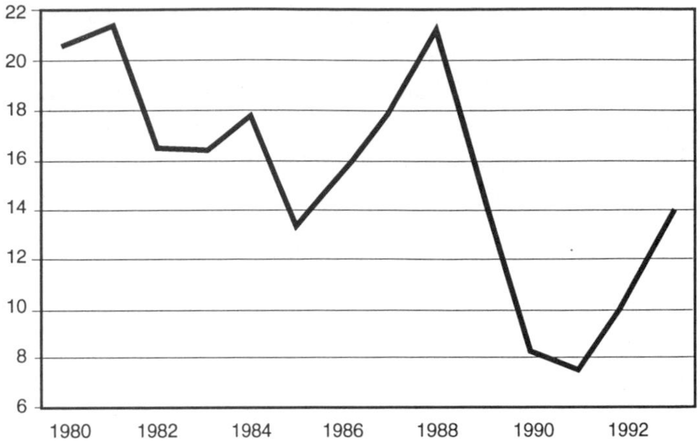

Source: IMF, *International Financial Statistics.*

central bank. During this period, Chile experienced only moderate inflation, and real interest rates on loans and deposits remained positive. As
mentioned above, an element of market discipline foreclosing an inflationary solution in Chile was the large percentage of bank liabilities to
foreigners, mostly to U.S. banks, denominated in U.S. dollars. Foreign
borrowings as a percentage of bank financial liabilities plus capital accounts on the eve of the crisis in Chile in 1982 was 53 percent, compared
to 24 percent in 1981 in Argentina.

If the foreign liability holders were to be paid, the Chilean restructuring program had to work. During the crisis, many borrowers who had
borrowed foreign currency from banks were unable to earn foreign currency to repay their loans. Hence, banks could not service their own
foreign liabilities. To help banks repay these liabilities, the central bank
absorbed the foreign exchange risk for the banks.

In the first step in this process, many foreign currency loans held
on the balance sheets of banks were converted into indexed peso loans,
to relieve borrowers of foreign exchange risk. However, this left the banks
with an imbalance of foreign currency liabilities. For example, in 1985
foreign currency loans remaining on bank balance sheets totaled $2.0
billion,[14] while liabilities to foreigners denominated in foreign currency

---

[14] All dollar amounts are in U.S. currency.

(mostly rescheduled loans from U.S. banks) equaled $6.3 billion. In other words, foreign currency liabilities were funding indexed peso assets.

The second step was to remove most of the risk created by this imbalance from the banks. The central bank issued foreign currency bonds to the banks, while simultaneously offering them loans denominated in indexed pesos. For example, in 1985 all banks held foreign currency-denominated bonds and deposits issued by the central bank equal to $3.6 billion on the asset side of their balance sheet. Meanwhile, the banks borrowed $5 billion in indexed pesos from the central bank, excluding loans sold to the central bank.[15]

This device was available to all three categories of banks operating in the market—foreign-owned banks, the state bank, and private domestic banks, but it was the private domestic banks, where the bad loan problem was focused, that most extensively used the program. In 1985, private domestic banks had indexed peso loans of $4.2 billion on their balance sheets and indexed peso deposits of only $1.1 billion. At the same time, these banks had foreign liabilities of $4.6 billion and foreign currency loans of $1.3 billion. Private domestic banks were net lenders of more than $3.1 billion to the central bank in foreign currency and net borrowers of $3.8 in indexed pesos, excluding loans sold to the central bank.

As Table 4.2 shows, the net position of domestic private banks in all currencies with respect to the central bank, including loans sold, was -$2.8 billion, indicating a net borrower position with the central bank. The two other categories of banks were actually net creditors of the central bank in 1985, although they were net borrowers in indexed pesos.

The data from this table allow us to estimate the cost of the restructuring effort and determine the role of domestic and foreign sources in paying for it. (As mentioned above, foreign funds did not come from private sources but were restructured loans from foreign banks plus additional funding from multilateral agencies.)

The cost is calculated based on 1987 balance sheets, since afterward the cost began to decline. As Table 4.2 shows, the net borrowing position of the domestic private banks with the central bank equaled $4.3 billion in 1987. About one-third of this amount, or $1.4 billion, was covered by loans to the central bank from the state bank and foreign banks, which had become net creditors of the central bank by year end

---

[15] In that same year, all banks were net borrowers to the central bank in all currencies in the amount of $2 billion, including loans sold to the central bank.

Table 4.2 Chilean Banks' Credit Position with the Central Bank
(In US$ billions)

	1985			1986			1987		
	All Currencies	Indexed Pesos	Foreign Currency	All Currencies	Indexed Pesos	Foreign Currency	All Currencies	Indexed Pesos	Foreign Currency
Net Position									
Private Domestic Banks	-2.8	-5.1	3.1	-2.8	-5.7	3.1	-4.3	-5.9	2.0
State and Foreign Banks	0.9	-0.5	1.4	1.1	-0.3	1.4	1.4	0.1	1.1
Gross Position									
Private Domestic Banks									
Loans to Central Bank	4.6	1.8	2.7	5.7	2.6	2.8	4.9	2.7	2.1
Liabilities to Central Bank	-4.4	-3.8	-0.3	-4.0	-3.7	-0.2	-3.6	-3.3	-0.2
Net Loans Sold to Central Bank	-3.0	-3.1	0.6	-4.5	-4.6	0.6	-5.6	-5.3	0.1
Net Position with Central Bank	-2.8	-5.1	3.1	-2.8	-5.7	3.1	-4.3	-5.9	2.0
State Bank									
Loans to Central Bank	1.3	0.5	0.7	1.1	0.4	0.6	1.1	0.6	0.5
Liabilities to Central Bank	-1.2	-0.8	-0.3	-1.1	-0.8	-0.3	-0.8	-0.6	-0.2
Net Loans Sold to Central Bank	0.6	0.0	0.6	0.6	0.0	0.6	0.6	0.0	0.6
Net Position with Central Bank	0.7	-0.3	1.0	0.6	-0.3	0.9	0.9	-0.0	0.8
Foreign Banks									
Loans to Central Bank	0.5	0.3	0.1	0.7	0.5	0.2	0.7	0.5	0.1
Liabilities to Central Bank	-0.4	-0.4	-0.0	-0.4	-0.3	-0.0	-0.3	-0.3	-0.0
Net Loans Sold to Central Bank	0.2	-0.1	0.3	0.2	-0.1	0.3	0.2	-0.1	0.3
Net Position with Central Bank	0.2	-0.2	0.4	0.5	0.1	0.5	0.5	0.1	0.2

Note: Total includes unindexed pesos.

Source: Superintendencia de Bancos e Instituciones Financieras (Chile), *Información Financiera* (various issues).

Figure 4.3b Ratio of Deposits to GDP in Chile, 1980-92
(Percent)

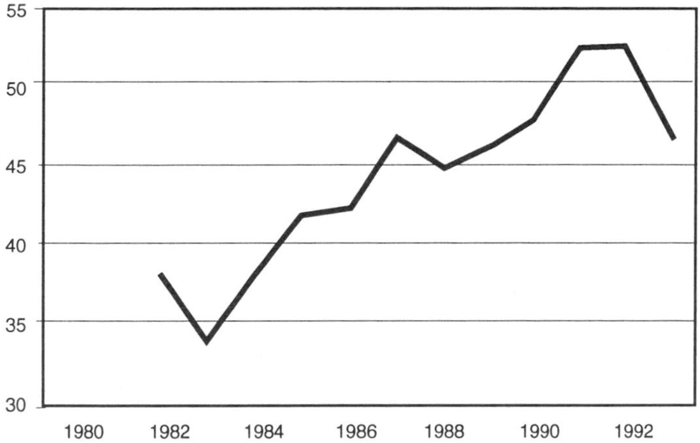

Source: Superintendencia de Bancos (Chile), various issues.

1987. Approximately $1.2 billion of the $1.4 billion was funded by foreign currency bonds issued by the central bank to the state bank and foreign banks.

The central bank funded the remaining $3.2 billion from its liabilities to nonbanks. In 1987, the central bank was able to issue $2.6 billion in domestic currency securities to the nonbank public. To avoid financing the remainder with inflation, it had to fund about $600 million from foreign sources, again mainly by borrowing from multilateral agencies. As a result, foreign sources covered $1.8 billion, or 42 percent of the cost, and the remaining $2.8 billion was funded in the domestic market.

The proportion of the cost funded by foreign sources in 1985 was much higher, 82 percent of the total, even though at that point the total cost appeared smaller. In that year, the central bank did not have sufficient access to the domestic nonbank funding market to cover much of its share of the cost. The rapid increase in nonbank domestic funding of Chile's restructuring program after 1985 demonstrates that, in contrast to Argentina, domestic investors gained confidence that the restructuring program would restore the banking system to solvency.

Some argue that this confidence was somewhat artificially created by Chile's mandatory pension system, which purchased much of the central bank's debt in 1987. On the other hand, if domestic investors had remained suspicious of the financial system, they would have fled the banking system to offset their mandatory investment in pension funds.[16] In fact, the opposite occurred: from 1984 onward, deposits increased rapidly as a percent of GDP (see Figure 4.3b).

While the loan restructuring program extended payment schedules for borrowers in financial difficulty, it adhered fairly closely to principle one. As of year end 1994, the banks were able to repurchase about half the restructured loans sold or placed with the central bank. However, two large banks still had large unpaid liabilities to the central bank. About half of this debt, equal to about 5 percent of GDP, probably will not be repaid.[17]

By the late 1980s, Chile achieved a stable banking system, with deposits increasing relative to GDP. Meanwhile deposits to GDP in Argentina had dropped precipitously to less than 8 percent, from 19 percent early in the decade (see Figure 4.3b).

As Chile's bank restructuring demonstrates, adequate real funding can buy sufficient time to prove to domestic investors that bank liabilities will be honored. To obtain this result, a program must encourage borrowers to meet their commitments and must provide incentives for bank managers to return their banks to solvency. However, even carefully devised programs succeed only if public policies promote low inflation and macroeconomic stability. When investors become convinced that their domestic financial assets are safe, they will be willing to provide a good portion of the real funds needed for a successful restructuring program.

Restructuring Systems in the Mid 1990s: Argentina and Mexico

Having implemented strong stabilization programs as well as financial and other economic reforms in the early 1990s, many Latin America countries experienced large capital inflows. In December 1994, however, large outflows of capital from Mexico resulted in a balance of payments crisis and a sharp devaluation of the Mexican peso.[18] The crisis of international investor confidence in Mexico expanded to several other Latin American countries, most notably Argentina. To stem capital flight, both countries

---

[16] There will always be people who save primarily through pensions and therefore will not be able to reduce deposits, and deposits are not perfect substitutes for pensions.

[17] For the basis of this calculation, see Rojas-Suárez and Weisbrod (1995).

[18] Analyses of the macroeconomic issues leading to the Mexican crisis are presented in Leiderman and Thorne (1995) and Sachs, Tornell, and Velasco (1995).

Figure 4.4 Interest Rates in Argentina and Mexico, 1995
(Percent)

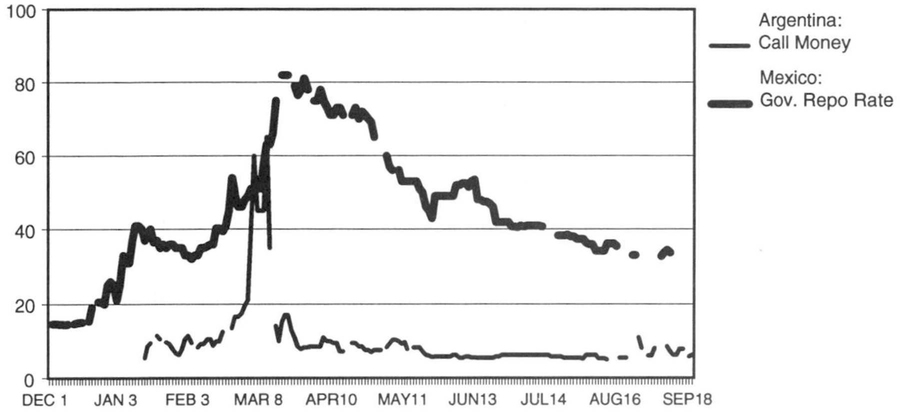

Source: Bloomberg Business News.

increased domestic interest rates, which led to concerns that bank borrowers would not be able to meet their obligations.

By early March 1995, the peso interbank interest rate in Argentina reached a peak of almost 70 percent, and in late March 1995, the repurchase agreement rate on government securities in Mexico reached over 80 percent (see Figure 4.4). The fears concerning the quality of the banking systems in these two countries were further fed by the impression that both systems contained institutions that were weak before the financial crisis. The loss in confidence, combined with tight monetary policies, resulted in banking crises that required major restructuring programs. The constraints that regulators faced in designing these programs, as well as their progress in executing them, are the subjects of this section.

Constraints

Despite investors' reduced confidence in their financial systems, regulators in both Argentina and Mexico face their current banking problems under much more favorable conditions for successful resolution than was the case in the early 1980s for a number of Latin American countries. Policymakers can design more effective restructuring programs, as a result of absorbing the lessons of success and failure from the 1980s. Also, although still below industrial country standards, bank reporting and supervisory conditions are much improved.

On the funding side, the fiscal situation in each country is much healthier than in the early 1980s. Moreover, since the fight against inflation has become a priority, each country has committed itself to solving the current crisis with noninflationary policies. Nevertheless, just as in the early 1980s, private funding for restructuring efforts practically vanished with the onset of the crisis, indicating that perceptions about country risk remained fragile in the early 1990s. Moreover, despite the reforms of the early 1990s, markets for long-term funds have not yet developed in many countries, and the market for insolvent banks remains thin. Although constraints on resolving bank problems have eased compared to the early 1980s, funding constraints are still relatively severe, compared with conditions in industrial countries.

Program Design

In determining whether a restructuring program follows the three principles, the analyst must consider the following aspects of the program: how it is funded, who bears the cost of resolution, and whether it controls the growth of impaired institutions. Conceptually, the restructuring programs in both Argentina and Mexico address each of these aspects in a manner consistent with adherence to the basic principles.

Consistent with principle three, the authorities in each country have promised to fund their recapitalization programs with noninflationary sources of finance. In Mexico, the capital injection program, known as PROCAPTE, or *Programa de Capitalización Temporal,* provides for the insurance fund, FOBAPROA, *Fondo Bancario de Protección al Ahorro,* to lend funds to the banks in the form of subordinated debt that will count as capital. These funds must be placed with the central bank to avoid monetary expansion and, therefore, inflation.

In five years, if this debt is not repaid, it is to be converted to equity, which will be transferred to FOBAPROA. In other words, banks with impaired capital can remain in business, but they face a specific deadline by which they must return to profitability. FOBAPROA can exercise conversion rights before the end of the five-year period if bank capital (excluding the subordinated debt) falls below 2 percent of assets or if, at any time, the regulators believe that the solvency of the bank is impaired—that is, if the bank continues to lose money during the restructuring program. Thus, the program enforces principle one.

In Argentina, the government has decided that a large part of the risk of adjustment will be borne by the private segment of the banking system. It has established a "safety net" fund, supported by large private banks and managed by *Banco Nacion,* which is used to provide liquidity assistance to banks losing funds. In addition, the central bank has provided liquidity assistance to banks through swap arrangements. The scope of these programs has been limited because regulations are in place that severely restrict the central bank's authority to act as lender of last resort to prevent the use of inflationary finance to solve banking problems.[19]

To channel noninflationary sources of funds to resolve banking problems, the government has established a trust fund to recapitalize banks. The fund is partially financed by the proceeds of $2 billion in three-year government bonds paying a below market floating interest rate, which are sold to domestic private investors and foreign financial institutions.[20] The remainder of the trust fund is financed by international multilateral agencies. The fund will purchase subordinated debt in banks with a maturity of three years, which will be converted to equity if a bank fails to repay interest and principal. As in the case of Mexico, this feature of the program enforces principle one.

In Argentina, to encourage depositors to keep their funds in troubled institutions while they are being restructured, the authorities have permitted banks to establish a private deposit insurance system, funded by the banks. Since the insurance fund is independent of the government, its commitment to insure deposits cannot be viewed as a potential source of inflationary finance.

While the design of capital injection plans was similar in the two countries, their policies to prevent banks from expanding bad credit during the restructuring phase (principle two) differed significantly in design.[21] Mexican authorities proposed two measures: strengthening supervision to force risky banks to reduce their capital and to restructure; and indexing loans along the lines used by Chile. Argentine authorities encouraged the sale of impaired institutions to new owners.

In Mexico, however, loan restructuring has not played an important role in the program. The government had intended to issue zero coupon bonds, paying interest indexed to inflation, to a trust fund established for the purpose of holding banks' nonperforming loans. To fund the government bonds, the trust fund was to issue liabilities to the government. The

---

[19] As of March 1995, it appears that the provincial banks had made very little use of liquidity facilities.
[20] The government has been able to raise funds at below market interest rates by appealing to private investors' stake in the success of economic reforms.
[21] Note that instituting policies preventing monetary expansion is not sufficient to control the growth of bad credit, because banks can reduce credit to good borrowers to fund bad ones.

trust fund was to exchange the government bonds for nonperforming loans currently held on bank balance sheets.

As a result of these transactions, the trust fund's assets were to become nonperforming loans, funded by liabilities issued to the government. To reduce the interest burden on borrowers, the principal of the nonperforming loans was to be indexed to inflation.[22] The indexed peso units are known as UDIs. One purpose of UDIs was to provide explicit criteria for defining a nonperforming loan, to aid regulators in stopping the expansion of credit to bad borrowers. Thus, as in the first stage of the U.S. savings and loan crisis, the Mexican program was designed to give banks time to return to solvency. However, in sharp contrast to the United States, Mexico's program intended to control the expansion of weak banks.

In Argentina, a significant portion of the resources from the fund established to inject capital into banks was planned to be used to finance mergers and acquisitions, which, by taking control of banks away from bad managers, would reduce the expansion of bad credit. Accomplishing this is likely to take time, however, and regulators must prevent risky banks from expanding credit to bad borrowers until buyers are found. The next section focuses on how this is actually being done in both Argentina and Mexico.

Evaluating the Restructuring Programs in Argentina and Mexico

As Chile's experience suggests, creating a restructured banking system that enjoys the full confidence of domestic investors takes time. Hence, it is too early to assess how closely the programs in Argentina and Mexico have adhered to their original designs. Whether principle one will be followed is not yet clear, because each program is designed to give the owners of problem institutions time to resolve problems before the authorities seize their banks. Indeed, even in cases where the program envisions the closure or sale of banks, such as in the case of provincial banks in Argentina, the institutions are allowed to remain in business while a buyer is found.

---

[22] During inflation, the principal of loan contracts with fixed nominal value depreciates in real terms. Lenders are compensated for this with high interest rates; however, the borrower must pay off real principal at a faster rate than in noninflationary times, since the high nominal interest rate in effect includes principal repayment. This increases the borrower's cash flow burden.

However, based on data for early 1995, there is already ample evidence that both countries have followed principles two and three in executing as well as designing their programs. Regulators acted quickly to constrain the growth of impaired institutions, and they have not resorted to inflationary finance to resolve banks.

Authorities in the two countries have relied on very different tools to accomplish these tasks. Argentina has used stringent controls on monetary base growth through the convertibility law and on bank deposit growth relative to the monetary base through reserve requirements; Mexico has enforced a capital-to-risk-weighted asset ratio standard.

To evaluate how these different methods of controlling the expansion of bank balance sheets have restrained the growth of weak banks and avoided inflationary finance, we consider the behavior of two groups of banks in each country between late 1994 and early 1995—those that are candidates for restructuring and those that are not. This subsection compares the behavior of the two groups of banks across the two countries to assess the progress of the two programs.

For Argentina, the banking data are divided into large provincial banks, which are relatively weak, and large private banks, which are relatively strong. To analyze the Mexican restructuring program, we categorized banks by whether, as of December 1994, they met supervisory standards for capital and provisions through their own resources, or whether they needed a capital infusion from PROCAPTE or from other sources, including FOBAPROA and private sources.[23] Provincial banks in Argentina and banks requiring a capital infusion in Mexico are designated weak banks; other banks in both markets are referred to as strong banks.

An important issue is whether the authorities in each country have prevented the weak banks from expanding credit—specifically, whether these banks are capitalizing interest on nonperforming loans into new loans. To answer this question, we must first determine whether loan portfolios are growing at a slower rate than the rate at which interest is being credited to the portfolio.

Table 4.3 presents annualized growth rates of loan portfolios for

---

[23] Whether a bank needs a capital infusion is determined as follows. Banks are required to have loan loss reserves to nonperforming loans equal to 60 percent. They are also required to maintain a capital-to-risk-weighted asset ratio of 8 percent. If reserves fall below the required level, and reported net income is insufficient to make up the difference, banks must withdraw funds from the capital account and place them in the loan loss reserve account. If this causes their capital-to-risk-weighted asset ratio to fall below 8 percent, a bank must raise additional capital. If it cannot raise funds, it must apply to PROCAPTE for assistance.

Table 4.3 Growth Rates of Bank Loan Portfolios in Argentina and Mexico, 1995

(Percent)

	Nominal Loan Growth	Interest Credited	Growth Net of Interest Credited
Argentina			
Strong Banks	6.5	12.9	-6.4
Weak Banks	-9.3	17.0	-26.3
Mexico			
Strong Banks	25.8	47.7	-21.9
Weak Banks	21.8	50.6	-28.8

Note: Growth rates and interest credited are annualized based on data through March 1995 for Argentina and through June 1995 for Mexico.
Sources: Superintendencia de Entidades Financieras y Cambiarias (Argentina), *Estados Contables de las Entidades Financieras;* and Comisión Bancarias y Valores (Mexico), *Boletín Estadístico de Banca Múltiple.*

Table 4.4 Growth Rates of Bank Liabilities in Argentina and Mexico, 1995

(Percent)

	Nominal Liability Growth	Interest Credited	Growth Net of Interest Credited
Argentina			
Strong Banks	4.0	5.9	-1.9
Weak Banks	-50.4	8.6	-59.0
Mexico			
Strong Banks	1.0	34.0	-33.0
Weak Banks	46.2	50.3	-4.1

Note: Growth rates and interest credited are annualized based on data through March 1995 for Argentina and through June 1995 for Mexico.
Sources: Superintendencia de Entidades Financieras y Cambiarias (Argentina), *Estados Contables de las Entidades Financieras;* and Comisión Bancaria y Valores (México), *Boletín Estadístico de la Banca Múltiple.*

each class of bank by country. Based on early 1995 data,[24] the rate of growth of loans at both categories of banks in both countries has been less than the rate at which interest was credited, indicating that credit growth has been severely constrained. In both countries, the negative growth rate in loan portfolios after accounting for interest earned is greatest at the weak banks, approaching negative 29 percent in Mexico and approximating negative 26 percent in Argentina. The strong banks in Argentina experienced a negative growth rate of 6 percent, whereas the strong banks in Mexico experienced a negative growth rate of 22 percent.

In contrast to the loan growth picture, the pattern of liability growth rates between strong and weak banks has been significantly different across the two countries. As indicated in Table 4.4, the growth rate of liabilities has been slower than the rate of interest credited at all institutions in both countries. However, in Argentina, the growth rate of liabilities net of interest credited was most negative at the weak banks, equaling -42 percent on an annual basis, compared to -2 percent at strong banks, whereas in Mexico it was most negative at the strong banks, equaling -33 percent on an annual basis, compared to -4 percent at weak banks. In both markets, weak banks paid substantially more for liabilities than strong banks (Table 4.4).

The Argentine pattern—strong bank liability growth and weak bank liability losses—parallels the loan growth data and is consistent with the perception that the supervisory program is restraining the growth of risky institutions. Because the Mexican pattern—weak bank liability growth relative to strong bank liability growth—does not follow the loan growth pattern, it requires some analysis.

A negative growth rate of liabilities, after accounting for interest credited, indicates that liability holders are withdrawing funds from banks, which requires banks to come up with cash to pay for this outflow by, for example, divesting cash assets. Before the crisis, Mexican banks held very little cash on their balance sheets since reserve requirements had been set at zero. Hence, banks would need positive cash flow if faced with deposit withdrawals, or they would have to bid aggressively for deposits to prevent withdrawals.

Since weak Mexican banks bid more aggressively for deposits than did strong banks (Table 4.4), the issue is whether this signifies that they

---

[24] The Mexican data are through June 1995, and the Argentine data are through March 1995. For Argentina, rates of interest credited are for all interest-earning assets, and for Mexico they are interest and fees received on loans.

Table 4.5 Growth Rates of Liquid Assets and Securities in Argentina and Mexico, 1995

(Percent)

	Liquid Assets	Securities
Argentina		
Strong Banks	-5.4	-43.0
Weak Banks	-67.9	-63.2
Mexico		
Strong Banks	2.3	-13.0
Weak Banks	28.8	38.4

Note: Growth rates are through March 1995 for Argentina and through June 1995 for Mexico. The Mexican growth rates are at a quarterly rate.

Sources: Superintendencia de Entidades Financieras y Cambiarias (Argentina).

did not have positive cash flow to pay for withdrawals. As indicated in tables 4.3 and 4.4, weak Mexican banks earned more interest on assets than they paid on liabilities. In addition, net income after provisioning for loan loss was positive for this group of banks.[25] Thus, the accounting data indicate positive cash flow; however, these data would be misleading if banks were capitalizing unpaid interest into new loans.

To determine whether interest earned on assets resulted from capitalization of unpaid interest on loans, it is necessary to determine what these banks did with their cash. For example, if they expanded their loan portfolios, we would not be able to rule out the possibility that they capitalized interest. As indicated in Table 4.5, weak Mexican banks expanded their cash and securities portfolios at a very rapid rate, whereas, as indicated in Table 4.3, the growth rate of loans was substantially less than interest credited. These data indicate that Mexican banks used interest revenue to purchase securities. Since investors who sold securities to these banks likely demanded to be paid with cash, the data indicate that the banks were actually earning cash on their loan portfolios rather than

---

[25] Positive net income implies that interest withdrawals by liability holders can be met by interest revenue on assets.

capitalizing unpaid interest. Thus, they had sufficient cash flow to meet liability withdrawals up to interest credited to these accounts.[26]

In contrast, weak banks in Argentina held a large stock of liquid assets as a result of high reserve requirements. As Table 4.5 shows, they divested liquid assets, which fell by 68 percent, to meet liability withdrawals.[27] The volume of liability withdrawals at weak banks exceeded the decline in volume of liquid assets, indicating that these banks had to pay out some interest revenue or call in some loans to meet liability holders' demands for cash. Hence, there is also no evidence that weak banks in Argentina capitalized interest on nonperforming loans.

Nevertheless, for two large provincial banks, the decline in liquid assets exceeded liability withdrawals. Since part of the decline in cash assets relative to liabilities was offset by an increase in loans at these institutions, it is possible that unpaid interest on some loans was capitalized into new loans.[28]

The evidence through early 1995 indicates that the restructuring programs in both countries have constrained the growth of bank balance sheets. Therefore, neither country is resorting to inflation to rescue weak banks. The evidence also indicates that both countries have made tremendous strides in controlling the growth of credit to bad borrowers by capitalizing interest payments. However, the possibility of unpaid interest capitalization at several large provincial banks in Argentina suggests that reserve requirements alone cannot control the growth of bad credit. Strong supervision is necessary as well.

Indexation of Financial Assets: Is It Always Necessary?

Chile's indexation program was an important vehicle for restructuring loans. A similar program was attempted in Mexico (UDIs), but as of June 1995, UDIs accounted for less than 0.5 percent of outstanding loans.[29]

---

[26] The absolute volume increase in the securities and cash portfolios was more than twice the growth in the loan portfolio. In addition, the increase in securities exceeded by a wide margin the increase in the capital account plus any transfers from the capital account to loan loss reserves. This implies that capital injections from the government did not entirely finance the increase in the securities portfolio.

[27] The decline in liquid assets at large provincial banks equaled 665 million pesos during the first quarter, compared with a decline of 760 million in liabilities. The remainder was accounted for by a decline in the loan portfolio. The 68 percent decline in liquid assets is for the quarter only; it is not annualized.

[28] From the accounting data, it is impossible to determine the extent to which good loans are called in to capitalize interest on bad loans. See Comisión Nacional Bancaria y de Valores (June 1995).

[29] See Comisión Nacional Bancaria y de Valores (June 1995).

Authorities have proposed a new loan restructuring program to index consumer and small business loans and to provide a subsidy for these borrowers.

The lack of success of the original program and the proposal of a new one raise two questions. First, why were borrowers reluctant to index loans under the original program? Second, can a restructuring program succeed without a successful indexation program?

As indicated earlier, indexation of principal reduces borrowers' loan payments, because paying nominal interest rates that include a substantial inflation premium relieves them of the responsibility of paying real principal. In Mexico, however, it is not clear that many borrowers would gain by accepting an indexed contract. As of June 1995, interest paid on loans relative to loans has been substantially below the inflation rate, indicating that real interest rates on many loans are negative.[30] Thus, many borrowers have received a substantial reduction in their real loan payments without the indexation program. In fact, the real cost of accepting an indexed loan contract would be higher over the life of the contract because the indexed contract, by assumption, carries a positive real interest rate.[31] Apparently indexation is not as effective in reducing loan payments for many borrowers as it was in Chile in 1984. This leads to the question of why the authorities are attempting to establish a new indexation program aimed at small borrowers.

According to some reports, banks have been more reluctant to reduce interest payments on small loans than on large ones. Hence, the new program is a response of the authorities to demands by small business and consumer borrowers for more lenient treatment, since their cash flow is not adequate to service their nominal contracts.

The creation of the new program is not necessarily a step backwards in the bank restructuring program, because banks are making a serious effort to collect on delinquent loans, which reflects positively on supervisory efforts. However, since the new program eases the impact of collection, it must be carefully circumscribed. There is a risk that subsidies could be extended to relatively large borrowers. If this happened, further pressure would be placed on the fiscal account. Therefore, authorities need to ensure that the new program remains limited, and that participating borrowers meet all their obligations.

---

[30] This conclusion is based on interest earned on performing loans.

[31] Borrowers can still face larger payments under the nominal contract paying negative real interest rates than under an indexed contract, as long as the nominal interest rate is above the rate on the indexed contract.

Conclusion

Five major lessons for successful banking crisis management emerge from the foregoing analysis. First, good banking crisis management begins with three basic principles: ensure that parties responsible for the crisis bear most of the costs of restructuring; prevent problem banks from expanding credit to delinquent borrowers; and avoid financing the program with inflation by making the restructuring program a high priority. A strong commitment to these three principles is essential if a bank restructuring program is to succed. Many efforts to reform Latin American banking systems, and Chile's experience in particular, have confirmed this.

Second, while the three basic principles for bank crisis resolution are the same for industrial and developing countries, constraints differ significantly: they are much more severe in developing countries. These constraints include the availability of funding, the availability of markets to dispose of nonperforming assets and institutions, and the knowhow to manage a restructuring program. Since the severity of constraints determines the shape of a restructuring program, the attributes of successful programs differ between industrial and developing countries.

Third, while Latin American policymakers face similar obstacles in resolving banking crises, there is no unique formula for success. For example, extension of loan maturities to give borrowers time to return to solvency is a common element of bank crisis management in the region. Since banks in the region face volatile markets for short-term funds, regulators must find ways of removing the risks created by maturity extension policies from the banks' balance sheets. However, the appropriate method to execute loan restructuring programs varies by country: indexation worked in Chile, but does not seem indispensable in the Mexican environment.

Fourth, the appropriate policy tool for controlling the expansion of risky credit must also be tailored to the conditions in the market. For example, the choice between two policy instruments—reserve requirements and supervisory standards such as capital-to-risk-weighted asset requirements—should be based on the quality of bank management and the experience of bank supervisors. Where both are weak, reserve requirements are often an appropriate tool for controlling bank expansion. As supervisors gain experience and the banking system has a core of sound banks, supervisory tools become much more attractive methods of controlling the expansion of risky credit. These tools can be refined to distinguish between credit growth at sound and unsound banks better than can reserve requirements.

Fifth, a crisis should be used as an opportunity to strengthen supervision and improve the quality of bank management. In the near future, Latin American economies are likely to be subject to periodic shocks that are large enough to generate banking crises. A sound banking system will speed the recovery process, however. In both Argentina and Mexico, conditions now are much more favorable to rapid recovery than they were in the 1980s.

A policy question that comes out of these conclusions is what authorities can do to ease constraints, to reduce the cost of resolving banking crises. The only certain means of loosening constraints in Latin America is to build credibility in policies and institutions, which takes time. Even efforts to reduce constraints directly, such as forced savings schemes, can only work when authorities pursue policies to build credibility. For example, mandatory pension funds can be useful as a means of relaxing funding constraints. However, these programs will succeed only if investors have some confidence in the economy. If policies are volatile and institutions weak, some investors will react to forced savings plans by removing funds from voluntary savings vehicles, such as bank deposits. Nonetheless, forced savings can improve funding options if introduced when institutions and markets are clearly becoming more stable.

How can authorities know that the constraints for resolving banking difficulties have been eased? A clear market signal for regulators is that funds markets do not dry up in a crisis—a feature present today primarily in industrial countries.

Liliana Rojas-Suárez is Principal Advisor, Office of the Chief Economist, Inter-American Development Bank. Steven R. Weisbrod is Consultant, Office of the Chief Economist, Inter-American Development Bank.

References

Baliño, Tomás J. T. 1991. "The Argentine Banking Crisis of 1980," in Sundararajan, V. and Tomas J. T. Baliño, *Banking Crises: Cases and Issues,* IMF.

Banco Central de la República Argentina. 1994 and 1995. *Estados Contables de las Entidades Financieras* (November and March).

Burkhard, Drees, and Ceyla Pazarbasioglu. 1996. "The Nordic Banking Crisis: Pitfalls in Financial Liberalization?" IMF Working Paper No. 95/65 (June).

Comisión Nacional Bancaria y de Valores (Mexico). 1995. *Boletín Estadístico de Banca Múltiple* (June).

Goldstein, Morris, and David Folkerts-Landau. 1993. *International Capital Markets, Part II. Systemic Issues in International Finance.* Washington, D.C.: IMF (August).

Folkerts-Landau, David and Takahashi Ito. 1995. *International Capital Markets.* Washington, D.C.: IMF (August).

International Monetary Fund, *International Financial Statistics,* various issues.

Leiderman, Leonardo and Alfredo Thorne. 1995. "Mexico's 1994 Crisis and Its Aftermath: Is the Worst Over?" Paper presented at the Conference on Private Capital Flows to Emerging Markets After the Mexican Crisis, jointly sponsored by the Institute for International Economics and the Oesterreichische Nationalbank, Vienna, Austria (September 7-9).

Rojas-Suárez, Liliana and Steven R. Weisbrod. 1995. "Financial Fragilities in Latin America, The 1980s and 1990s." Occasional Paper No. 132. IMF (October).

Sachs, J., A. Tornell, and A. Velasco. 1995. "The Collapse of the Mexican Peso: What Have We Learned?" Working Paper. Harvard University (May).

Superintendencia de Bancos e Instituciones Financieras (Chile). *Información Financiera* (various issues).

Superintendencia de Entidades Financieras y Cambiarias (Argentina). *Estados Contables de las Entidades Financieras (various issues).*

Velasco, Andrés. 1991. "Liberalization, Crisis, Intervention: The Chilean Financial System," in Sundararajan, V. and Tomas J. T. Baliño. 1991. *Banking Crises: Cases and Issues,* Washington, D.C.: IMF.

World Bank, *World Debt Tables* (various issues).

Commentary to Part IV

Roque Fernández

My comments are organized according to the three principles for managing banking crises that Rojas-Suárez and Weisbrod have outlined. I agree with the authors' first principle, which is to ensure that, in the wake of a crisis, those parties that have benefitted from risktaking bear a large portion of the cost of restructuring the banking system. This is the way we deal with banking problems in Argentina. The charter of the central bank was changed in the early 1990s to establish new procedures for dealing with problem banks. These new procedures are designed to ensure that the stockholders, directors, and managers of the insolvent bank bear a large portion of the restructuring costs.

Prior to these changes, the process for dealing with insolvent banks had two stages: intervention and liquidation. In the first stage, the central bank removed the managers and the board of directors and appointed an *intervenor,* who was put in charge of managing the bank and had the authority to transfer assets and liabilities to restore its viability. If this intervention failed to restore the bank to health, the process moved on to the second stage. Here the central bank appointed a *liquidator,* who was authorized to liquidate the bank's assets in order to cancel its liabilities, and to start bankruptcy procedures. Both the liquidator and the intervenor could manage the payment of deposits, and if the bank's assets were insufficient to cover these withdrawals, the central bank provided the necessary funds.

Although under these procedures the stockholders were supposed to bear the costs of mismanagement, in practice this was not always the case. Even in cases of outright bankruptcy, where the institution had to be liquidated, the judicial system provided stockholders one last chance to gamble for resurrection. In some instances, judges forced the central bank to compensate the stockholders on the grounds that the bank was solvent at the time the central bank decided to intervene, and that the insolvency resulted from mismanagement during the intervention.

The new central bank charter limits the ability of stockholders to reclaim funds once a bank is found to be insolvent. First, and most important, the central bank does not act as either intervenor or liquidator of an insolvent bank. The new procedure establishes that, once the central bank considers a bank to have liquidity or solvency problems that cannot be resolved within a reasonable time frame, it can revoke the bank's license and submit the case to a judge, who will decide whether to start a liquidation process or initiate bankruptcy proceedings. This new procedure protects taxpayers' money by limiting the liability of the central bank.

In addition, Argentina's prudential regulations make the managers and/or the directors of the bank legally responsible for decisions about portfolio allocation and the assumption of risk. However, even the threat of legal liability and the possibility of the stockholders losing control of the bank might not be very effective in forcing managers to be prudent— at least not as effective as having to face angry depositors in the case of bankruptcy. Indeed, we found that many bankers would have been glad to surrender their shares if the central bank would have only taken charge of their operations. In such cases, assuming ownership of the stockholders' shares would have been a favor to them, not a punishment.

The authors' second principle can be summarized as preventing "gambling for resurrection." This type of behavior, well documented in the U.S. savings and loan crisis, has been discussed extensively in the literature on liability management. If a bank is facing financial stress or has become insolvent, and if there is an implicit or explicit guarantee on deposits, the bank will tend to raise the deposit interest rate just to stay alive, hoping that by a stroke of luck the situation will turn itself around. The bank can continue to attract deposits under these circumstances because the government deposit insurance scheme does not impose a cap on interest rates.

The other part of the bet, on the asset side, involves investing in high-risk, potentially high-return projects. The managers and stockholders have an incentive to make these gambles because, having already lost their own capital, they are now gambling with other people's money. Gambling for resurrection thus becomes a one-way strategic bet: if the managers and stockholders are lucky and the bet pays off, the bank is back in business; if it does not, the stockholders are not any worse off than before, since they placed the bet from a position of insolvency. In essence, gambling for resurrection with other people's money is a cheap strategy to follow. There is no way to save an institution once it has turned the corner to insolvency, but one can do a lot to prevent this kind of reckless behavior through prudential regulation and effective banking supervision.

The authors' third principle is perhaps the most controversial. Not everyone will agree on the need to use the government's fiscal resources for bank restructuring. Argentina undertook a massive bank restructuring effort as a result of a crisis in the early 1980s, at a high fiscal cost. Having paid that cost once, the Argentine congress is unlikely to consider repeating such a bailout in the future. Moreover, even to discuss publicly the precarious situation of troubled financial institutions could aggravate the problem one is trying to solve. Imagine what might happen if a country's authorities spoke candidly to the media using some of the following technical terms gambling for resurrection, adverse selection, rational runs on the bank, herd behavior, and so on. In public debate, their use would be as likely to create mistrust as understanding.

Even if public understanding and political will exist to resolve or avoid a banking crisis, and to use fiscal resources to restructure the financial system, several difficulties remain. First, how does one determine, in the absence of clear criteria, whether a problem at one bank will have systemic implications? Second, if liquidation of a financial institution poses a systemic risk, how does one manage the situation? Does one protect small depositors, transfer the assets of some institutions to others, or transfer the losses in some way to the taxpayers? My impression is that there is no institution "too big to fail," and no monetary authority with unlimited lender-of-last-resort capabilities. But state resources sometimes provide an unlimited incentive to play the game of gambling for resurrection.

Looking toward the future, we should continue to work toward an overall consensus on prudential regulation, minimum capital requirements, and full disclosure of information. This is essential for two reasons. First, we need effective, consolidated prudential regulations so that good supervision in one country cannot be neutralized by operations offshore. Even if a bank's position is sound in its home country, its foreign affiliate in another country might have a serious problem that domestic authorities know nothing about. Second, if we can achieve such a consensus in regulation, regulators will have an easier task of managing the political economy of banking regulation. It is difficult for one country to enforce strict reserve requirements, capital-asset ratios, or other tough banking policies if its neighbors are not doing the same. Without internationally consistent regulation, political economy will work against the country doing the right thing, because bankers can simply move across the border.

I have two final points. The first concerns to what extent the central bank should disclose the rules it intends to follow in managing a financial crisis. The optimal strategy is probably to disclose the basic principles without being too specific about exact rules. A term I like is "constructive ambiguity." Bankers have to know that the authorities might let the bank fail, which is very important to give them the right incentives. At the same time, however, one needs to maintain some room to maneuver, to deal with extreme circumstances.

Second, as Argentina's recent financial crisis made clear, a country cannot diversify systemic risk. Here there is room for cooperation with the international financial community and financial organizations experienced in dealing with such problems. Cooperation is also necessary with countries in other regions of the world. For Argentina, a cooperation agreement with Mexico would probably not be very useful, because the two countries tend to face similar external financial shocks at similar times (there is a positive covariance of the shocks). However, such agreements could be made with countries in other parts of the world that face different types of financial shocks at different times. In this area the multilateral organizations can be extremely useful.

Roque Fernández is the Minister of Economic Affairs of Argentina.

E. Gerald Corrigan

My response to the paper by Rojas-Suárez and Weisbrod is based on my experience of managing financial crises in the 1980s and early 1990s. That has left me with some definite views as to what central banks should do in the face of a major financial disruption, and equally strong views as to what they should not do. My approach is more pragmatic than theoretical, because theory provides only limited guidance in this area. Indeed, the dominant theme that emerges from my experience is that each crisis is unique and that crises should be managed on a case-by-case basis.

To cover broadly the major elements of this complex subject, I will address three topics: the institutional framework needed for the central bank to prevent and manage crises, the traits of troubled financial institutions, and how to manage long-fuse and short-fuse episodes.

The Institutional Framework

For any central bank to manage a financial crisis successfully, a broad institutional framework is needed to provide the tools, authority, and flexibility to deal with problems as they arise. Properly structured, this institutional framework also plays an important role in preventing crises by helping to identify and anticipate problems before they become serious. The framework has seven key elements.

First there must be laws that clearly define the basic structure of the banking and financial system. The laws should deal explicitly with the important question of ownership and control of banking and other major financial institutions.

Second, regulations must establish a legal and administrative framework that sets forth the roles of the various government authorities in overseeing financial institutions and markets. Especially important in this regard is the system of bank supervision. In my view, the central bank should always play a major (but not necessarily exclusive) role in bank supervision, and that process should be fully independent of any political influence or involvement. The following elements must be developed for a system of effective bank supervision: core supervisory policy in such areas as capital standards; detailed procedures for licensing banks and for reviewing and approving major changes in their structure, activities, and ownership; an effective, efficient, and mandatory system for banks to regularly report key statistical information; central bank capacity to undertake rigorous, ongoing analysis of these statistics, to better anticipate problems; a comprehensive program of on-site examination of banks; regular procedures for reporting to banks the results of examinations and other supervisory initiatives; and procedures for remedying problem bank situations.

The third key element in an effective institutional framework is a deposit insurance system with a suitable limit or cap on the level of individual deposits that will be guaranteed. The deposit insurance fund should be financed by premiums paid by the banks, but where such insurance funds are new or relatively new, the initial capitalization will almost always have to come from the central bank (as in the United States) or from some other government source.

Implicitly or explicitly, the government will stand behind the deposit insurance fund, but as a practical and philosophical matter it is important that the government be as far behind the curtain as possible. On the other hand, central banks and/or governments must retain the flexibility to do the right thing in the face of a truly systemic problem without raising moral hazard to a dangerous level. To strike the right balance here, central banks and governments should follow the doctrine of constructive ambiguity, which implies that the authorities will never commit themselves in advance to what specific measures they will take in the face of a financial crisis. As a general matter, for example, uninsured depositors or other creditors should not be protected against loss. Circumstances can arise when concerns about the stability of the system may make such protections necessary and appropriate. However, as a matter of strict public policy, shareholders and top management should never be protected.

The fourth element is clear authority on the part of the central bank or the bank supervisors—subject to national standards of due process— to force a problem bank to take certain steps to remedy its problems. Those steps might include changing directors and management, reducing or eliminating dividends, or selling assets. In the extreme, the authorities should also have the ability to take over and manage a failing institution until a permanent solution can be found. And the authorities should have the ability to inject fresh capital into seriously troubled institutions.

The fifth element is that the central bank should always have in its possession the formally executed documents establishing the terms and conditions under which banks will have access to its lender-of-last-resort facility. These documents should be reviewed and updated periodically, and most important, the central bank should—to the fullest extent possible—have in its possession the collateral necessary for discount window borrowings. In addition, if markets are sufficiently deep and liquid, the central bank should have plans to provide large-scale liquidity to the system as a whole using open market operations.

The sixth key element in an effective framework is an established institution outside the central bank with the authority and responsibility to liquidate failed banks. This task requires a competent professional staff whose integrity and fairness are beyond question.

The final element is that the central bank must have a strong but informal intelligence (as distinguished from information) network to aid its decisionmaking during a crisis. This means that top officials of financial institutions and other market participants must know about and trust their counterparts in the central bank, and they must know that the central bank has the competence to be able to weigh and evaluate such intelligence as part of its decisionmaking process.

Traits of Troubled Financial Institutions

Financial disturbances that can turn into crises come in all shapes and sizes. In managing financial crises it is essential to understand the characteristics of an emerging problem that could complicate the task of management. The traits of seriously troubled financial institutions that will make matters more or less difficult are as follows.

First is the issue of the ownership of the institution and the associated problem of contagion. That is, to the extent that a failing financial institution is owned and controlled by another entity, such as an industrial concern, the problems of the failing bank will almost always spill over to the owner, making damage control more difficult. This is an even more serious problem in the reverse case, that is, when the failing financial institution owns other, nonfinancial entities.

The second set of important characteristics is the maturity mix, ownership mix, and currency mix of the bank's deposits and other liabilities, especially its liabilities to other banks, financial institutions, exchanges, clearing corporations, and foreigners. From a systemic point of view, obligations to other financial institutions, which can often be very large, are of particular concern because of the chainlike credit linkages they entail.

A third concern is the extent of the failing institution's's direct involvement in local, national, and international payments, clearance, and settlement systems. The central bank should always know and understand the nature of these arrangements for all of its banks, all of the time.

The fourth set of characteristics is the presence, size, and financial condition of a bank's foreign branches and/or subsidiaries, with emphasis on the currency mix of the liabilities of those foreign establishments. When foreign establishments of a seriously troubled bank encounter large-scale deposit outflows, the complexities of managing the situation rise geometrically.

A fifth concern is the scale and complexity of the bank's's activities. The complexity factor is relevant on several grounds. For example, the strategy chosen for dealing with an institution will depend on the central bank being able to make an informed judgment as to how large the prospective losses are, and the extent to which those losses are likely to exceed the bank's capital. Such judgments are never easy, but they are extraordinarily difficult in the case of an institution with far-flung and complex activities, in a setting in which a major misjudgment (in either direction) as to the nature of the losses can lead to the wrong choice of strategy, at potentially great cost. Beyond that, the task of merging or liquidating a bank with highly complex activities becomes much more convoluted simply because the valuation process becomes so much more difficult and lengthy. For example, large and complex off-balance-sheet positions, including but not limited to derivatives, can be a major obstacle to the valuation and resolution process.

The sixth relevant characteristic is the corporate structure of the failing or failed bank. Corporate structure can be a particular problem for large, internationally active financial institutions, most of which are made up of dozens of legal entities that may be subject to different regulatory and/or bankruptcy regimes.

The final characteristic to be considered is the speed with which the crisis develops. Financial crises may be characterized as either "long-fuse" or "short-fuse." In long-fuse episodes, authorities can see a problem as it develops and take steps to minimize its potential consequences. As for short-fuse episodes, the very worst are not expected until the moment they occur. The unanticipated crises are far more difficult to manage and pose the greatest danger, because they require action based on scant information.

Managing a Long-Fuse Episode

When the authorities have an opportunity to correct or at least contain financial problems before they reach a crisis stage, there are certain steps they should follow. First they should encourage a troubled institution to raise fresh capital and to reduce or eliminate dividends. Next, they should advise the institution to shrink its balance sheet in order to reduce promptly the most sensitive liabilities; to sell affiliates or subsidiaries and/or selective lines of business, in order to either raise capital or reduce points of vulnerability; and actively to explore merger possibilities, even those that might entail some interim governmental financial assistance in the form of capital injections.

While carefully monitoring the situation on a daily basis, regulators should maintain strict confidentiality. Eventually they may need to encourage, and perhaps force, changes in management.

Managing a Short-Fuse Episode

The central bank's efforts to engage in early intervention depend on two things: its capacity to pinpoint specific trouble spots before they get out of hand; and some reasonable set of criteria that, when triggered, will allow the central bank to act aggressively as required by the early intervention strategy. Since there will be cases that meet neither of these conditions, control might not always have the same flexibility as in the long-fuse episode.

A short-fuse crisis involving a failing financial institution is the most difficult and demanding problem for any central bank, because the consequences of a wrong decision can be so serious. In the worst case, the central bank might have to decide in a matter of hours whether to take overt steps to contain or cushion the situation. Often the central bank will have to make this decision without knowing whether the institution is facing a liquidity problem or is, in fact, insolvent. The decision will also have to be made in the context of an informed judgment as to whether the possible failure of one or more institutions has systemic consequences.

What makes this situation so difficult, of course, is the consequences of the initial decision. For example, if the central bank decides that no systemic threat is present and the decision turns out to be wrong, the consequences—including for the credibility of the central bank itself—could be devastating. On the other hand, if the decision is that systemic risk is present, and the authorities respond by taking extraordinary and successful actions, they might still be harshly criticized, even though no one could ever know for certain what would have occurred had the authorities not stepped in. In other words, any decision in this situation has something of a no-win character.

In essence, faced with a short-fuse crisis, the central bank must recognize that a great deal of criticism and second guessing will follow its action. But if it fails to act, judging wrongly that no systemic risk is present, the consequences can be catastrophic. That is why any central banker—as a human being—will tend to approach these matters very cautiously.

The following are suggestions for dealing with a short-fuse crisis. First, doing nothing, either by design or by default, can sometimes be the best response, at least in the short run. Second, there are no formulas for dealing with a crisis. Although contingency planning has a role, crises, by their nature, must be approached on a case-by-case basis with maximum flexibility, and with a steady eye on the danger of setting precedents that could be counterproductive over time. Third, every crisis will be accompanied by a vacuum of information. No matter how sophisticated the analytical and intelligence-gathering capability of the central bank, there will be important gaps. Needless to say, when a crisis breaks, the central bank does not have the option of commissioning a study. Although it must try to close the information gap, the central bank almost certainly will have to act with less information than is desirable.

Fourth, in these circumstances the crucial elements of effective crisis management will almost always be communication and cooperation among the government, the top officials of the troubled and other financial institutions, market participants, and fellow central bankers in other countries. Communication and coordination are the most effective ways to gather intelligence—and to instill confidence. They presuppose a high degree of trust. For that reason the credibility of the central bank and its absolute assurances of confidentiality are vital.

Fifth, the central bank should never leave itself without a fallback position. Sixth, the central bank should be very guarded about what it says publicly, and when it says it. Premature pronouncements or press statements can be counterproductive.

Seventh and last, the central bank should always leave itself the option of the ex post review, which will help protect it against having to answer questions at a time when there are no answers.

Managing a Market-Driven Crisis

All of the above considerations relate to managing crises that center on seriously troubled or failing institutions. There is, of course, another form of a financial crisis, namely, a market-driven crisis, such as the stock market crash in the United States in 1987 and the "run on country" phenomenon in Mexico in 1995. In managing such crises, three points are important.

First, it is almost always the threat or reality of credit problems—including credit losses induced by the market crisis—that triggers the kind of behavior on the part of individuals and institutions that creates systemic difficulties. Without credit problems, it is unlikely that individuals would withdraw all their funds or that institutions would hold back on executing transactions—thus, without credit problems it is unlikely that gridlock in the payments, settlement, and clearing systems would occur. This holds true even if there were a major drop in the price of financial assets. In other words, to the extent that a market crisis has the potential to cause systemic problems, the danger point is likely to manifest itself in concerns about the creditworthiness of individual financial institutions.

Second, within the category of market crises, the Mexican-style "run on country" is a special case. The most important approach to these problems is to avoid them altogether by having all nations follow sound and disciplined fiscal, monetary, structural, and microeconomic policies.

Third, whether a crisis has its origins in a major market move or in failing financial institutions, the single most important way to ensure that it does not take on systemic proportions is for all nations to aggressively ensure that they have well-managed, safe, sound, and efficient national banking and financial systems. Even in the most advanced industrial countries, these goals are very elusive. However, the following characteristics of national banking systems can help to meet these goals:

- the presence of a strong and independent central bank that relies, to the fullest extent possible, on indirect monetary policy instruments for the conduct of monetary policy;
- broadly distributed private ownership of banks and other major financial institutions;
- the absence of internal or external credit controls;
- market-driven interest rates for both loans and deposits;
- a unified exchange rate system, whether the exchange rate mechanism itself is fixed, floating, or something in between;
- efficient, effective, and highly liquid money, equity, and debt capital markets, starting with state-of-the-art interbank and national government securities markets;
- efficient, safe, and trusted payment, delivery, and settlement systems that ensure the finality of transactions and payments in the shortest time frame possible;
- transparency and public disclosure in all things, especially market practices;
- equal treatment for foreign and domestic institutions; and
- a strong but flexible system of prudential supervision of markets and institutions.

Achieving everything implied by these traits is a long and difficult process, and even then surprises and shocks will occur. When they occur, central banks must provide leadership and be ready to act appropriately. The suggestions presented here—consisting as they do largely of lessons learned in the school of hard knocks—may be of some help in framing approaches to surprises and shocks when they arise. But at the end of the day it is that great intangible of the credibility of the central

bank and its leaders that will be decisive. That is why continuity, competence, independence, and integrity in the ranks of the international community of central bankers are so crucial.

---

*E. Gerald Corrigan is Chairman, International Advisors, Goldman, Sachs
and Company.*

Stefan Ingves

Sweden is said to represent one of the success stories of bank crisis management. As one who was deeply involved in the Swedish banking crisis
of 1992, I must say that it did not feel like a success story at the time. It
was more the kind of experience that Gerald Corrigan described: what do
you do when the crisis breaks, and at two in the morning you have to
make a decision based on the numbers that you know are wrong? Well,
you survive the next couple of weeks until you figure out the *right* numbers.

However, let me begin with a more basic question: Why should the
government intervene to restructure the banking system in time of crisis
at all? Part of the textbook answer is that restructuring is done to protect
the payments system— a familiar public argument. The other part is that
restructuring is for the sake of protecting depositors. Depositors should
be protected for various reasons, not the least of which is to avoid serious
wealth effects in the broader economy. An additional reason nowadays is
that a country with a small, open economy must protect its present and
future access to international capital markets.

The paper by Rojas-Suárez and Weisbrod identifies three principles
for the design of support measures in a banking crisis. My own formula-
tion contains a total of eight principles, which cover largely the same
ground. Here I will illustrate these general principles with examples of
how Swedish authorities attempted to implement them in practice.

The authors' first principle is that a distressed bank's stockholders
and delinquent borrowers should pay: if the bank fails, the stockholders
should lose their capital, and borrowers must make good on their obligations to the extent that they are able to. Stockholders are not to be protected from the risks of their own behavior. In the end, this means the
government has to be prepared to take over banks in one way or another.

In Sweden's bank crisis, the Parliament in December 1992 made an unlimited guarantee to meet the banking system's commitments, but that guarantee did not cover owners' equity capital. In those cases where the government provided financial support, owners lost their equity capital correspondingly.

As for delinquent borrowers, one way to deal with them—and this is another of my eight principles—is to set up specialized debt workout units that are organizationally separate from the distressed banks. The reason for the separation is that unlike banks, which like all going concerns want to maintain customer relationships, workout units are not supposed to have any customers left when their work is completed. Indeed, they want to get rid of their customers as quickly as possible, so they have completely different incentives than do healthy banks. Separating debt workout activities then allows the good banks to resume their normal business without being overburdened by a large volume of workout cases. The debt workout units—sometimes also called bad banks or asset management companies—can recruit for themselves the specialized expertise needed to transform the assets involved into something that can be sold. In Sweden the Bank Support Authority (which the Ministry of Finance created to manage the crisis) funded the insolvent banks in which the debt workout units were housed—before being separated—and thus became the owner of these banks.

The authors' second principle, about which there is again no dispute, is the need for prompt and decisive action. Several things can enhance the authorities' ability to react promptly and effectively in a crisis. One is a common yardstick for assessing the health of banks: supervisory authorities should have prepared in advance a set of procedures for working their way through the balance sheets of distressed banks and a set of criteria for evaluating them. The same procedures and criteria should be used throughout the system.

In Sweden the common yardstick was founded on the capital adequacy ratio. This was used to distinguish those banks that had only temporary liquidity problems from those that would not return to profitability, and to the minimum capital-to-risk-weighted asset ratio of eight percent of cash-weighted assets, within a reasonably short period. Banks in the first category received the support they needed to survive the crisis; those in the second were merged with healthier banks or radically restructured. Government support to surviving banks varied according to each bank's circumstances and included credit loss guarantees, capital ratio guarantees, injections of equity capital, and outright loans. These loans were extended at market rates of interest, so that the banks received no subsidy. Likewise the banks paid fees for any guarantees extended to them.

In assessing the condition of troubled banks, it is important to assess all assets at their proper value and to do so openly, even if this means paying more to support these banks in the short run. The Swedish authorities imposed clear and unambiguous guidelines for, among other things, determining when a loan has become nonperforming and setting aside provisions for losses. Strict valuation of real estate holdings was harmonized through a Valuation Board of real estate experts, who themselves evaluated a large number of individual holdings in the banks. Teams sent in by the Bank Support Authority assessed the value of the loan portfolio of each bank seeking support, as well as the value of the collateral for each loan.

Another of my eight principles is that when authorities must intervene, they must also be able to impose various conditions on banks. A fundamental condition is usually the demand that the distressed bank upgrade its internal controls and risk management systems. (During the Swedish crisis these were inadequate in most cases.) Authorities must also have the power to demand complete access to all of a bank's files. Without such access they cannot hope to determine the true state of the balance sheet. In such an evaluation it is useful to employ a bottom-up analysis (start with a loan-by-loan analysis and then aggregate) rather than a top-down analysis (start at a high level of aggregation), because using a top-down approach will cause the inevitable hole in the balance sheet—the gap between assets and claims—to grow during the process. At the same time, however, the crisis management authority must avoid becoming involved in the bank's day-to-day management.

The authors' third principle is that political consensus on the form and extent of government intervention is better than no consensus. Countries that do not achieve such a consensus generally experience greater difficulties, both in resolving the failure of individual institutions and in restoring broad confidence in the financial system. Sweden was fortunately able to build a political consensus to deal with its bank crisis: the Parliament's decision to provide an unlimited guarantee was made with the consent of all the major political parties, and the guarantee may be revoked only by parliamentary action.

Political consensus helps because it reduces uncertainty. Confidence has to be regained in one way or another if restructuring is going to work. When political leaders of opposing parties can appear together in front of the cameras and tell the press and the general public that they have agreed on a plan of action, then people know the plan is going to hold.

To restore confidence requires that the banking authorities bring the system's problems out into the open. Therefore an information or public relations strategy is essential. Lack of information increases volatility in the financial markets and causes them to malfunction—and, unfortunately, markets tend to behave the worst when they are most needed. The necessary information should be provided in many different ways, because one is dealing with different audiences: the political community, the depositors, and the international financial community.

Sweden adopted a policy of complete openness in response to its banking crisis. All nonconfidential information (that is, that did not relate to specific strategic conditions within a particular bank) was disclosed. The details of the government's support measures—and their implications for depositors, investors, and others—were extensively reported, both domestically and abroad. The Swedish authorities made a special effort to inform the international financial markets of what was happening in the country, even holding briefings at major international financial centers. They also maintained a flow of information to members of the opposition party and provided them with opportunities to influence decisions, both those of a general nature and those concerning support for individual cases. The opposition is in fact represented on the Board of Directors of the Bank Support Authority. This policy of outreach to the political opposition greatly strengthened the political consensus that proved so important to resolving the crisis.

Another important principle—and here I strongly agree with Gerald Corrigan—is the need for a well defined institutional framework. Without appropriate institutions and a clear division of labor among them, one does not know at two o'clock on the morning of the crisis who is in charge. The division of institutional responsibility falls largely along three lines: solvency, liquidity, and supervisory issues. Clearly one agency has to take responsibility for issues regarding bank solvency, because in any banking intervention one will always find that there is some kind of hole in the balance sheet. A second agency must be in charge of liquidity issues, although in most cases that involve real problems in the system, the problem is principally one of solvency, not liquidity: it is rare to encounter a situation where banks are solvent but merely illiquid. The array of bank supervisory issues should be left to a third agency.

Which agency should undertake which responsibilities? And what skills and expertise should be housed in which institutions? In my experience, neither central banks nor bank supervisors nor even ministers of finance have the skills to deal with solvency issues. Usually the government ends up owning something—whether it is a forty-story hotel in Atlanta, Georgia, a helicopter company in Zimbabwe, or a vintage Rolls Royce car in the south of Sweden. In such cases, people and institutions with the right skills to manage those assets must be found. It is particularly important to keep solvency issues out of the central bank, so that it can attend to its most important task, namely, conducting monetary policy. Another reason for keeping the central bank out of deep involvement in solvency issues (or rather, insolvency issues) is that the amounts of money that must be put up to resolve the problems of insolvent institutions could consume almost its entire balance sheet.

In Sweden, the Ministry of Finance, the Riksbank (the central bank), the Financial Supervisory Authority, and the newly established Bank Support Authority all were assigned specific roles, but a close network of formal and informal communications was maintained among them as well. All of these institutions had a voice both in establishing general principles and in deciding individual cases. It was deemed necessary to set up a separate agency—the Bank Support Authority—under the Ministry of Finance, because the ministry lacked both sufficient personnel and the specialized expertise needed for the new task. Adding a bank crisis management division within the ministry's existing structure would have interfered with the ministry's other tasks, such as preparing and proposing new legislation. It was also considered prudent not to assign the task of bank support to the Financial Supervisory Authority or to the Riksbank, again to avoid interfering with other responsibilities.

Finally, when one is engaged in the unpleasant tasks that I have described, it is important that the overall macroeconomic environment be working with you, not against you. If macroeconomic conditions are going against what the authorities are trying to do, the hole in the balance sheet is sure to increase. This can put the government, the banking sector, and the financial system in a terrible bind.

Sweden's crisis occurred in the midst of a deteriorating macroeconomic environment, and indeed it was the plunge in real estate prices during the decline in the business cycle in 1990-91 that precipitated the problems in the banking sector. In 1993, however, Sweden's macroeconomic conditions improved considerably. Following a large depreciation of the krona, exports boomed and economic activity rose. Interest rates came down, and real estate prices stabilized, although at a low level.

Business confidence, including that in the financial sector, was restored. The earnings of the banks improved considerably, and some major banks were able to return to the equity markets, adding to their capital and thereby improving their capital adequacy ratios. The banks returned to almost normal profitability in 1994 and 1995, and credit losses are down to normal levels. The Bank Support Authority issued no new support payments in those years, and none are expected in the future. Although the weaker banks retain extensive real estate holdings in a thin real estate market, and therefore will probably remain vulnerable for some time, Sweden can say that the most critical phase of its banking difficulties are behind it.

Stefan Ingves is Deputy Governor, Riksbanken, Sweden.

Part V

Crisis Avoidance

Ruth de Krivoy

Commentary

Andrew D. Crockett
Andrés Bianchi
Manuel Guitián

Crisis Avoidance

Ruth de Krivoy

Avoiding banking crises should be established as an explicit, high priority goal by policymakers and institutions throughout Latin America. Sound banks and efficient financial intermediation have always been important for a country's development, but today, the problem has reached new dimensions.

Severe banking crises occurred in many Latin American countries in the 1980s. The more recent problems not only threaten stability, growth, and modernization in the region, but also harm emerging markets around the world. That is why the international community is concerned with Latin American banking crises.

Reform programs implemented in Latin America have generally underestimated the risk of banking crises. The authorities pursued financial deregulation with vigor, but did not address sound and safe banking with equal determination. As events have demonstrated, bank insolvencies can play a role in financial system crises. After the experiences of Venezuela, Mexico, and Argentina in 1994 and 1995, we can hardly overestimate the importance of healthy financial systems.

Banking crises are extremely disruptive. The damage can be felt in the economy, in the political system, and in public attitudes. The cost of a crisis to the taxpayer is unavoidable: it might be limited if authorities bring problems quickly under control, but can be enormous if they do not handle the crisis properly. In its inevitable sequel, the crisis fuels recession, unemployment, and inflation. It erodes market confidence in the government's commitment to economic reforms and to sound macroeconomic management. In the extreme case, a crisis can derail economic reforms, as happened in Venezuela. Furthermore, the banking crisis obstructs the country's relationship with the international financial community. When these markets begin to exclude a country, its prospects for monetary stability and economic development suffer a severe setback.

Because democratic institutions come under great pressure during a banking crisis, it can also affect the political system. Banking problems usually arise in close association with outdated and mostly inappropriate financial and business legislation, and the legal system is unprepared to deal with the complexities of the crisis. Legislative reforms become not only necessary, but also very difficult because social tensions escalate and might lead to measures that accentuate distortions or set bad precedents. The judicial system confronts strenuous challenges and property rights may be impaired. Overall, a crisis harms every government institution dealing with financial issues, regardless of its specific duties.

Finally, a banking crisis damages the people's trust in banks and in private enterprise. France took a century to overcome the suspicions generated by John Law and his Banque Royale, which collapsed in 1720. Following a crisis, it can take a long time to rebuild confidence.

An Agenda to Avert Banking Crises in Latin America

Strong economies can withstand a banking crisis and solvent banks can survive macroeconomic shocks. Conversely, if the economic is fragile and the banking system weak, the risk of a crash is high and the effects can be devastating. Strong economies and healthy banks can be achieved only by *good economic policies* and *effective banking supervision.*

Several Latin American countries are currently dealing with severe banking sector insolvencies and need to move out of crisis situations. In these circumstances, how banking failures are handled become especially important. Adequate crisis management can help contain the losses, restore confidence in the banking system and the country, and turn the crisis into an opportunity. Thus, an agenda to avert banking crisis requires not only good economic policies and effective banking supervision, but also special efforts to resolve immediate problems.

Economic Policies to Avert Banking Crises

Financial euphoria and speculation are always involved in the origins of financial crises. Since the Dutch tulips, societies readily give in to the temptations of new investment opportunities or financial instruments that offer attractive investment opportunities. The objects of speculation, be they securities, land, or other property, rise in price and are expected to continue rising, building their own momentum. But when the fall inevitably comes, in Galbraith's words, it bears "the grim face of disaster."

A macroeconomic strategy to avert banking crises in Latin America must therefore focus on the goals of monetary stability and real growth: avoiding speculative bubbles, management of cross-border capital flows, close coordination between the central bank and the government, and a sustained commitment to economic reforms.

Avoiding Speculative Bubbles

Speculative bubbles are highly damaging to the banking system. During a boom, banks tend to lend imprudently, invest heavily in assets whose prices are rising, and enter into new business without assessing the risks involved. When the bubble bursts, asset values fall and the decay of borrowers' financial positions undermine banks' solvency and may lead to failure.

Conventional wisdom can help to provide a sound economic environment for banking, which means a good economic program, fiscal restraint, and prudent monetary policy, backed by a strong institutional framework to support monetary stability. An independent central bank is crucial in this process, since it serves to counteract the influence that politics and elections, the single most important cause of speculative bubbles in Latin America, have on monetary policy.

Another important source of instability can be found on the fiscal side, especially when governments are the direct beneficiaries of windfall export revenues or receive substantial income from privatizations, as in many Latin American countries. Extra efforts towards fiscal discipline are needed to protect the economy from these shocks. Success will be more likely if these efforts are sustained by sound budget approval and accounting rules, by stabilization mechanisms embodied in the fiscal system, and by prudent public sector borrowing. The political authorities must be committed to the goal of price stability and to laying the groundwork for effective coordination between fiscal and monetary policy.

Cross-border Capital Flows

Latin American economies have relied excessively on short-term foreign borrowing and have underestimated the disruptive effects of volatility on world financial markets. Heavy capital inflows generated a boom in many countries in the 1980s and early 1990s. Subsequently, problems arose as the euphoria came to an end. Political turbulence affected several leading countries in the region and almost drove up interest rates in the developed world. Heavy capital outflows and high interest rates hurt the banks, and the fear of a massive bank collapse further fueled capital flight.

Volatile financial flows are especially harmful to banks in developing countries. Capital markets are thin, investment opportunities are limited, and shocks easily translate into runs on deposits and speculative attacks on the currency. Adequate management of cross-border capital flows is therefore important to protect the banking system.

As a general rule, it is desirable to allow capital to move freely into and out of a country. However, discussions about the virtues of controls have resurfaced in Latin America as part of the search for protection from volatile capital flows. The degree to which a country can sustain financial liberalization will ultimately depend on the soundness of the macroeconomic fundamentals, the health of its banking system, and the quality of banking supervision.

Deregulation without strong bank supervision leads to imprudent banking, since bankers will be tempted to get into new businesses and take unwarranted risks. However, exchange controls are not the solution either. Experience has proven, again and again, that exchange controls lead to distortions and corruption. To avoid using them, a government should maintain an appropriate level of international reserves and take early action to deal with macroeconomic imbalances and potential banking problems. Once these controls become the only option, as happened in Venezuela, the need for proper policies is even greater to be able to move away from the controls quickly.

Most Latin American countries have totally abolished direct controls. Under such circumstances, the mere possibility of reimposing controls to cope with capital outflows—or simply putting sand in the gears—can be extremely destabilizing. These actions could be taken to mean that the situation is getting out of hand, and the market's reaction will worsen the problems.

Some advocate high reserve requirements as a tool to prevent the destabilizing effects of cross-border capital flows. However, high reserve requirements are an inefficient tax on the banking system, and they encourage the substitution of bank deposits with other liquid instruments. Financial transactions tend to move out to offshore banking centers, thus introducing further complications. As banking operations become less transparent, supervision becomes more difficult.

To deal with cross-border capital flows and to withstand speculative attacks on the exchange rate, countries must develop a coherent set of foreign exchange and monetary policies that rely on market-oriented mechanisms. More important than direct controls or high reserve requirements are the methods a country uses to correct fundamental macroeconomic imbalances and ensure that its banks remain solvent.

Close Coordination Between the Central Bank and the Government

Speculative attacks on a country's currency can trigger a widespread banking crisis when the financial system is weak. Bank deposits tend to fall sharply and the banks may find it increasingly difficult to honor their obligations to depositors. Weak banks are usually hurt the most.

A central bank's ability to withstand attacks on the exchange rate depends on the soundness of the foreign exchange rate regime and the strength of the banking system. Often these policy areas are beyond the powers of the central bank. Thus the government and the central bank must collaborate in resolving conflicts. By cooperative efforts, they can avert and manage attacks on the exchange rate, promote restabilization of the financial markets, and prevent major damage to the financial system.

The foreign exchange regime contributes to reducing financial uncertainties and thus allows for lower real interest rates. The critical factor lies in the decisionmaking process with respect to foreign exchange policy, an area where responsibilities are usually shared by the government and the central bank. No single prescription will fit all countries, but one thing is clear: a country cannot deal with cross-border capital flows and achieve financial market stability if the foreign exchange policy ties the hands of the central bank. If foreign exchange policy is decided by government, not by the central bank, the rules must ensure that the decisions are made after proper consultation with the central bank and are implemented by mutual consent.

Volatility and speculative attacks on the exchange rate seem to be a chronic problem in Latin America. Therefore, efforts to build a cooperative relationship between the government and the central bank will render enduring benefits.

Sustained Commitment to Economic Reforms

Good economic policies provide an environment in which real interest rates can be low and stable. They also serve to promote sustainable growth, which, in today's world of open capital markets and free financial flows, can only be achieved through a sustained commitment to economic reforms. There is less room than ever for policies that do not adhere to sound economic principles and lead governments to resort to direct controls. To succeed, governments have to establish their accountability in the markets, and this cannot be attained by moving away from market-oriented policies.

Effective Banking Regulation and Supervision

Alan Greenspan has summarized the goals of banking supervision: to maintain the stability of the financial system, enhance the efficiency and competition of banking and financial markets, protect consumers of financial services from fraud and deceptive business practices, and protect taxpayers from the risk of loss associated with the safety net for insured depositories (Greenspan, 1995).

Banking supervision serves a country's interest best when it prevents problems. Therefore, the first line of supervisory defense is to ensure prudent risk management by the banks themselves. As Latin American countries move towards market-oriented policies, open trade, and free financial flows, banking supervisors should establish incentives for safe and sound banking and move away from the direct controls used—and abused—in the past. The regulatory system must also eliminate the "rituals" of banking supervision, which for years have allowed formal compliance with regulations without addressing the crucial issues of bank solvency, profitability, and competition.

Banking supervision entails three basic functions: *setting the rules* for sound and safe banking, *supervision* to ensure proper compliance, and *monitoring* to optimize the results.

From experience, the key issues to address in Latin America are the following:

- strong bank supervisors
- implementation of the Basle banking rules
- supervision of insider lending
- home country consolidated supervision
- a comprehensive and effective monitoring system
- implementation of "fit and proper" standards in banking criteria, and
- competent handling of bank failures.

The Need for Strong Bank Supervisors

Effective bank supervision requires strong and independent bank supervisors. They must have political support to perform their role, thereby shielding them from special interests. To this end, bank supervisors must be accountable to both government and Congress, and there must be an institutional framework with appropriate checks and balances. Bank supervisors must also be empowered with the resources needed to accomplish their goal. Weak bank supervisors, lacking funds and political support, will be unable to enforce regulations that effectively address the sources of bank weakness.

In Latin America, with few exceptions, banking supervision has been a low priority task. Often it is performed by agencies within the Ministry of Finance that lack proper authority and are understaffed and underbudgeted. Therefore, giving authority and accountability to bank supervisors entails bold public sector reforms. Budgetary and labor rules must allow the creation of a force of respected and skilled civil servants with a strong identity and commitment to supervisory tasks.

Should banking supervision be placed in the central bank or a separate body? Independent central banks in Latin America can contribute significantly toward effective banking supervision, either directly or by actively participating in the national supervisory system. The central bank will have stronger concerns for safe and sound banking than any other government agency; it can also attract and train qualified people and establish the technological infrastructure required for modern banking supervision.

If the central bank has no supervisory powers and cannot act directly to prevent or contain a banking crisis, as was the case in Venezuela, its charter to pursue the goals of monetary stability and an efficient payment system will be difficult to fulfill. Therefore, if bank supervision is weak, an independent central bank vested with supervisory powers can become part of an overall strategy to avert banking crises. But strong, accountable bank supervisors, while necessary, are not enough to ensure safe and sound banking. Appropriate rules must also be established and enforced, and compliance must be monitored.

Implementation of the Basle Banking Rules

Banking supervisors around the world are adopting the rules established by the Basle Committee. The philosophy of the Basle Accords is to allow for healthy competition in banking while improving discipline through sufficient capitalization. These principles, once implemented, will serve all Latin American countries well. Bringing Latin American banking regulation and supervision into line with what is currently being done in other parts of the world will also build confidence in the domestic banking systems, and hence, in the countries themselves.

As these rules were originally designed for international banks, they need to be adapted to the Latin American milieu. The necessary changes include simplifying the banking system; establishing capital adequacy ratios that reflect higher risks; relying mainly on Tier 1 capital; using few risk-weighting categories; avoiding distortions in credit allocations; and adjusting the risk factor for government bonds.

Simplification of the Basle Regulations

Enforcement is the key issue for banking supervision in Latin America. It is risky to rely on regulations that are beyond the real enforcement capacity of the supervisors. Sophisticated, cumbersome capital requirement regulations can easily become an excuse to procrastinate. Policymakers and supervisors risk becoming trapped in a lengthy implementation process when new rules are being established. Vested interests might easily use the excuse of technical difficulties to avoid complying with higher capitalization requirements or avoid moving away from imprudent risk taking, especially if the investment climate in the country is unfavorable. Therefore the system should be simple, easy to comply with, and easy to supervise, so as not to compromise the fundamental goal of solvency for the sake of technicalities.

Establishing a Higher Capital-Asset Ratio

The Basle regulations require capital to be equal to at least 8 percent of a bank's total assets (including its off-balance activities) after applying risk-weighting coefficients to the assets. The 8 percent figure resulted from studies geared to international banks and performed in industrial countries with stable and diversified economies, developed capital markets, and a long tradition of strong banking supervision. It is based on the assumption that the quality of the assets is well known to the supervisors and is accurately measured. However, this is not the case in many Latin American countries. In this region, banks operate in a volatile environment, capital markets are thin, and many years of weak bank supervision have led to bad assets and hidden losses in the banks' balance sheets. Banks also have important "off–balance sheet" risks that raise the level of uncertainty as to the accuracy of the balance sheet.

Until Latin American countries attain world class banking supervision and can feel at ease about the strength of their banks, it might be appropriate to target the capital adequacy ratio above the 8 percent level. Not only would this compensate for weaknesses and accounting deficiencies, it would be more prudent than relying on a magical figure that the members of the Basle Committee probably never intended to create.

Critics of higher capital requirements argue that such requirements impose costs on the bank. However, theory and empirical evidence suggest that capital costs are independent of capital structure (debt-equity ratio). Latin America has many well-capitalized banks that are also profitable, and these banks were best able to withstand the trauma of Venezuela's recent banking crisis.

While moving towards higher capital requirements, bank supervisors must be aware that capital cannot be increased overnight. This is true in normal circumstances and much more so in times of crisis. Increased capital requirements must be announced well in advance, and ideally, timed to coincide with the expectations of good earnings in the banking sector. It is worth remembering that bank capitalization should be actively undertaken while investor confidence is high. This becomes an almost impossible mission once the economy enters a recession and a crisis emerges, as was the case in Venezuela.

The most effective way to recapitalize banks is to attract new capital, because problems are rarely solved simply by reinvesting profits. To this end, Latin American countries may opt to eliminate restrictions on foreign investment in banks or to adjust prevailing restrictions on owner-

ship concentration. In times of crisis, some extra effort might be necessary to induce owners or new investors to invest in banks through tax
holidays, debt-equity conversions, or other means.

The government may contribute to the recapitalization of banks in
times of crisis, either by putting up funds and taking control of the banks,
or by buying bad assets and accepting some losses as an incentive for
investors to come in. Government recapitalization of problem banks has
been the rule in many Latin American countries. However, this worsens
moral hazard and should therefore be avoided. To the extent possible, the
government should not be involved in bank recapitalization, but should
instead direct its efforts to attracting private investment and establishing
a favorable investment climate.

Reliance on Tier 1 Capital

To improve the capital adequacy ratio in Latin America, it is advisable to
focus on Tier 1 capital (equity and reserves created by appropriations of
retained earnings, share premiums, and other surplus). This does not
require the issuance of sophisticated financial instruments for which the
country might not have proper legislation or markets, and it is also relatively easy to use in reconstructing a bank, as in the Nordic countries.

Tier 2 capital is supplementary; it includes subordinated debt, un-
disclosed reserves, perpetual securities, and shares redeemable at the
option of the issuer. For developing countries, Tier 2 capital is an interesting improvement and will ultimately allow for more highly capitalized
banks through a variety of market mechanisms. At this point, however,
its main virtue—flexibility gains through market mechanisms—is not a
real advantage in thin and underdeveloped capital markets. If the implementation of Tier 2 capital requires major regulatory changes that otherwise are not needed, it is even less attractive. Many countries around the
world are trying to fulfill solvency requirements without relying on Tier 2
capital; this option may also be valid for Latin American countries at this
stage.

Use of Few Risk-Weighting Categories

In developed countries, it is appropriate to identify as many risk categories as possible, and to fine tune the risk-weighting criteria, to prevent
regulations from interfering with efficient asset/liability management and
competition. However, this approach demands more from supervisors,

since it makes it more difficult to ensure compliance and prevent the system from being abused. Fewer risk-weighting categories render the system easier to implement and supervise.

Avoidance of Credit Allocation Distortions

Now that direct controls over banks' loan portfolios are (fortunately) no longer in fashion in Latin America, bank supervisors should avoid using risk-weighting criteria to influence credit allocation. Risk-weighting co-efficients should reflect the riskiness of the operations and not the microeconomic priorities of the government.

Adjustment of the Risk Factor for Government Bonds

The Basle Accords consider government bonds to be riskless. This is an incentive for banks to invest in government debt and leads to question of whether we will truly have stronger banks in Latin America if financial intermediation shifts further in favor of lending to the government.

Two issues arise in this context. First, government bonds carry a market risk, as shown by the behavior of market prices for developing country debt. Second, if banks hold substantial amounts of government bonds, they might become too dependent on government and prone to credit events of a political origin. Thus, there is also a credit risk. It is useful to remember that when governments face financial difficulties, there are political incentives to stop paying interest (and even capital) on debt before cutting other expenditures. It is also easier to accumulate arrears with domestic banks than with foreign creditors. In Venezuela, the buildup of arrears in internal debt service payments has been a recurrent phenomenon and has always affected the banking system. Banks were further harmed by the Treasury's increasing arrears in 1993, while the country was heading towards the crisis.

The merits of inducing banks to invest in government bonds can also be questioned from a macroeconomic perspective, especially when the government runs a high deficit and is crowding out the private sector. Assigning zero risk to government debt will contribute to worsening the situation of private borrowers and will increase pressures towards monetization of the fiscal deficit. Both the banks and the government will have an incentive to push for an expansionary monetary policy, especially when the country is in a deep recession.

Focus on Asset Quality

As a complement to adapting the Basle banking rules in Latin America, supervisors must look closely into the quality of the banks' assets. The main goal is to prevent potential problems due to insider lending and imprudent asset valuation criteria. Frequent, effective on-site inspections are the best way to achieve this goal.

The Problem of Insider Lending

With few exceptions, ownership of financial institutions in Latin America is heavily concentrated, and banks are controlled by small groups of individuals. Markets are also very concentrated, since a few banks account for a high share of total deposits. The typical Latin American banking system is overly dependent on the fate of a few banks, which in turn depend on the decisions of a very small number of people. Insider lending and individual problems can easily trigger systemic banking crises. For example, private ownership of banks and financial groups in Venezuela is highly concentrated, and the largest six banks, all of them closely held, accounted for more than 50 percent of total financial system assets by the end of 1993, shortly before the crisis broke out. The link between the financial difficulties of *individual* bank owners and the generalized banking crisis is easy to demonstrate. This poses a special challenge for bank supervisors: how to ensure prudent lending in closely held banks.

To effectively monitor insider lending requires supervising a conglomerate that includes financial intermediaries. Latin America has a long tradition of close links among banks, industry, and commerce, usually through common ownership. Because most financial systems are based on a legal and regulatory framework in which institutions specialize in certain types of business and are legally prevented from engaging in other types, financial institutions have formed conglomerates of legally independent financial entities. These conglomerates are controlled by common shareholders and are closely linked to industrial conglomerates—a set-up analogous to universal banking but less transparent, and burdened by rigidities and inefficiencies. Commercial banks are usually the core of these financial groups, which include mortgage banks, investment banks, finance companies, insurance and leasing companies, brokerage firms, money market and trust funds, and offshore banking operations.

The main concern of bank regulators with respect to conglomerates is that a bank—with insured deposits—might suffer if forced to rescue a nonbank affiliate from failure. Direct transfers are usually seriously limited by law, but many types of transactions are more difficult to monitor. Furthermore, complex arrangements involving third parties, often in offshore jurisdictions, can obscure the nature of the transfers. Lending to affiliates has been a source of serious problems in the Venezuelan banking crisis. The dimensions that such operations acquired and their impact on bank balance sheets were grossly underestimated due to the lack of consolidated supervision.

Consolidated supervision by the home country, enforced by independent banking supervisors, is the means to address the issue of insider lending in Latin America.

Asset Valuation Criteria

Market value accounting generally produces an accurate measure of a bank's tradeable assets. However, there are some caveats to using this method in Latin America, such as the volatility of markets. Asset values in times of transition are unstable, and valuing assets to market could increase the risk factor in the bank's balance sheet. In the boom phase, prices rise sharply, and market practices do not take into account the effect that a downturn might have at any time. Moreover, many assets are illiquid, either by nature or because of exceptionally difficult market conditions during a crisis. In Latin America, prudent asset valuation could be achieved by applying cost or market value, whichever is lower—to avoid relying on a banker's prudence or a bank supervisor's opinion.

As financial innovations gain ground in Latin America, bank supervisors must move swiftly. Accounting and valuation rules for the tradeable portions of the bank's portfolio must allow proper measurement of the exposure to this new set of risks. This is a complex and quickly evolving matter in which Latin American bank supervisors could benefit from experiences in other parts of the world.

No matter who sets the rules, all government agencies involved in banking matters (the Ministry of Finance, the central bank, the deposit insurance fund, and bank supervisors) must approve the bank accounting principles, and the asset valuation rules. This will contribute to a smooth decisionmaking process, and strengthen prudential supervision and early action if a bank runs into problems. Disagreements or lack of participation could lead to information gaps or controversies that might delay the measures required to remedy bank insolvencies.

On-site Inspections

Information on the quality of bank assets cannot be based exclusively on bankers' reports, since these often mask problems. Skilled bank supervisors can usually identify hidden problems, but their job is difficult when the supervisory framework is weak.

Effective on-site inspections must be conducted on a regular basis by skilled professionals who operate under clear rules and follow rigorous procedures. These inspections are highly demanding tasks: they cannot be accomplished by understaffed and underbudgeted government agencies, which usually lack the necessary political support. Thus, on-site inspections reinforce the need for strong bank supervisors.

Home Country Consolidated Supervision

Consolidated supervision is the only effective means to ensure accurate information and allow for effective prudential supervision. Bank supervisors in Latin America must establish this as a goal.

Venezuela did not establish consolidated supervision until 1994. As the crisis emerged, insider lending, off-balance sheet liabilities, and offshore operations became sources of substantial losses. Furthermore, the first bankruptcy of a Venezuelan offshore bank in early 1994 revealed the existence of a substantial mass of hidden off-balance sheet deposits with virtually no asset coverage. This fueled runs on the international operations of many other Venezuelan banks, which worsened the crisis. The use of offshore operations as an outlet for problem assets could have been discovered sooner, had there been home country consolidated supervision.

The authorities responsible for the vast majority of Latin American offshore banking operations should strictly enforce accounting and disclosure rules and demand full compliance with external auditors. The information available to home country supervisors will then be substantially more accurate.

A Comprehensive and Effective Monitoring System

To improve bank monitoring capabilities in Latin America, we must strengthen accounting and disclosure rules, use liquidity as an early warning system, and expand the role of external auditors and private rating agencies.

Accounting and Disclosure Rules

Global markets are advancing steadily towards the internationalization of accounting rules. Companies that seek to do business worldwide would be well advised to adopt international rules. For banks, this is a necessity, since financial markets are rapidly integrating.

To meet international standards, Latin America must first establish uniform bank accounting rules at a national level to improve the value of available data. It is not enough for bank regulators to ensure the accuracy of balance sheet information; the public must also have timely access to relevant information. To this end, the rules must establish appropriate disclosure of bank financial data and of external auditing reports. The goal is not more information, but *better* information—information that is objective, accurate, complete, relevant, timely, and comparable across banks and countries.

Liquidity as an Early Warning System

Illiquidity is usually an early warning of insolvency. In Latin American markets, liquidity is the primary proof of solvency, partly because of the lack of transparency in the legal and accounting infrastructures (Rojas-Suárez and Weisbrod, 1996). Since investors cannot rely on the legal infrastructure to aid in evaluating borrower solvency, they force borrowers to remain liquid by restricting their loan opportunities to short-term funds and carefully monitoring their cash flow. Another reason for the emphasis on liquidity is the macroeconomic uncertainties in Latin American economies. In this context, investment decisions have very short-term horizons, since economic policy turnarounds and political turbulence can raise long-term risks to unbearable levels.

Latin American banks operate under these constraints. Short-term deposits are the rule, but most of the assets have long—sometimes too long—maturities. Compulsory long-term lending to priority sectors (agriculture, industry, or low-income housing) has accentuated this mismatch and made assets less liquid.

Therefore, the picture of a bank's assets and liabilities provided by solvency ratios must be complemented with objective measures of liquidity that can serve as an early warning system. Liquidity ratios are the most widely used tool for this purpose. However, a more detailed analysis of the bank's short-term assets might be a useful complement. Relevant information may be obtained by looking at refinancing dates and the projected cash flow needs of the issuers of securities that the bank is holding. Eventually, proper measurement criteria that include these factors in the liquidity ratios could be established.

The nature of bank lending in Latin America must also be taken into account when assessing bank liquidity. Bank loans are usually booked as short-term operations, but this is not the true picture. Due to the virtual absence of long-term funding, short-term loans are frequently used to fund medium and long-term investments. Under such circumstances, it can be misleading to assume that the maturities of the loan portfolio are really short term, even if the loans are current. The mismatch of maturities can sometimes reach extreme proportions. In Venezuela, 90-day loans are normally used for medium and long-term funding. Some of the banks even funded 12 to 14-year projects with 8-day funds. Not surprisingly, these banks failed.

The Role of External Auditors

As an arm of banking supervision, external auditors can perform a useful role by conducting on-site inspections on behalf of the authorities to ensure that information provided by the bank accurately reflects its financial position. However, such efforts may have limited effect, especially when bank supervisors are perceived to be weak. In Venezuela, the information provided by external auditors in many cases was ineffective and misleading.

To render the work of external auditors more effective, rules making them accountable to bank supervisors must be effectively enforced. After recent experiences in Latin America and elsewhere, bank auditors clearly understand that they may be liable for bank failures. Therefore, cooperative efforts between auditors and supervisors are becoming more common.

The Role of Private Rating Agencies

Independent rating agencies improve market information and awareness and complement official information. Depositors will refuse to put money in a bank or will demand a higher interest rate if the bank has a low solvency rating, and thus reward banks that are well managed. However, bank supervision by the markets—the depositors—does not prevent runs on banks. On the contrary, even a slight drop in a bank's rating could give rise to serious liquidity problems, especially when the market is unstable or influenced by a crisis. Furthermore, these private ratings could be self-fulfilling. A good rating reduces the interest a bank needs to pay and might cause shareholders to behave conservatively, while a bad rating increases the interest rate and induces shareholders to choose riskier strategies.

The role of independent agencies has been deemed so powerful that proposals have been made in other parts of the world to fully deregulate banks that agree to post a debt rating by an independent agency. Although Latin America is hardly in a position to waive official banking supervision and rely solely on private rating agencies, the role of such agencies should be enhanced and rules should be established to ensure the objectivity and accuracy of their judgment. To this end, the governance of such agencies must be clearly established in order to prevent misconduct and promote competition. The key is to ensure that private rating agencies are free of conflicts of interest, a frequent source of problems in Latin America.

"Fit and Proper" for Banking

One of the most important requirements in banking regulation is to ensure that those who control and manage banks have the skills, prudence, and ethics required for sound and safe banking. Some countries, such as the United Kingdom, apply a screening and approval process to those who seek to enter the banking business. In other countries there are legal, institutional, or political barriers to adopting such a practice.

Regulations to determine whether an applicant is fit and proper for banking are difficult to implement but are worth the effort. Fit and proper criteria address the core of a bank's strength or weakness: the people who operate it. Explicit regulations can protect citizens who want to enter banking from being abused by bureaucrats, while also protecting the taxpayer from undesirable bankers. To this end, appropriate disclosure of the applications submitted to authorities is useful. Fit and proper principles should be implemented in Latin America within the framework of the region's culture and laws.

Competent Handling of Banking Failures

Many Latin American countries currently face substantial bank insolvencies. Numerous banks have recently failed, and further failures are expected if special efforts are not made to move them out of crisis situations. The way a bank failure is handled will largely determine its effect on the financial system.

Banking failures in Latin America should be handled in accordance with the following guidelines:

- appropriate bankruptcy rules for banks,
- early remedial actions,
- clear responsibilities in crisis management,
- determining in advance how to distribute the costs of a crisis,
- ensuring the availability of timely and accurate information,
- avoiding disruptive bank closures,
- avoiding prolonged government involvement in banking, and
- protecting the payment system.

Bankruptcy Procedures for Banks

Bankruptcy procedures for banks must accommodate the existence of many creditors and allow for proper resolution. Because a failure can have a domino effect, regulations must allow supervisors to take control of the bank before it reaches the point of defaulting on its obligations.

Early Remedial Actions

If a bank failure is imminent, early action is the only way to achieve an orderly solution, avoid a contagion effect, minimize the impact on the payment system, and reduce cost to the taxpayer.

Resolution procedures should be imposed on weak institutions before they fall below a critical level, whether through liquidation and pay-off, government loans and open bank assistance, nationalization, or merger. Proactive authorities contribute to strengthening the banking sector and reducing potential costs to the taxpayer. Market uncertainties created by delayed decisions contribute to an overall loss of confidence in both the banks and the currency. Venezuela is a clear example of the harmful consequences of delayed decisionmaking.

Clear Responsibilities in Crisis Management

In times of crisis, expeditious decisionmaking and a clear voice can help restore the confidence of depositors. Thus, the institutional framework must provide clear authority to deal with a systemic crisis. This is crucial when the responsibility for handling banking failures is shared by several government agencies.

When public institutions are weak, a single, accountable authority with an unequivocal mandate is needed to deal with a major crisis. As the Venezuelan case demonstrates, conflicting authorities frequently lead to contradictory decisions that add to the general confusion and may accentuate the depositors' loss of confidence.

Sharing the Cost of a Crisis

Banking crisis management will be more efficient if early decisions are made as to how the cost of the crisis will be shared among shareholders, depositors, and taxpayers. Improvisation as the crisis unfolds will likely lead to the most damaging outcome for taxpayers, as happened in Venezuela. The Venezuelan experience also proves the need to establish from the outset that the banking crisis must be properly accounted for in the fiscal budget.

Timely and Accurate Information

The availability of timely, reliable information on the banking system—and especially on problem banks—is of utmost importance for adequate crisis management. Reliable information on large loans, equity and real estate investments, trust funds, proprietary funds, loans to affiliates, and offshore operations is also crucial for implementing private sector solutions and thus minimizing the cost to taxpayers.

Avoiding Disruptive Bank Closures

Bank closures can have devastating effects, as happened in Venezuela. Furthermore, if a bank is to be closed, the fate of depositors must be clearly defined at the outset and the rules consistently applied. Persistent depositor uncertainty while banks were being closed in Venezuela damaged their confidence, increased the contagion effect, and fueled capital flight.

Limiting Government's Involvement in Banking

Governments should not be bankers. If they become involved in banking as a consequence of bank failures, they must move away from it quickly and in as orderly a fashion as possible.

The "good bank–bad bank" approach has been increasingly used as a way to speed up market-oriented solutions. In this case, the government or deposit insurer accepts some losses or assumes risks of future losses in order to facilitate the transfer of deposits, other liabilities, and some or all assets to new owners that have real capital at stake.

Selling off the good bank is the easy part of the equation. If the bad bank can be sold, government involvement will be further reduced. However, the price will be low, since investors will face uncertainties regarding the value of the bank and potential legal risks. If the price of the bad bank is too low, it will most probably be kept on the government's books, as happened in the Nordic countries and in Latin America. But because this solution has a potential impact on money supply, and bad banks have to be financed, sometimes for substantial amounts, it should be avoided if possible.

To contain the losses and prevent government agencies from becoming the eternal managers or liquidators of failed banks, early reprivatizations are essential, as is the prompt sale of marketable assets in the case of liquidations. Privatizations are an opportunity to set rules and establish incentives that will prevent future banking crises.

Protecting the Payment System

Along with conducting monetary policy and overseeing banking and financial markets, the central bank has a mandate to protect the payment system. In meeting this mandate, the central bank helps to maintain public confidence in a country's financial system, even during times of stress (Spindler and Summers, 1994).

As a general rule, authorities must seek to minimize the disruption to the payment system that would occur if one or more major banks are unable to meet their obligations. In certain unusual circumstances, the central bank might extend temporary credit to a troubled bank so it could meet its obligations during a crisis. Thus the bank might weather a period of adversity until it regains the strength (and the confidence of depositors and other counterparties) to operate independently in the marketplace, or until authorities can arrange a more permanent and orderly solution to its problems. The central bank, as lender of last resort, can limit the spread of financial problems from a troubled institution to the payment and financial system more generally; however, that does not address the institution's solvency problems.

Protecting the payment system should be the highest priority in crisis situations, because the damage that could result from the collapse of the system could greatly exceed the negative effects on inflation. A central bank is sometimes confronted with conflicting objectives, but if a banking crisis is properly handled, conflicts can be resolved with minimal trauma. Venezuela's experience shows that if bank supervision is weak, there is need for an independent central bank vested with supervisory powers.

Deposit insurance should be geared to protecting the payment system while minimizing moral hazard. Deposit insurance schemes throughout Latin America should focus on bank liabilities, which are the core of the payment system. Protection should be limited to small depositors. All other liabilities of banks and nonbank financial institutions should be uninsured, and the rules should be clearly defined and widely publicized. Educating depositors is a way of protecting them from misleading information and fraud, and thus avoiding the threat of political pressures that lead governments to undertake massive bailouts.

International Financial Institutions and Latin American Initiatives

After recent Latin American banking crises, international financial institutions have improved their surveillance, lending, and technical assistance in the region. New means of averting and of managing banking crises have been identified and are being employed. This is a never-ending process that will continue to put governments and institutions to the test.

On a national level, there are now encouraging signs that both Argentina and Mexico have managed the most critical phase of their recent financial crises and averted the risks of systemwide banking failures. Although many problems still exist, these experiences strengthen the case for early remedial actions in both macroeconomic and banking areas.

Regional initiatives are needed to strengthen and stabilize Latin America's banking systems. There are many similarities in various national agendas for avoiding banking crises, and much insight can be gained through the exchange of experiences.

Ruth de Krivoy is President, Síntesis Financiera, Venezuela.

References

Greenspan, Alan. 1995. Opening Remarks, Thirty-first Conference on Bank Structure and Competition. Federal Reserve Bank of Chicago (May 11).

Rojas-Suárez, Liliana and Steven R. Weisbrod. 1996. "Achieving Stability in Latin American Financial Markets in the Presence of Volatile Capital Flows," in *Volatile Capital Flows: Consequences for Latin American Economic Reform.* Washington, D.C.: IDB/Johns Hopkins University Press.

Spindler, J. Andrew and Bruce J. Summers. 1994. *The Central Bank and the Payment System.* Washington, D.C.: IMF.

Commentary to Part V

Andrew D. Crockett

In many countries today, both developed and developing, growth has been retarded, monetary policy undermined, and budget deficits enlarged by bank solvency problems. In other countries the banking system appears fragile, and its resilience to disturbances is doubtful.

In all these cases problems could have been reduced or avoided altogether, if precautionary measures had been taken to at the right time. Especially important in this regard, as Ruth de Krivoy suggests, is increasing the resilience of banking systems—by creating the right incentives for prudent banking behavior, providing a healthy macroeconomic environment, and strengthening supervision.

Proper incentives must be created for the three groups most directly affected by bank failures: shareholders, management, and depositors. Most analysts would agree that shareholders should bear the losses from bank failures. To generate the proper incentives, however, shareholders must have both a stake to lose (that is, banks should have adequate capital) and the means to exert control over managers. This raises questions of transparency and corporate governance. It also seems fair that managers should lose from failures, presumably by forfeiting their jobs—except when the losses arise from government-inspired lending or when management experience is needed during the workout period. Balancing the goal of setting appropriate incentives with the need to retain valuable experience is not always easy. As far as depositors are concerned, it is also difficult to strike a balance between avoiding moral hazard and preventing bank runs. My view is that an element of coinsurance is healthy for all depositors, but particularly necessary for large depositors. (Here a useful distinction can be made between retail and wholesale markets, although the line between them is not always easy to draw.)

Concerning the macroeconomic environment, de Krivoy emphasizes the importance of sustained commitment to economic reforms, proper management of cross-border capital flows, and avoidance of speculative bubbles. It is particularly important not to allow an exchange rate misalignment to build up, because that could provoke a currency crisis. An exchange rate policy that at times requires a sharp increase in domestic interest rates can weaken even a relatively strong banking system. When the system is fragile, such a policy can be fatal. That is why exchange rate policy decisions must be consistent with the central bank's domestic monetary policy objectives.

Cross-border capital flows often cause problems in macroeconomic management. When economic reforms and stabilization take hold, large amounts of capital may enter the country, inflating the real value of the currency in foreign exchange and inducing a false sense of comfort in policymakers. If and when those flows are reversed, the resulting problems are difficult to handle. So despite the advantages of free capital flows, too great a dependence on foreign savings signals a potential danger. Possible cushioning mechanisms include strengthening of the fiscal position (perhaps to the extent of running budgetary surpluses), building up foreign reserves (despite the quasi-fiscal costs), and pacing domestic and external financial deregulation, to discourage rapid growth in potentially volatile short-term capital inflows. There are potential benefits from foreign lending, a useful type of diversification by domestic financial institutions: this could offset the upward exchange rate pressures resulting from capital inflows.

Effective supervision requires for strong bank supervisors, who are independent of pressure to soften controls. De Krivoy suggests putting the supervisory authority within the central bank, to ensure the independence of supervision from political pressures and help make the objectives of monetary and financial stability consistent. This is a different twist to a familiar debate. In industrial countries some have argued that supervision should be taken out of the central bank, to avoid a conflict of interest between monetary stability and financial stability. This argument is far from straightforward; but certainly supervision should be performed by an organization that is professionally competent and politically independent.

A related point concerns the enforcement of capital ratios. Too often, capital ratios are observed more in letter than in spirit. Bad loans sometimes go unrecognized because they have been extended to public sector bodies or priority sectors, and dubious accounting techniques are used to justify raising the numerator or reducing the denominator of the ratio. I therefore fully agree with de Krivoy's emphasis on more consistent and conservative accounting standards, on avoiding preferential credit categories, on Tier 1 capital, and on the use of a capital ratio well above the 8 percent minimum recommended by the Basle Committee on Banking Supervision. In the larger industrial countries the 8 percent ratio is used as a minimum, and national supervisors very often require higher minimums for banks in their jurisdiction. Given the uncertainties, both macroeconomic and microeconomic, in the markets in which they are active, Latin American banks should also aim for a capital ratio above 8 percent.

The only part of de Krivoy's analysis of supervisory techniques I question concerns the simplification of capital adequacy rules. The analysis of a balance sheet is a complex matter, and we should beware of trying to simplify it too much. Assets do carry different credit and market risks, and asset concentration has traditionally been one of the main sources of unforeseen loss. While I accept the goal of simplification, the medium-term objective must be to develop a supervisory system with the sophistication to deal with complex balance sheets.

Finally, I fully agree that we must improve transparency by strengthening disclosure. This includes both providing information to supervisory authorities through home-country consolidated supervision (and better information sharing among supervisors) and disclosing information to the market. As off-balance sheet activity grows, that is becoming more difficult. But this makes it all the more essential to develop accounting practices and establish rules for market disclosure.

Andrew D. Crockett is General Manager, Bank for International Settlements, Basel, Switzerland.

Andrés Bianchi

The paper by Ruth de Krivoy identifies two basic factors in the avoidance of banking crises, namely, sound economic policies and effective bank regulation and supervision, and considers whether such crises are due mainly to failures of the former or of the latter. The paper then lays out in a very orderly fashion the specific practical requirements of sound economic policy and efficient bank supervision and regulation. These requirements are quite varied and complex, and the paper lists a large number of them. It is easy to agree in theory that most of these requirements are important; nevertheless, I have two principal reservations about the paper's overall approach.

The first has to do with the obvious imbalance that exists between the quantitative and taxonomic abundance of the measures described and the almost total absence of any analysis that would suggest which of these measures are technically, institutionally, or politically more feasible, and therefore should be implemented first. The lack of such an analysis is a serious omission, because it implies that the host of measures proposed could be adopted more or less simultaneously, or that the sequence in which they are adopted is of no great consequence.

Either conclusion would be wrong for at least two reasons. The first is that any set of policy measures will include some that are more important, technically less complex, and less likely to provoke political resistance, than others—and this is all the more true the greater the number of measures being contemplated. Those are the steps that should be taken first. The second reason is that at a given moment, any government has limited capacity to introduce, and society has limited capacity to absorb and effectively process, a great number of reforms simultaneously. This limitation on the capacity of both government and any society inevitably requires one to pick and choose—in a word, to set priorities. Not to identify or suggest which reforms or policy changes ought to be introduced at the outset, and which should be deferred, is to imply that government's capacity to bring about change or reform is unlimited. This implication is especially lacking in realism when the initial circumstances are as unfavorable as those of the bank regulation and supervision system that the paper describes.

Indeed, if, as the paper asserts, the agencies charged with bank regulation and supervision have grossly inadequate human, physical, and financial resources; if they lack authority and prestige; if they do not receive in timely fashion the information they need to fulfill their responsibilities; and if in addition they are vulnerable to political pressure and influence, they will be in no position to introduce and implement a large number of reforms simultaneously. Under these conditions, even if these reforms were established by law or decree, they would not be efficiently enforced in practice. Especially in such cases, decisions will be needed about which measures are most essential from a technical perspective and most politically and institutionally feasible.

In fact, real improvement in a country's system of financial regulation and supervision requires a cumulative process of incremental but sustained change. Such an approach can accomplish the transition from the existing system, with all its weaknesses, to a new (although still less than perfect) system. Most important, this process of incremental change can lay the groundwork for introducing more complex changes in the future, as knowledge and experience are gained, as the technical capacity of the supervisory agency is strengthened, and as the new system begins to show good results.

My second reservation about the paper relates to its proposal that the functions of bank regulation and supervision should be transferred to the independent central banks that have been established in several Latin American countries in recent years. This proposal, also advanced elsewhere in this volume by David Folkerts-Landau, is based on two observations. The first is that the present institutions of regulation and supervision are technically weak and subject to political pressures. The second is that central banks are better able to attract and keep the qualified personnel needed to put in place the technological infrastructure on which modern banking supervision depends, and are also more capable of resisting political pressure.

Reasonable technical arguments can be advanced for assigning supervisory functions to either the central bank or some other independent institution. I doubt, however, that there are any real advantages to be gained from such a transfer, given the circumstances in those countries where laws establishing the autonomy of the central bank have been recently enacted. Indeed, I doubt that such a transfer of responsibility would consolidate that autonomy and wonder whether it might, instead, inadvertently undermine it.

Two basic considerations relating to the independence of central banks can help us understand why and how the latter might happen. First, legal or formal independence for a central bank is one thing; effective independence is another. Second, granting political autonomy to a central bank has undeniable and important political implications.

Legal independence is a necessary but not sufficient condition for real independence. Real independence requires that the notion of central bank autonomy itself gain political legitimacy—that is, that it be supported by the administration, the legislature, the political parties, and by public opinion generally.

Such legitimacy does not establish itself immediately with publication of the central bank autonomy law in the legislative record. Quite the contrary, it has to be earned with the passage of time, through the bank's consistent success in achieving its objective, which is essentially to keep inflation firmly and constantly in check. Needless to say, accomplishing this task is not an easy matter technically, and it takes time.

But there is another reason why central bank autonomy has such a hard time gaining acceptance. Conceding independence to a central bank is not merely a technical economic policy decision—it represents a transfer of considerable power from the government to the central bank.

Accepting such a transfer of power does not come easily to politicians, and it comes scarcely more easily to ministers of finance. In fact, many of the former and not few of the latter resent the very existence of an autonomous central bank, where unelected and virtually irremovable technocrats, receiving much higher salaries than the ministers themselves, are allowed to make fundamental decisions about economic policy over long periods of time. For these reasons, until an independent central bank has built up a conspicuous record of successful economic stewardship, it remains vulnerable to the threat of losing part or all of its independence.

Only in the past few years have central banks anywhere in Latin America been granted legal independence. In part because of this, they have not yet demonstrated clear and lasting success in reducing inflation. Consequently, none has solidly established its real autonomy, although I believe that Chile's central bank is well on its way. Under these circumstances, to transfer the functions of bank regulation and supervision to legally independent central banks may be to give them something they do not or should not particularly want.

For a central bank to assume such functions implies the possibility that it would have to take strong action against certain banks should a crisis occur, possibly including closure or liquidation. When that happens, the political pressures that the banks formerly exerted on the bank supervisors would now be aimed squarely at the central bank. The decisions that the central bank often has to make to fulfill its primary tasks, combating inflation and maintaining balance of payments equilibrium, are disagreeable enough and expose the central bank to considerable and often broad-based political opposition at a time when it is striving to legitimize its autonomy. To add the much more intense hostility of the affected banks and the interests associated with them might tilt the overall political balance against the central bank while its independence is still fragile. This, in my judgment, would be a clear step backward for the central bank as an institution.

A far more prudent and more effective approach would be to strengthen the capacity of existing bank supervisory agencies to fulfill their regulatory and supervisory functions. Some countries in Latin America today have bank supervisory agencies that are well endowed with human and financial resources, technically efficient, and immune from political pressure. Their existence shows that the reforms I have suggested are possible.

On the other hand, the costly banking crises that some of our countries have suffered in recent years—and the poor showing of existing bank supervision and regulation in those crises—may, paradoxically, enhance the political viability of reforms aimed at substantially improving the quality of existing supervisory agencies. The hyperinflation experience signaled the need for central banks to control the money supply. In parallel, the current crisis demonstrates the clear need to strengthen the ability of the supervisory agency to control bank risk. It would be unfortunate if the current crisis does not lead to the realization that these agencies need to be reformed.

Andrés Bianchi is President, Banco Credit Lyonnais, Chile.

Manuel Guitián

Ruth de Krivoy's paper is interesting, instructive, and timely: it makes clear that banking sectors are today exposed to growing risks, but also that they can benefit from new opportunities. It stresses that avoiding banking crises is a priority—a message that holds beyond Latin America.

The author lays out an excellent roadmap to avoid such crises, highlighting the need for a sound macroeconomic policy setting and the importance of effective bank supervision. Both these elements should serve to prevent crises. But bank problems will emerge even in the best of circumstances, and the paper suggests methods of handling them. Since there is little here with which to disagree, I will focus on a few subjects that underlie the analysis.

The first is the notion that some problems in the banking and financial sectors reflect the significant economic progress made over the past years. One important channel for such progress is the drive toward financial sector deregulation and liberalization, which is occurring in many countries. This of course, has contributed significantly to the globalization of capital markets.

Essentially, such a policy decision involves taking the government out of the financial sector and allowing market forces to play a larger role in financial intermediation. This enhances both efficiency and competition in the sector, internally as well as externally. As a result, both risks and opportunities increase. The risks are evident from the proliferation of banking sector difficulties in Latin America, as well as other regions.

Taking the government out of the financial sector soon creates demands to bring the government back in as the issuer of prudential norms, to ensure the soundness and safety of banking in a setting of higher risks. In essence, the issue becomes one of redefining the appropriate role and scope of government action, and of market forces, in financial activities. The challenge, then, is to keep the government from interfering with private activity (e.g., administrative control of financial transactions) and to focus it on the provision of public goods (e.g., banking sector safety and soundness). This challenge is but one aspect of the perennial issue in economic policy of defining the proper boundaries of government.

The consensus on this question has moved toward having government focus on establishing and implementing an appropriate supervisory framework to ensure the soundness of the banking sector at large. I should add, though, that there are voices in favor of letting market forces be the agent of supervision.

The general view, however, is that clear, transparent, prudential norms help the operation of market forces. Therefore, establishing a fundamental supervisory framework that focuses on the substance of risk assessment and management rather than on formal compliance is a legitimate government activity—indeed, a responsibility.

The difficulty is to ensure that supervision and prudential regulation support market discipline rather than hinder it. This is easier said than done: after all, the market will tend to keep benefits for itself and pass the costs to others. Or to put it differently, the market will tend to take advantage of the opportunities and shift the risks to the taxpayer.

It is important, then, to be as explicit as possible about government's role in the process, which is to ensure that the public good of systemic financial soundness is protected while keeping the government from interfering with market solutions to the problems of particular financial institutions.

Good policies, good supervision (including the adaptation of Basle rules—and I agree with Dr. de Krivoy that the Basle capital-asset ratio is a minimum that should in many cases be exceeded), and commitment to reform, all go in this direction. But all these measures are preventive. They must be in place before a crisis both to avert it and to help when it arises.

The second subject in the paper on which I would like to focus concerns capital flows, an area where liberalization has also been followed by a renewed interest in controls. I agree with Dr. de Krivoy's reservations about the usefulness of controls on capital transactions. What would be the point of liberalizing and deregulating capital movements, only to then revert to capital controls? As Alan Greenspan recently said, "To thwart technological advance and new knowledge and innovation through the erection of barriers ... would, as history amply demonstrates, have large, perhaps adverse, unintended consequences .... We cannot turn back the clock ... and we should not try to do so." In opening up the economy to capital movements, though, important issues will need to be considered, such as the pace and sequence of liberalization, as well as its preconditions, which include proper supervision and prudential norms. These supervisory prudential norms, as opposed to controls, are important. Open capital and financial markets entail potentially higher risks, and the code of banking behavior should be adapted accordingly.

My third topic is the approach to handling bank failures. Dr. de Krivoy's advice to avoid moral hazard and adopt early remedial actions can hardly be disputed; both are necessary and desirable. But I would stress the importance of establishing clear responsibilities and focusing on the distribution costs of such actions. These are critical for a proper approach to resolving the banking sector's difficulties. And while avoiding bank closures is desirable, there are other considerations to keep in mind. After all, closing insolvent banks not only demonstrates the firmness of supervision but also provides the right signal that market discipline will be allowed to work, and thereby help contain the tendencies toward unsound banking practices.

In sum, an important consideration in handling banking crises is to avoid reversals of appropriate policy decisions already taken, for example, through reregulation (as distinguished from appropriate supervision), or counter-liberalization (capital controls). The emphasis on market forces in the economy has generally served countries well, and there would not be much point in backtracking on this hard-won front in times of crisis. It would hardly be persuasive to argue that market forces will be allowed to play when they do what suits us but not when they do not.

What is most important is to keep policy on its proper course and not reverse it arbitrarily. In the specific area of supervision, nationally what is needed is a set of sound, clear, and effective prudential norms; and internationally, consistency and harmony among those norms to contain the scope for supervisory arbitrage or the search for minimum common denominators, which can only increase the probability and frequency of crises.

Andrés Bianchi makes a persuasive argument against giving supervisory responsibilities to central banks. However, there are still pragmatic arguments in favor of giving such responsibilities to central banks. First, the two most important criteria for successful supervision are professional competence and independence, which are often the attributes of a central bank. Second, a sound banking sector is necessary to properly transmit the signals of monetary policy; a central bank that does not exercise oversight may be unable to achieve its primary objective of price stability. In effect, central banks can hardly avoid a monitoring role over the banking system, even where supervisory authority lies outside their mandate.

Manuel Guitián is Director, Monetary Exchange Affairs Department, International Monetary Fund.

Part VI

Lessons from Country Experiences

A Regional Overview
Michel Camdessus

Mexico
Lawrence H. Summers
Guillermo Ortiz
Miguel Mancera

Argentina
Pablo Guidotti

Chile
Eduardo Aninat

Venezuela
Antonio Casas

United States
Richard Spillenkothen
Timothy Ryan

A Regional Overview

Michel Camdessus

In recent years banking and financial crises have imposed heavy costs: in the United States savings and loan crisis, in Nordic countries, the European Union, and Japan. Elsewhere we have seen the impact of such crises on economic growth and development. Several countries in Latin America now face the challenge of resolving difficulties in their banking systems. For a better understanding of these difficulties, we should view them in the context of the recent crises in Mexico and other Latin American countries, and the rapidly changing nature of international capital markets.

The increased challenges today in preventing and resolving both domestic and international financial crises are paradoxically a consequence of economic progress. The globalization of capital markets and the rapid mobility of funds that technology allows have contributed to this progress. Latin America's recent problems illustrate this point, for they can only be understood in light of the region's economic progress over the past decade. Mexico's remarkable advance between 1988 and 1993 is an example. During this relatively short period, Mexico strengthened the process of macroeconomic stabilization and structural transformation that it had begun in the wake of the 1982 debt crisis. On many fronts these efforts were remarkably successful: Mexico entered 1994 with a stronger economy, more deeply integrated into global markets. Because of this deeper integration, Mexico needed to be even more disciplined in its policies, to attend to its weak saving performance and large current account deficit, and to improve its external competitiveness. In 1994, however, Mexico suffered a number of unfortunate domestic disturbances, and policy discipline slipped. Between the beginning of the official presidential campaign and the new president's inauguration occurred one of those long intervals that are propitious to policy slippages, and indeed are a constitutional calamity in many Latin American countries. The result is well known.

The crisis in Mexico has been described as the first financial crisis of the twenty-first century, meaning that it was the first major crisis to hit an emerging market economy in our new world of globalized financial markets. The increasing international integration of financial markets has brought great benefits, by fostering a more efficient allocation of global saving and boosting investment and growth in many countries. But there is a downside to greater integration: vastly increased financial flows across national borders also make countries more vulnerable to changes in investment portfolios. As we have seen, concerns about economic fundamentals and policy shortcomings can lead to sudden, massive, and destabilizing adjustments in these portfolios. Disturbances in one country can be rapidly transmitted to others. Thus financial globalization, both a product of and a contributor to the economic progress of our time, has increased our need to prevent financial crises and to resolve them quickly when they occur.

The Mexican crisis showed clearly that openness to international financial markets today imposes an obligation of unfailing discipline in economic policy. Financial market integration may ease financing constraints, but domestic savings is still the key to investment and growth. Large-scale capital inflows, particularly when they are easily reversible and when they finance domestic consumption, provide no grounds for relaxing adjustment and reform efforts. In fact the opposite is true. The events in Mexico demonstrated the high costs that can arise when a country lowers its guard and markets exercise their discipline instead. Mexico's crisis was resolved through a strong policy program and large-scale financial support from the international community.

Argentina's quick and vigorous response to the spillover effects of the crisis also showed the effectiveness of strong policy efforts. By transforming the crisis into an opportunity to address weaknesses that had developed, for example in the financial position of its banking system,

Argentina—with strong support from the Inter-American Development Bank, the World Bank, and the International Monetary Fund—has done a great service not only to itself but to the region and the world at large. Brazil also responded quickly with policy measures. With the situation under control in Mexico, Argentina, and Brazil, spillover effects were quickly contained. Many of the countries that suffered least were those with sound policies, good reputations for fiscal and monetary discipline, and—I emphasize—strong banking systems. Markets are appropriately discriminating.

I have said that Mexico's crisis was resolved by Mexico's own strengthening of its adjustment and reform effort and through large-scale international financial support. The IMF arrangement with Mexico is the largest ever approved for a member country, both in absolute amount and in relation to the country's quota in the Fund. Why such exceptional support? The reason is very simple: it is called for by the IMF's basic mandate. Article I of our Articles of Agreement states that it is the IMF's mission "to give confidence to members by making the general resources of the Fund temporarily available to them under adequate safeguards, thus providing them with opportunity to correct maladjustments in their balance of payments without resorting to measures destructive of national or international prosperity." On January 31, 1995, this was the problem: if the IMF did not contribute quickly and substantially to a major international financial package for Mexico (and the IMF was the institution in a position to react promptly), Mexico may have had no other solution than a moratorium on foreign debt or a reimposition of trade and exchange restrictions. Such steps would have met Article I's description of "measures destructive of national or international prosperity," and taking them would have posed a major risk of such measures spreading to a number of other countries.

In the weeks following the eruption of the crisis, stock markets and currency markets came under pressure, particularly in Latin America but also in a number of more distant emerging market economies, including in Asia. These immediate spillover effects indicated that Mexico's crisis could raise doubts, unwarranted by the fundamentals, about the viability of policies in other countries as well. A major interruption in the flow of capital to developing countries could have ensued, and thus one of the driving forces of global growth could have vanished.

Following Mexico's adoption of its strong adjustment program, its markets stabilized, but economic activity has contracted sharply. Beyond a doubt, however, the decline would have been much larger and more prolonged in the absence of a strong program and international support. If the Mexican authorities continue to implement the program steadfastly and consistently, Mexico's economy is headed toward recovery in the near future. Given the acceleration of reforms in the program, Mexico should emerge from the crisis stronger than before. Thanks to the resolution of the crisis, earlier expectations of a marked and prolonged slowdown of private capital flows to Latin American countries and other emerging markets have not been borne out. The renewed access of several Latin American countries to international bond markets has been striking, and activity in new international equity issues has resumed as well.

In fact, the region has recognized that these new economic challenges are an inevitable consequence of economic progress. The countries of Latin America are fully aware, as evident from their responses to the Mexican crisis, that they cannot avoid such crises by reverting to closed economic systems, with exchange controls and less open markets. To do so would turn the clock back and forego the benefits of globalization.

With the crisis behind us, the challenging work must begin of strengthening the financial systems in those countries that are becoming increasingly integrated into international capital markets. In most emerging market economies, banks are responsible for intermediating a predominant share of financial resources. Therefore an increased importance attaches to the efforts of several Latin American countries to resolve their banking problems, which were more apparent in the wake of the crisis.

As has been observed on many occasions, the financial position of a country's banking system can severely constrain the country's ability to manage crises, and in particular an exchange rate crisis. The classic policy response of a central bank to an attack on its pegged exchange rate is to use its foreign exchange reserves to buy its own currency and to tighten domestic credit conditions. The effect is to raise domestic interest rates. The problem, however, is that higher interest rates may put critical pressure on the financial condition of the banking system, especially in countries where capital markets are just emerging. If these countries are to allocate resources efficiently and to withstand the pressures associated with being full-fledged participants in international capital markets, including the effects of large-scale and volatile capital flows, their banking systems will need to be strengthened and put on a sound footing. This can be accomplished by ensuring that banking systems are adequately capitalized, with appropriate accounting, legal, and supervisory infrastructures and effective mechanisms for the enforcement of regulations on a consolidated basis.

Banking problems often arise as a result of poor credit allocation decisions, inadequate supervision, and ineffective enforcement of financial regulations. But such problems also take place against the background of macroeconomic developments and efforts at structural reform, including financial liberalization—and banking crises are often triggered by macroeconomic imbalances. In some cases imbalances are created by policy mistakes, and in other cases by external developments beyond the control of national authorities. The IMF can help countries to avoid banking problems, and to resolve them when they occur, through both its surveillance activities and technical assistance. The IMF concentrates its surveillance efforts on trying to achieve the proper mix of macroeconomic and structural policies oriented toward private sector-led growth. Partly in response to the Mexican crisis, the Fund's efforts to strengthen country surveillance have been stepped up considerably. In particular, the Fund is paying greater attention to capital account developments and to financial flows and their sustainability. And the Fund's technical assistance in the area of central banking is intended to help countries design and put in place the financial infrastructure—including sound regulations and proper supervisory arrangements—that provides the backbone of sound financial systems.

In the end, of course, countries are responsible for managing their own economies. Latin American countries well understand that they must maintain their access to international capital markets if they are to achieve their potential for economic growth and development. Although some of the recent financial crises constituted a setback in terms of economic growth and access to capital markets, tremendous progress has been achieved since the days of the 1982 debt crisis. As long as adjustment and reform efforts are maintained, these recent setbacks will be temporary and short-lived.

We must prepare for important and difficult challenges that lie ahead. To maintain access to international capital markets, the countries of Latin America need to reestablish and sustain their macroeconomic stability and make further progress toward financial market liberalization. They must also continue to strive to establish and maintain sound banking systems, and sound financial systems in general. This volume confirms the essential linkages among these objectives.

Michel Camdessus is Managing Director of the International Monetary Fund.

Mexico

Lawrence H. Summers

The form of Mexico's crisis was shaped by the financial innovations of recent years, and advances in information and communications technology caused it to be propagated globally in a way that is without precedent. Thus Michel Camdessus has called it the first crisis of the twenty-first century. Yet after the crisis, Mexico returned to the private capital market far more rapidly than most observers expected. This is a tribute to the sound policies its leaders adopted and the rapid and substantial international support it received. While recent turbulence reminds us that Mexican economic recovery will take time, the critical phase has passed. Certainly this is true for emerging markets in general, which no longer move in tandem with events in Mexico, as they did in early 1995.

The Mexican crisis is not yet history, but it has been so widely discussed and analyzed—at the Halifax Summit, within the IMF and other international financial institutions, and among market participants— that some lessons can now be distilled.

Obvious, but Easily Forgotten

The first lesson is plain and simple: sound government policies are of fundamental importance. One flippant remark heard about the international economy these days is that because capital moves so quickly and so freely, government policies have little influence. In reality, precisely because of greatly increased capital mobility, the difference between having the right or the wrong government policies has never been greater.

Twenty-five years ago it was almost inconceivable that many countries might grow at rates of 7 to 9 percent a year. Yet in some places such growth rates are now almost ordinary. Countries with open economies can attract enough capital to make this possible by pursuing sound policies that ensure profitable opportunities for investors that also benefit their own economies. And just as good policies are rewarded more richly than before, mistaken policies are punished more severely. Other countries have made the mistake of pursuing ultimately incompatible monetary and exchange rate policies, as Mexico did in 1994. Rarely, if ever, were they brought to grief as quickly as was Mexico.

That illustrates a second lesson: that unsustainable policies cannot be sustained. This is a cliché, but it is nonetheless important. With a tighter monetary policy implemented early enough in 1994, Mexico could perhaps have sustained its exchange rate regime. But the particular combination of Mexican monetary and exchange rate policies was not sound, and these policies were certain to collide, sooner or later.

Mexico's experience points up a broader issue. There is a natural human tendency, magnified by the political process, to regard good news as permanent and bad news as temporary. When capital flows taper off, the temptation for government officials is to dip into reserves, sterilizing their intervention to avoid a contractionary effect on monetary policy. On the other hand, good news is often treated as permanent—and an excuse for big spending programs.

The reality is that capital inflows often reflect transitory changes in the international environment, while outflows are usually a sign of an enduring problem. Hence a third lesson: emerging-market economies should treat capital outflows as permanent, allowing themselves to be pleasantly surprised if the capital flows back.

A fourth lesson with longer-term implications is that, even with the increasing sophistication of international capital markets, high rates of domestic savings are essential for healthy development. The difference between Latin American and Asian economic experience over the past several decades brings this out clearly. In Asia, where savings rate are high, discussion of growth starts at 5 percent. In Latin America, where savings are low, growth aspirations are low too. Chile is the one country in Latin America with an Asian saving rate, and it has an Asian growth rate as well.

With the benefit of hindsight, critics can argue that Mexico was asking for trouble in 1994 by running a current account deficit of 8 percent of GDP. Had the authorities chosen not to permit such a large current account deficit, and still maintained the same low level of domestic savings (an estimated 14 percent), Mexico would have lacked the finance to maintain investment at even its relatively modest estimated rate of 21 percent of GDP. That would have meant it was failing to lay deep enough foundations for future growth.

As the Mexican authorities now recognize, if Mexico is to grow at a reasonable rate without returning to dependence on an unsustainable current account deficit, longer-term measures are needed to increase domestic savings. These include reducing the rate of inflation (so that savers are more certain they will get positive real returns), reforming the pension system, maintaining fiscal discipline, and working to ensure that a well-functioning financial system provides adequate returns even to small savers.

Regarding current account deficits, Nigel Lawson once remarked that they are dangerous only when caused by government budget deficits. However, as Mexico's experience shows, even deficits that arise alongside a sound fiscal policy can cause serious difficulties. Policymakers should remember that current account deficits, however they were created, represent borrowing on a national scale. They are dangerous if they are too big, or if the terms on which they are financed are too sweet for the creditor, or if the proceeds are not used to generate extra capacity to repay.

These principles and the Mexican experience suggest a fifth lesson: that close attention should be paid to any current account deficit in excess of 5 percent of GDP, particularly if it is financed in a way that could lead to rapid reversals. A current account deficit financed indirectly by government guarantees to creditors, such as happened through the currency risk insurance provided by Mexico's dollar-denominated tesobonos, or through deposit insurance on foreign deposits in domestic banks, should also be watched carefully. Particular scrutiny is needed if increases in capital inflows are not matched by increases in investment in traded goods sectors.

To condemn excessive current account deficits is easier than to prescribe what countries should do when they face large inflows of short-term capital. Working to raise domestic saving rates is an important first step. Another is to avoid measures that provide government guarantees, whether explicit or implicit. If these measures do not work, governments should be ready to accumulate reserves. As Mexico found out, reserve levels that look very substantial can dwindle quickly.

Transparent for All to See

A sixth lesson may be harder for developing country governments to accept: the need for greater openness. Transparency is essential to a well-functioning international capital market. Just as the generally accepted accounting principles (GAAP) have made an enormous contribution to American capital markets, so standards for reporting and disclosure can improve the international capital market. Such standards are especially important in today's securitized world.

Full disclosure will attract capital by reassuring the investment community. Moreover, it will promote market discipline, generating a faster response from private analysts and public institutions when trouble looms on the horizon. Most important, the discipline of disclosure fights policymakers' temptation to believe that they can somehow slip and slide their way through problems by making use of clever reporting.

Contrary to much that has been said, figures on Mexican tesobono debt were freely, immediately, and publicly available throughout 1994. And while foreign exchange reserves figures were provided irregularly, contemporaneous market reports contained quite accurate estimates. Nonetheless, as the Mexican authorities have recognized by putting their official statistics up on the Internet, fuller, prompter disclosure can only help. Recent steps taken by the IMF to set standards for countries' disclosure and to identify countries that meet them should make an important contribution to improving the functioning of the world capital market.

The seventh lesson from the Mexican crisis, however, is that even when armed with all this extra information, the international financial community should become better at surveillance. This is a task for private analysts, as well as for the IMF. But it is also a task for national finance ministries. Indeed, mutual surveillance is a central function of G7 finance ministers' meetings. Two secretaries of the Treasury, Lloyd Bentsen and Robert Rubin, have sought to spread the net through the APEC finance ministers' group, which will hold its third meeting in Japan next spring, and through a Latin American finance ministers' group that met for the first time in May 1996.

The IMF's present surveillance efforts, and other analyses by many of the world's finance ministries, were appropriate for the current account–centered world of 20 years ago. They are not sufficient in a capital account–centered world, however. Today one must also analyze the composition of capital flows, the risks of liquidity problems, and the possible reaction of capital markets to political shocks.

The style as well as the substance of surveillance exercises needs to be changed. Sending teams of analysts once a year to interview national officials and examine the books fit the rhythms of earlier eras, but it is not appropriate today. Following the Mexican crisis, the IMF has announced changes in its surveillance procedures. They are a valuable first step. But even more important will be the lessons learned by governments and the markets.

The international community must develop a greater capacity to respond to financial emergencies. The Mexican crisis reminds us of the classic banking distinction between liquidity and solvency problems. Just as a prophecy that a sound bank will fail can become self-fulfilling once a run starts, a country that is fully solvent can experience great difficulties as prophecies of default prove to be self-fulfilling. And just as bank runs have serious contagion effects on other banks, so the response of emerging markets around the world to Mexico's crisis shows that country runs can do the same.

As with domestic bank runs, any last-resort lending also raises questions of moral hazard. Planning too well to deal with failures may encourage countries to behave irresponsibly, and also undermine market discipline as investors rely on the international community rather than monitoring country risks. On the other hand, not planning in advance runs serious risks too. The Mexican emergency could easily have happened in a country that did not border on the United States, or at a time when the IMF was less well positioned to act.

To use an analogy, fewer people would smoke in bed if there were no fire departments. But this is not usually taken as a serious argument against fire departments. In the same way, the G7 leaders in Halifax were right to call for the development of IMF emergency financing procedures—the eighth lesson from Mexico—and for increasing the General Arrangements to Borrow to support these procedures. To minimize moral hazard, however, it remains essential that these procedures should not be spelled out in detail; and that it be universally understood that any financial assistance will come only with rigorous conditionality.

In the future, the international community must explore the possibility of orderly workout arrangements for situations in which debt cannot be paid. An international system for debt workouts already exists for sovereign creditors through the Paris Club, and for bank creditors through the London Club. Such systems have worked passably well because the number of key actors has been relatively small, so free rider problems could be overcome. In the case of banks, regulatory suasion assisted in working out arrangements that were mutually satisfactory for debtors and creditors.

The major shortcoming in the international system for handling sovereign crises is securitized debt. Tens of thousands of mutual funds and bondholders have replaced bank syndicates as the dominant source of private finance to developing countries. Not only are such groups of creditors too large to identify and organize; governments have far less power over them.

Bondholders had a free ride throughout the debt crisis of the 1980s, but that will not be possible in the future. At a time when many emerging market debt instruments carry yield spreads of 500 or even 1000 basis points above LIBOR, it is foolish to suppose that there will never again be a default. While nothing should be done to license any country's decision not to meet its obligations (so no Chapter 11 for countries), some planning is necessary to anticipate future crises.

In Halifax, G7 leaders called for study of this difficult issue. Any possible workout procedure is bound to have problems, but the present nonsystem is unsatisfactory.

Invest for the Future

In the end, however, fundamental solutions must always begin at home. The basic solution, a ninth lesson, is to promote long-term investment. Capital flows to Asia and Latin America differ in two important respects. One is that Asia has less need for capital flows, due to its higher savings rate. The second involves the fraction of capital flows that take the form of direct investment. Direct investment flows are higher quality because they usually represent a longer-term, better-informed commitment to an economy. The quality of capital flows can be as important as the quantity.

Latin America needs an estimated $60 billion a year in capital flows to pay for infrastructure investment. Asia certainly requires at least $200 billion a year to the end of the century. International financial institutions such as the World Bank should accept that their role is to support, not supplant, private finance. They can improve the quality of capital flows by enhancing their use of guarantees to catalyze longer-term investments. In particular, the institutions could guarantee (with government cross-guarantees) the political risks associated with long-term investment projects. For example, they could insure power plant firms against punitive future regulation of electricity prices, thus eliminating one of the biggest disincentives to such investment.

Even so, there is a tenth lesson: given the momentum of reform in the developing world, the work of economic integration must continue. Some try to interpret Mexico's difficulties as evidence that NAFTA was a mistake for the United States. The opposite is the case. The argument for NAFTA is that people are living on America's border in a society moving firmly towards democratic capitalism. NAFTA has locked in that trend, making it irreversible even when it was most sorely tested.

There is nothing more hopeful for humanity now than the trend toward market institutions in the developing world. This will be tested by more financial crises in the future. Countries will have to export their way out of financial difficulties. In the meantime, it is important that the march continues toward lower trade barriers—unilaterally, regionally, and multilaterally.

None of these ten lessons represents a radical departure from past knowledge. The circumstances of Mexico's crisis may indeed belong to the twenty-first century, but its themes are eternal verities of finance. Thanks to Mexico's reforms and the efforts of the international community, the Mexican crisis probably will not figure prominently in history books 50 years from now. Nonetheless, there is much that can be learned from it. And if those lessons are learned, they will enable the history books to tell a happier story.

Lawrence H. Summers is Deputy Secretary, U.S. Department of The Treasury.

Guillermo Ortiz

Even now it is difficult to say what went wrong with Mexico in 1994. Until the end of 1993 at least, it was widely acknowledged that Mexico had been pursuing sound economic policies. Several years previously Mexico had embarked on an ambitious program of economic stabilization and restructuring: opening the economy to the world, deregulating, reducing the size of the state, and much else. True, by the end of 1993 Mexico was experiencing a period of slow growth, and the current account deficit was creeping upward, but few believed then that a major devaluation of the peso was called for. In fact, by early 1994 there were many signs that the Mexican economy was becoming more competitive. Export growth had accelerated in 1993 and early 1994, productivity growth was higher than in Mexico's leading trading partners, country risk was gradually decreasing, and capital flows were sufficient not only to finance the current account deficit but to allow a substantial buildup of international reserves as well.

During 1994, however, Mexico suffered a succession of shocks, both domestic and external. On the home front there were political events: the uprising in the state of Chiapas and, most damaging of all, the assassination in March of the leading presidential candidate, Luis Donaldo Colosio.

The accumulated effect of these events eventually shook the confidence of investors. This uncertainty, together with the effects of rising interest rates abroad and a diminished pool of funds available to emerging markets generally, sharply reduced capital inflows to Mexico. However, Mexican authorities believed these shocks to be temporary; they responded by raising interest rates only moderately, allowing the peso to depreciate within its flotation band, and issuing short-term, dollar-denominated debt—the *tesobonos*—in vast quantities.

In hindsight it is apparent that the decision to accommodate these shocks was based on a wrong assumption, namely, that once the election was past and the political coast was clear, capital inflows would resume and the opportunity would arise later to engineer a smoother adjustment. What should have been done was to assume a permanently more difficult environment and adjust accordingly.

When finally, in late 1994, the peso was sharply devalued, that maneuver was less than impeccably executed. With the resulting sequence of events Mexico soon found itself facing a twofold crisis. At first the problem appeared to be a high current account deficit that had led to excessive spending so that an orthodox adjustment program, with tightening of both fiscal and monetary policy, would correct any imbalance in relative prices. As the days went by, however, Mexico found itself confronting a crisis of a more profound nature: a precipitate loss of confidence on the part of investors about Mexico's ability to repay its short-term debt. This second crisis had to be overcome with a substantial financial package to reassure investors that Mexico would indeed honor its short-term obligations.

What have we learned from this episode? One lesson is that a stabilization (or disinflation) program based on using the exchange rate as a nominal anchor has its limits. In the early stages of a disinflation process, when monetary and exchange rate policies are accompanied by a strong fiscal stance, inflation can diminish rapidly. The limits are reached when a substantial appreciation of the real exchange rate begins to develop. In this age of electronic, global markets and massive international capital flows, markets respond very quickly to the perception of an overvalued currency. Thus a policy based on an exchange rate anchor works best in the early stages of adjustment. Later on one must pursue antiinflationary policies through conventional tight fiscal and monetary policies, without relying disproportionately on such an anchor.

The second lesson from the Mexican crisis is that financing a current account deficit largely with short-term capital inflows puts a country in an extremely vulnerable position. By 1994 Mexico had substantially reduced its total domestic and foreign debt, as a proportion of GDP. All the standard indicators—the debt-GDP ratio, the debt service ratio, and the rest—pointed to solvency. In fact Mexico ranked near the top of the list within the OECD club it had recently joined. But so much of that debt was short-term that when the government was forced to devalue the peso in late 1994, the almost instantaneous result was, as it were, a run on the bank—the bank in this case being the Mexican economy itself, as Mexico's "depositors" rushed to get their money out.

How can such crises be avoided in the future? Clearly, if countries choose to rely on short-term capital inflows, they must be extremely virtuous: policy must be impeccable in both conception and execution. But beyond that, and contrary to the Biblical injunction against sounding a trumpet when one does good deeds, countries must transmit ample and timely information to the markets about the righteous path they are pursuing, and they must patiently and thoroughly explain and justify their policies to investors. Even then they must pray that no external shocks befall them, for countries that rely on short-term inflows are still greatly exposed to sudden changes in the external climate and to investor misperceptions of their actions.

How can countries reduce their dependence on short-term inflows? The key is to increase domestic saving, to create a source of demand for longer-term, local currency-denominated assets. In Mexico, domestic saving actually fell quite sharply, by 6 percent of GDP, from 1988 to 1995—the counterpart to that decline was, of course, a rising current account deficit. Mexico is now devoting its efforts to raising domestic saving through tax reform and reform of the pension system.

The serious shocks that Mexico's economy and financial system suffered in late 1994 required a rapid policy response. Mexico did respond rapidly, and after the earlier mistakes, appropriately, by implementing short-term measures to regain market confidence and to adjust the balance of payments. For the future, Mexico has pursued policies aimed at lessening dependence on short-term inflows by raising domestic saving and making structural changes in the economy to raise its productivity.

On the productivity front, Mexico's policy has changed considerably. When the economy first opened to trade, productivity rose rapidly in the tradeable goods sector. Today the government is focusing on privatizing and restructuring infrastructure, telecommunications, and other nontradeable sectors that are key to overall economic efficiency but may not necessarily benefit from open markets. Meanwhile the worst of the crisis is past, and in fact Mexico has begun to repay the emergency funds borrowed in 1994 from the U.S. government. The challenge now is to establish the conditions at home that will guarantee robust and stable economic growth.

Guillermo Ortiz is Minister of Finance, Mexico.

Miguel Mancera

Trust is the cornerstone of a country's financial system. When confidence in the system is threatened or eroded, those charged with preserving its integrity must act swiftly and effectively. Although there are no general formulas for managing financial crises, a basic set of principles must be observed, which include the following:

- prevent the development of systemic risk;
- avoid undue expansion of the central bank's net domestic credit;
- resist political pressures to bail out the stockholders of financial institutions, while protecting the legitimate interests of both creditors and borrowers (in other words, save the banks, not the bank owners);
- minimize the fiscal costs of policies adopted to overcome the crisis, and if feasible, distribute those costs over a number of years; and
- interfere as little as possible with the normal functioning of markets.

Preventing or containing a financial crisis is not an end in itself. The ultimate goal of the authorities should be to protect the real sector of the economy. However, the immediate objective is to maintain and strengthen the financial system, so that banks can perform their essential function of credit intermediation, without which the development of a modern economy is virtually impossible.

The devaluation of the Mexican peso in December 1994 had a severe impact on an already strained banking system. This event came after nonperforming loans had been increasing for at least a year. A number of factors had influenced the supply and demand of loanable funds, leading to an extraordinary expansion of bank credit to the private sector between 1991 and 1993.

During that time, prudence was not always the guiding criterion for Mexican banks in granting credit, or for their clients in soliciting it. For years the nationalized banking system directed financing mainly to the public sector. This produced organizational and information systems that could not adequately assess credit and market risks or monitor loan performance. In addition, as banks were reprivatized in 1991 and 1992, some new management teams, not in all cases experienced, took charge of the banks' lending function.

In the early 1990s, Mexican authorities liberalized interest rates and deregulated the banking system. These factors, together with favorable prospects for the Mexican economy, a reduced demand for funds by the public sector, and, most important, an enormous inflow of foreign capital —unleashed forces that led to a rapid expansion of credit to the private sector.

The net indebtedness of the private sector became burdensome with the slowdown of the economy, deteriorating employment opportunities, and persistently high loan rates in 1993. Although adjustment of the private sector's balance sheet position was underway, and commercial banks had adopted more prudent policies for granting credits to firms and individuals, by the second half of 1993 the problem of nonperforming loans had started to exceed normal dimensions. By the second quarter of 1994, higher interest rates and the modest depreciation of the peso following the assassination of presidential candidate Luis Donaldo Colosio put further pressure on an already complex situation.

The direct impact of the December 1994 devaluation on Mexico's commercial banks was limited. The Bank of Mexico had previously imposed a ceiling on the amount of foreign currency–denominated liabilities that banks could assume. This measure, adopted in early 1992, assumed that the central bank is limited in its ability to act as a lender of last resort with respect to banks' liabilities in foreign currency. Moreover, limiting banks' capacity to contract foreign debt was expected to help moderate the expansion of domestic demand and the current account deficit. These regulations kept the run on banks' external obligations in early 1995 from being worse than it was. The harmful effects of the devaluation were also contained by a longstanding ordinance that imposes a ceiling on banks' open foreign exchange positions.

Nonetheless, the devaluation led to other problems had other damaging effects: inflation and interest rates skyrocketed, economic activity collapsed, the burden of servicing credits denominated in both foreign and domestic currency increased, and banks' capital ratios deteriorated.

To deal with these problems, the government formulated a comprehensive package of programs, which are described below.

The first part of the package was a dollar liquidity facility, the aim of which was to stop and eventually reverse the run on the external liabilities of commercial banks. Relief to commercial banks took the form of dollar loans by the Bank of Mexico, channeled through the Banking Fund for the Protection of Saving (FOBAPROA). The high interest rates charged on these loans encouraged commercial banks to pay them back as quickly as possible.

At its peak in early April 1995, the outstanding credit granted through this facility reached $3.8 billion. By September, all the banks using this facility had paid their outstanding debts in full, so the program was very successful.

The second part of the package was the establishment of a Temporary Capitalization Program (PROCAPTE). The devaluation of the peso drastically increased the domestic currency value of bank loans denominated in foreign currency, causing the capital–asset ratios of many Mexican banks to fall below the 8 percent minimum. To remedy this situation, FOBAPROA purchased subordinated debt instruments issued by commercial banks with capitalization ratios below 8 percent. These debentures must be converted to capital after five years, or when a bank's capitalization ratio deteriorates beyond certain parameters. FOBAPROA acquired these debt instruments with resources obtained from the central bank. To prevent unwarranted expansion of the Bank of Mexico's net domestic credit, commercial banks must deposit the resources thus obtained with the central bank. This plan allows banks a relatively long grace period to obtain fresh capital and pay their debts, but it also means that stockholders could lose their investment or see their participation diluted if FOBAPROA should become an owner. If so, it would be only a temporary shareholder and would proceed immediately to find suitable new shareholders.

Five commercial banks obtained support through PROCAPTE, and the value of loans reached 7 billion new pesos in June 1995. By the end of August this amount had been reduced to 3.6 billion pesos, after one of the banks paid its subordinated debt in full.

High inflation causes a serious problem that is little understood, particularly in countries that have experienced long-term price stability. This problem is the accelerated and contractually unforeseen amortization of credits in real terms. To solve this problem, Mexico introduced the UDI (a Spanish acronym for "investment unit") to be used in denominating credits. The UDI is a unit of account with constant real value; its daily value reflects movements in the consumer price index, with a short lag. Consequently, the value of credits denominated in UDIs remains practically constant in real terms with regard to both principal and interest. In other words, credits denominated in UDIs are safe from the accelerated amortization caused by inflation.

Furthermore, UDIs are a valuable tool for promoting saving, especially medium and long-term saving, because the real value of resources invested in bank deposits, bonds, or other financial instruments denominated in UDIs is protected from erosion caused by inflation.

Problems have arisen in implementing the UDI program, because both bank officials and borrowers initially had great difficulty understanding the economic effects of the new unit of account. As a result, the authorities had to step in to facilitate the restructuring of a large number of viable loans and encourage their redenomination in UDIs. At present, a massive loan restructuring process is underway involving both FOBAPROA and commercial banks. The commercial banks bear the credit risk, while FOBAPROA bears the interest rate risk stemming from the conversion of credit into UDIs. These UDI–denominated restructured loans have medium and long-term maturities, so the potential fiscal impact is spread over a number of years.

Some restrictions on participation in the capital of commercial banks have been eased to attract new investors, both foreign and domestic. Participation by Mexican legal entities in the ownership of banks was liberalized, and some of the obstacles that prevented banks in other NAFTA member countries from acquiring control over Mexican financial institutions have been removed. The new law does not, however, permit full foreign ownership or control of the three largest Mexican banks.

Other schemes have been implemented to ensure that institutions remain sound, with adequate provision against losses and adequate capitalization. The Mexican federal government, through FOBAPROA, provides an incentive for banks to remain sound by offering to acquire a fraction of the banks' loan portfolio: FOBAPROA will purchase two pesos' worth of these loans for every peso of new capital paid in by stockholders. In exchange, banks must buy long-term government bonds with the proceeds. The banks retain responsibility for managing the loans and share in any eventual losses.

A number of steps were taken to improve financial supervision: the National Banking Commission and the Securities Commission were joined together and, most important, the staff of the new commission was strengthened. In addition, the International Monetary Fund, the World Bank, and the Inter-American Development Bank are providing technical advice and assistance.

In August 1995, to alleviate the difficulties faced by a large number of debtors due to high interest rates and the steep drop in economic activity and employment, the Mexican government introduced an unprecedented, one-time debt relief program targeted at credit card, small business, agricultural, and mortgage borrowers. This program, which complements and strengthens existing arrangements, aims to encourage additional loan restructuring, avoid the development of a culture of default, provide interest relief, and offer a legal truce to debtors.

The cost of the program, based on conservative assumptions about the level of interbank interest rates, is an estimated 7 billion new pesos, or 0.4 percent of Mexico's projected 1995 GDP. The total fiscal cost of all schemes to support debtors and the banking system is expected to be around 2.3 percent of 1995 GDP and will be spread over a period of years.

Mexico has a long way to go to fully address the problem of nonperforming assets in bank portfolios. The fundamental elements for a permanent solution are in place, however, and Mexico expects that these steps, in combination with complementary measures in other sectors, will in time overcome the problem. It is noteworthy that none of the schemes implemented to deal with the problem of nonperforming loans and to support the banking system implies the net expansion of primary credit.

Miguel Mancera is Governor of the Central Bank of Mexico.

Argentina

Pablo Guidotti

Argentina's experience during 1995 may prove instructive to other emerging markets, in particular regarding the role of bank regulation and mechanisms to resolve problem banks. My comments will focus on the role of regulation and the resolution process of problem banks rather than supervision. In my view, the Argentine financial system's brush with the so-called tequila effect was essentially a problem of liquidity, not solvency. Effective regulation and resolution enabled our banking system to withstand the test imposed on it by the Mexican crisis. A few facts illustrate the seriousness of the liquidity problem. Over a period of three months, the Argentine banking system lost 18 percent of its deposits; five months later, however, more than two-thirds of those deposits had returned. In the few cases where banks were liquidated or their assets sold, losses to depositors were minimal, amounting to under 1 percent of the deposit base.

To be sure, the benefits of prudential regulations, as well as the effectiveness of the bank resolution process, depend fundamentally on a strong supervisory system. Bank capital and capital requirements, for instance, mean little without a reliable system of loan classification and provisioning. How Argentina's financial system operated during the tequila effect shows that supervisors need to look at banks' operations on a consolidated basis, because that is precisely how the market looks at them. Some banks experienced heavy losses largely because the market did not know the extent of their offshore activities, or whether they had fully informed the central bank of all their operations.

Before discussing the specifics of regulation and resolution, I will address two common views mentioned elsewhere in this volume: first, that banks are special, and second, that public funds have to be used in resolving banking problems.

Why are banks special? When one looks at the multiple aspects of banking, what is special comes down to one key characteristic: high leverage. And since high leverage can only be attained by issuing short-term liabilities (i.e., deposits), this explains why, in essence, banks tend to be illiquid. Why then are banks allowed to operate with much higher leverage than any other industry? The conventional view is that there is always some government institution explicitly or implicitly standing by to provide funding to the banking system whenever the market tests this illiquidity. In fact, if such institutions were perfectly credible, the argument goes, there may not be market tests at all. This framework applies to industrial economies and is, in fact, the basis for the prudential recommendations of the Bank for International Settlements (BIS).

With regard to emerging market economies, however, it is by no means clear whether a government can assist banking systems when they come under severe stress, because governments themselves are often under stress at the same time. The relevant issue here is not unwillingness, but, rather, inability to provide the required liquidity assistance. The different abilities of industrial and emerging market economies to assist the banking system has, in my view, enormous implications for the design of bank regulations in the latter. In particular, regulatory systems in emerging market economies may need to be significantly more conservative than called for by the minimum standards of the BIS.

Of the many prudential regulations that are important for emerging markets, let us consider liquidity and capital requirements. The resilience of the Argentine banking system in the face of the tequila effect was in large measure due to strong reserve requirements, or more generally, liquidity requirements. Banks in Argentina are required to invest a significant share of their deposits in liquid assets, a large proportion of which must be international liquid assets, not domestic government bonds. When the private sector in an emerging market economy comes under a financial squeeze, often so does the government. Government bonds can therefore lose their value very rapidly. Thus, while domestic government bonds at the individual bank level may be regarded as liquid, they are not so in the event of systemic illiquidity. Hence the central bank must impose liquidity requirements, in order to prevent systemic crises.

Argentina's experience shows that the presence of liquidity requirements of this kind significantly enhances the central bank's ability to manage monetary and financial conditions under stress, when there are limitations to the use of the discount window or the lender-of-last-resort functions. Such limitations may derive from the legal framework governing the central bank, as in Argentina, but they also may come from adverse market conditions. Following the 18 percent decline in deposits during the recent crisis, only about 10 percent found its way through to the asset side in the form of a credit crunch. This indicates the power of the instruments at the central bank's disposal to act as a shock absorber. About half of these regulations concern the management of liquidity requirements.

Many argue that high reserve or liquidity requirements make a country's banks less competitive vis-à-vis foreign banks that are not subject to those requirements. This comparison of banks in emerging markets with those in industrial countries is inappropriate, however. In the U.S. banking system, for example, nearly 25 percent of assets consist of government securities. This makes the assets of U.S. banks highly liquid, quite apart from reserve requirements. Banks in emerging market economies as a rule do not choose to hold such a large share of their assets in government securities, or indeed, any domestic securities, because their prices are more volatile than those of similar securities in industrial countries. At the same time, banks have little incentive to hold internationally liquid assets, given the prevailing spreads earned on domestic over foreign assets.

Consequently the portfolios of banks in emerging market economies tend to be more illiquid, with a greater share of loans, than are portfolios in industrial country banks. Stringent liquidity requirements of the kind applied in Argentina are therefore needed simply to bring the overall level of bank liquidity in line with what is universally considered sound bank management.

Let me now turn to capital adequacy. Capital requirements are effective only to the extent that one can accurately value bank assets. That can be done only through on-site examinations. Assuming that asset valuation is reasonably accurate, however, what should the capital requirement be? In particular, how should bank supervisors in emerging market economies interpret the 8 percent standard proposed by the BIS for industrial countries? The capital requirement has essentially two main roles. One is to ensure that, under normal economic conditions, adequate capital will act as a shock absorber on asset quality, so that banks preserve their solvency during the business cycle. In particular, bank capital should be high enough so that management never has the incentive to engage in the kind of desperate behavior common to institutions whose equity has fallen close to zero or has become negative. On this account alone, given the high volatility to which emerging markets are exposed, high capital requirements are appropriate. In Argentina, capital requirements are set at about 16 percent of risk-weighted assets, and the banking system holds a capitalization level of about 18 percent.

Capital requirements also play an important role in crisis resolution. As explained below, this role is of particular relevance when dealing with systemic liquidity crises such as the tequila effect. As we have observed in Argentina, even when banks have positive capital, a liquidity squeeze of a systemic nature may provoke a complete loss of public confidence, and hence, failure. In such events, when a failing bank needs to be sold or taken over by another bank, the acquiring institution will typically place a significant discount on the value of assets being acquired. Such discount reflects the risk premium placed by the buyer on account of two factors: first, bank loans are typically difficult to value in stress scenarios, and second, the speed of the transaction forces buyers to make decisions with seriously inadequate information.

Thus, if the use of public funds is limited during the resolution process, then its outcome may depend on how much capital is left in the bank to absorb the above-mentioned risk premium. This suggests that capital requirements should be set at even higher levels than those implied by the need to cover the credit risk.

These considerations also imply that supervisors should have a clear legal mandate to initiate the resolution process. In this respect, the lower the amount of public funds available during resolution, the higher the level of bank capital at which the resolution process should be initiated. The sort of legal mandate I propose would closely resemble that contemplated in the FDIC Improvement Act in the case of the U.S. banking system, with higher capitalization thresholds being applied in emerging markets.

I will now turn briefly to the resolution process itself, and discuss the recent Argentine experience. When supervisory authorities must intervene in the banking system, it is best to move quickly, if they have sufficient funds available to take over the failing banks and pay off the depositors. But what if sufficient public funds are lacking, as often happens in emerging markets? If funds are limited or nonexistent, supervisors can only be patient. As Aristóbulo de Juan argues elsewhere in this volume, one must keep in mind the alternatives to any supervisory action, and sometimes the only alternative to forbearance is to force the problem bank into bankruptcy. From the perspective of depositors, that is most likely to be the worst alternative, because bankruptcy proceedings are typically protracted processes that end up consuming all the banks' asset value.

In 1992 Argentina passed laws that severely limited the central bank's capability to inject funds into the banking system, putting the failure resolution process in the domain of the judicial system rather than the central bank, and eliminating deposit insurance. Thus, entering 1995, we had little experience with bank crisis resolution within this new context. As the tequila effect evolved, new legislation was required to improve the central bank's effectiveness in the resolution of problem banks, keeping the general philosophy of the 1992 law intact.

Under Argentine banking law, the main protection afforded to depositors is essentially the right to seniority in bankruptcy proceedings against the failed bank. Moreover, to enhance the protection of small depositors, a special privilege is granted up to five thousand dollars per person. Based on this background, the legislative changes introduced in 1995 allow the central bank to segregate assets along with the senior liabilities (i.e., those with small depositors and the central bank) and hence, sell off those parts of the failing bank that can be kept in operation. In this way, the process achieves efficiency while being consistent with the eventual seniority rights embedded in the bankruptcy legislation.

The preliminary results of applying this methodology during 1995 are encouraging. So far the experience shows that funds obtained from the sale of a small amount of assets can go a long way: in the few cases in which banks had to be closed, more than 75 percent of depositors have been repaid in full by selling around 10 percent of the bank's assets.

In some of the more complex cases, only a limited amount of bank assets could be sold—enough to repay small depositors, and when applicable, part of the bank's obligations to the central bank. There we established trust funds or mutual funds to receive the remaining assets and senior liabilities, with the voluntary assent of a critical mass of creditors. With this procedure, it is expected that more than 50 percent of the bank's remaining liabilities will be repaid. This is quite a favorable outcome under the circumstances, and interestingly, is consistent with losses incurred in other banking crises, where the resolution involved significant use of public funds. For instance, Rojas-Suárez and Weisbrod find that, in the case of Chile, it is expected that half of the central bank's outlays for resolution assistance will not be recovered. Similar orders of magnitudes are quoted by Timothy Ryan elsewhere in this volume, to the effect that the bailout of the savings and loan industry extended to 700 institutions with assets of $400 billion, whereas the cost to the taxpayer was approximately half that, or $200 billion. Thus, a primary advantage of the resolution process I have outlined is that it keeps taxpayers' cost to a minimum.

Pablo Guidotti is Secretary of Finance, Ministry of Economic Affairs and Public Works, Argentina.

Chile

Eduardo Aninat

Banking crises and their relation to macroeconomic policy are timely topics, given the financial instability in Latin America and other emerging economies in recent years. We in Chile can now claim that after a long struggle to implement difficult structural reforms, we have finally overcome much of that tendency toward instability. Today the Chilean banking system is operating normally, soundly, and with the support of a domestic saving rate of about 27 percent. This strong performance, however, comes a after a period of extreme turbulence in the early 1980s, during which Chile suffered the same costs and experienced the same turmoil that other countries did during the debt crisis of those years. Chile went through both a severe banking crisis and a severe indebtedness problem during the 1980s, and that experience has taught us lessons that may prove valuable for others today.

Chile has learned one lesson in particular about financial markets in developing countries: at certain points in the business cycle, these markets can become highly unstable. They must be carefully monitored and expertly regulated if they are to support the intermediation of saving and long-term investment that a country needs in order to develop. This lesson has become deeply ingrained both among Chilean authorities and in Chilean institutions, across the spectrum. There is unanimous agreement that we must avoid repeating the financial crises of the recent past.

The anatomy of financial crises is by now familiar. Each crisis has three phases: a speculative boom, followed by a loss of confidence and distress in one part of the system, and ultimately by systemic failure and collapse. The first phase begins when a significant number of key market participants upgrade their expectations, adopting an overly optimistic view of the economy's overall prospects. People come to expect rapidly increasing profits and take for granted the opportunity to reap large capital gains with little risk. Eventually there is a strong "perceived wealth" effect: households as well as businesses begin to consume beyond their reasonable limits; that is, beyond what any prudent assessment of their future income would warrant.

The shift in expectations that gives rise to such behavior can occur for a variety of reasons: the discovery of valuable natural resources, a surge in productivity in one or more sectors of the economy, a positive shock to the terms of trade, and so on. The demand for credit increases substantially to finance capital investment and to acquire assets of all sorts, from real estate to stocks and bonds to office buildings. Asset prices soar, and the increase in the country's perceived wealth becomes a major factor in the economy's overall dynamism. As these assets rise in value, businesses and households are led to offer them, and banks to accept them, as collateral against which to borrow to acquire still more assets. The asset side of the balance sheet of the banking system grows rapidly and is perceived as improving, while liabilities—deposits as well as other claims both domestic and foreign—expand briskly as well. The overall picture is one of high investment, strong demand, high prices, and growing private wealth. Meanwhile, the behavior of bankers during this boom phase is the exact opposite of the familiar saying: instead of always being two steps behind the times, bankers race ahead of the curve, driven by their Keynesian animal spirits to build up their loan portfolios at an ever more frantic pace.

The distinguishing feature of such a speculative boom is that the demand for credit, the rise in asset prices, and indeed financial conditions in general are in no way justified by the underlying structural forces that govern the growth of GDP and the long-term rise in productivity of economic factors. Lacking a firm anchor in economic fundamentals, the boom becomes unsustainable.

At this point the economy moves into the second phase, and confidence dwindles as key macroeconomic signals—interest rates, exchange rates, wages, inflation—become misaligned. Growth in various sectors and in some of the fiscal accounts begins to lag. In this situation of increasing uncertainty, some small news item—a minor political embarrassment, signs of distress in a few banks—can trigger a rush to sell in one or another part of the market, reinforcing the uncertainty and worry. This eventually precipitates a larger selloff of stocks and bonds, or a slump in real estate markets, or in whatever group of assets was enjoying a speculative runup. This sudden turnabout causes a seismic shift of relative portfolio values, with immediate consequences for financial institutions. The market value of banks' assets declines sharply as the loans they have made become riskier (or rather, as their existing risk is exposed) and as the collateral supporting those loans plummets in value. Loan-loss provisions are discovered to be far short of what is needed in the changed situation. Meanwhile, the leverage of the banking system has expanded to unsustainable levels, and loan portfolios begin to give off the unmistakable odor of putrefaction.

The third phase is financial failure and collapse. If the drop in confidence becomes generalized, an open crisis in the banking system develops. Loans become nonperforming and collateralized assets difficult to recover. Financial institutions discover that the supply of foreign funds is no longer infinitely elastic as it had seemed during the euphoria. In fact, it has gone infinitely inelastic—the promise of higher interest rates is no longer enough to induce foreign investors to stay. The typical aftermath is one of high interest rates, widespread bank failure, a credit crunch, and other forms of distress across all sectors of the economy.

Historically, Latin American countries have responded to such crises through various pragmatic means, seeking to restore the solvency of the financial system through liquidation of failed banks and other intermediaries, by the merging (voluntary or forced) of financial institutions, and by direct aid to borrowers at preferential interest or exchange rates, the rescheduling of loans, and central bank purchases of nonperforming or risky assets. This is almost a universal recipe for resolving bank crises. But all these maneuvers involve high fiscal and efficiency costs, and more important, massive redistributions of wealth among various sectors. Bailouts, whether partial or total, are always unpopular and are a blemish on the reputation of the country's economic system as a whole. That is why countries attempt to minimize the costs of such episodes and to avoid them wherever possible.

Chile's central bank was given the task of handling the bank crisis of 1981–83. The central bank then implemented various special programs, including support for borrowers, the merging of financial institutions, reform of supervisory institutions and practices, and, most important, the purchase of a large share of the banking system's nonperforming assets. The government provided guarantees of the external debt that the private sector had contracted, and became involved in a series of reschedulings and restructurings of that debt. The cost of this rescue to the central bank was high: the quasi-fiscal deficit rose to as much as 0.7 or 0.8 percent of GDP, and the resulting debt is a liability that the central bank still carries on its books.

However, the financial system was rescued, and the cost of that rescue, although high, is proving to be manageable. Despite the drag on the fiscal balance, the state accounts as a whole are highly positive. For its part, the financial sector has emerged from the crisis in good health and is even on the verge of expanding into cross-border operations, with the new international banking law that is before Parliament.

The history of Chile's banking crisis, and those of other developing countries, raises several important issues. The first concerns the special characteristics of economies that are growing rapidly and trying to catch up to more developed countries, not only in terms of income but also in terms of technology and fixed capital stocks. There is a close and special interaction between the evolution of a gradually liberalizing world financial system and the growth of emerging, developing economies. But in a rapidly growing country where, by definition, savings are scarce and capital is scarcer, how does one value newly created assets? How, in particular, does one evaluate intangible assets, which are especially prone to irrational pricing? The valuation problem is complicated by the fact that these economies are especially prone to external shocks of various kinds. And how does one develop many of the assets that now have to be evaluated on a cross-border basis? How does one develop valuation methods for specific sectoral assets that have now become heavily intermediated through a rapidly developing banking system? Clearly what happens inside the banking sector is critical to meeting these challenges.

Here the main obligation of policymakers and regulators is to discourage markets from pricing assets emotionally instead of rationally. The key is to pay attention to the phases of the economic cycle described and to interpret the behavior of market participants accordingly.

Another lesson concerns the bankers' role in this cycle of boom and bust. If one were to map the distribution of expectations of the various participants in the economy, bankers would be the outliers. They are always in the vanguard, out ahead of the curve during both the euphoric expansion and the chaotic retreat. The skeptical, more conservative institutions must therefore counter them in a system of checks and balances. This is an appropriate role for the central bankers, who must therefore be very conservative and, I am sorry to say, even boring people.

My final comment relates to the quantitative and qualitative shift in banking portfolios that occurs with the turn of the boom-bust cycle. A bank's portfolio of loans is, as it were, the mirror of reality that banks use in deciding whether and where to lend next. Given the importance of their decisions to the overall economy, any distortions in this mirror must be detected and repaired as early as possible. This means upgrading the information technology available to the supervisory agencies—liquidity indicators, solvency indicators, concentration indicators, and so on—to allow them to regulate the financial sector in a more pragmatic and responsive way. The financial history of many Latin American countries shows that quality of information often falls and supervision and regulation are often relaxed during financial booms—whereas that is precisely when they should be strengthened.

As Harry Truman's two-handed economist, or indeed any mainstream economist, would surely emphasize, long-term development in Chile and any other developing economy requires both sound banking supervision and responsible liberalization of financial markets. Neither of these, however, is what ultimately drives and sustains economic growth of the kind that Chile is now enjoying. In the end, it is the mathematics of the underlying structural forces—of businesses on the investment side, of households on the saving side, and of the equilibrium between them—that keeps the economy moving forward. No financial miracle and no macroeconomic policy, however sophisticated, can substitute for a sound investment and saving profile.

Eduardo Aninat is Minister of Finance, Chile.

Venezuela

Antonio Casas

Banking crises are complex because they have multiple causes and are triggered by events in different countries. In some cases the intervention in a particular bank has been the principal cause. In others it has been a sharp change of key monetary policy instruments, such as interest rates. Another cause can be external economic factors, such as speculative movements of capital. Often a change in noneconomic conditions, such as a political or social crisis, has been the precipitating event. Any of these causes, alone or in combination, can give rise to a generalized situation of illiquidity and insolvency that ultimately affects the bulk of a country's financial and payments systems.

These phenomena have become important in both highly industrialized and developing countries, because their harmful effects are generally not limited to a country's financial institutions. Instead, the breakdown of the payments system that results from lack of confidence in banks, in the domestic currency, or in the general economic stability has implications that extend to real economic activity and beyond. Phenomena such as inflation and unemployment, with their resulting social and political disturbances, have in many cases been the direct consequence of banking crises.

A crisis develops through a long and deep process that is not easily traced. But when a crisis does erupt, its impact is quick and violent and spreads to the full range of human activity. Its corrosive influence is not limited to the economic world; the trauma suffered by defrauded depositors also has an immediate and strong destabilizing impact on social and political life.

Since January 1994 the management of monetary policy by Venezuela's central bank has been strongly influenced by a crisis in the financial system. The crisis has severely restricted our ability to carry out policies consistent with our fundamental objective of reducing the rate of inflation.

In early 1994, inflationary pressures resulted from the difficulty of financing Venezuela's growing fiscal deficit, as well as from uncertainty about the economic policy of the new government to be inaugurated in February. Such an environment called for a restrictive monetary policy. The eruption of the banking crisis did not force the central bank to abandon entirely its stabilizing objectives. But because financial support was required to preserve the stability of the financial and payments system, the central bank—in keeping with its role as lender of last resort—had to grant financial assistance to troubled banks, in some cases directly but in most others through FOGADE, the deposit guarantee fund.

This massive injection of credit, which amounted to 800 billion bolivars (more than $4.7 billion), immediately increased monetary liquidity. Accordingly, the central bank had to use other measures to offset the inflationary impact of the increased money supply. With this goal in mind, the central bank lowered the reserve requirement on commercial banks to encourage those with surplus funds to channel those resources to financial institutions with liquidity problems.

At the same time, the central bank redoubled its open market policy, using the only instrument available that was acceptable to the market: zero coupon bonds. These were later replaced by monetary stabilization securities (TEMs by their Spanish acronym), which, unlike zero coupon bonds, are issued at a fixed interest rate. Whereas open market operations in many countries are carried out with Treasury securities, in Venezuela these operations had to be performed with central bank securities. The capital markets regarded Venezuelan Treasury securities as unattractive because of their long maturities and low yields.

The choice faced by the central bank was unpalatable: either risk abandoning the financial and payments systems or accept an undesirable expansion of the money supply. The central bank's decision to increase the money supply was thoroughly scrutinized by its Board of Directors, widely discussed with other government officials, and carried out in an autonomous and responsible way. The decision also reflected the will of the Venezuelan people.

The central bank's monetary policy since that time has been strongly influenced by the 1994 crisis. The central bank has tried to maintain the integrity of the banking system, because it is only through the banks that the monetary authority can exercise its moderating or expansive influence on liquidity. Banks are also the most efficient channels of communication between the central bank and the private sector.

Naturally, any crisis of this scale has international ramifications. Several Venezuelan banks have offices in the United States and other countries. In addition, two U.S. banks, one in the Miami area and another in New York, were controlled by Venezuelans. Fortunately, despite the severe problems of some Venezuelan banks, the impact on their U.S. operations was limited. There was some withdrawal of deposits in early

1994, but these were manageable and handled without difficulty, because the U.S.-based branches all had sufficient liquid resources on hand. Later in the year, the authorities did have to intervene in two important Venezuelan banks with offices in the United States. However, the impact on their deposits was absorbed without problem, and there was little effect on the U.S. operations of other Venezuelan banks.

The fact that there was only a modest spillover effect on operations in the United States reflected the confidence that depositors had in the supervisory and regulatory roles of the Federal Reserve, the Office of the Comptroller of the Currency, and the New York and Florida state banking departments. These U.S. authorities insist on high levels of liquidity and capitalization, which banks recognize as important to preserving their own strength and credibility. During the crisis, U.S. authorities, working in close cooperation with Venezuelan banking regulators, quickly raised the liquidity levels of the U.S.-based affiliates, which enabled them to weather a difficult period. These banks are now healthy because of the work of the American regulatory bodies.

We learned a number of lessons from the crisis. The first is that complete, agile, and effective coordination among the various agencies responsible for solving banking problems is essential. Efforts at coordination were complicated in the Venezuelan case by a number of recent changes in the laws governing the banking system. Just a year before the crisis, in 1993, a new law granting broad autonomy to the central bank had been passed. Then, on January 1, 1994, the new general banking law went into effect. It contained important innovations such as giving functional and financial autonomy to the banking system's regulatory agency, the Banking Superintendency, and to FOGADE.

To strengthen the autonomy of these institutions, the new laws required the Venezuelan Senate to authorize the appointment of the presidents of the central bank, the Banking Superintendency, and FOGADE. To enhance coordination among these bodies, the general banking law provided for a coordinating mechanism called the Superior Council of the Superintendency, comprising the Minister of Finance and the presidents of the central bank and FOGADE, with the participation of the banking superintendent. This body is for resolving such important matters as the licensing and, when necessary, the closing of financial institutions.

Nonetheless, subsequent events demonstrated the limitations of the new law. within five months, nine financial groups holding one-third of the public's deposits were closed. Most of the officers charged with managing the crisis were temporary appointments unfamiliar with the new legal instrument. Moreover, the recent inauguration of the administration elected in December 1993 and the lack of adequate, timely information created continuous pressure, which resulted in a series of poorly coordinated and sometimes contradictory actions by the various public agencies. In July 1994 a Financial Emergency Board was appointed to absorb the functions of the Superior Council. The new board enabled the Banking Superintendency and FOGADE to each concentrate on its specific area, removing them as far as possible from the public debate. This finally allowed the government to deal effectively with the crisis.

Similarly, a bank supervisory group was established by the Banking Superintendency, with the logistical and technical support of the central bank. This group is currently developing an intensive training program for Superintendency officials, and should also satisfy the Financial Emergency Board's need for accurate and timely information.

The second lesson of the crisis is that banking authorities must have adequate legal tools to deal with systemic and generalized crises. Although the current law moves the banking system toward healthy financial practices, its provisions are not adequate to manage a crisis as widespread as that of 1994. The current law deals with banking problems as they develop, and since it improves banking supervision, it will surely contribute to preventing crisis situations. On the other hand, it was not designed to manage systemic crises, because the magnitude of the system's insolvency problems was not known when the law was written.

Similarly, recent commercial legislation will not prevent the transfer of properties, which in many cases represent guarantees on problem banks. When such banks became subject to intervention or were taken over by the state during the crisis, the presumably guaranteed parts of their loan portfolios were in fact uncollectible. Thus Congress enacted the Financial Emergency Law in mid 1994, a few months after the general banking law went into effect. This law allows banking supervisors to address the insolvency problems of troubled banks and prevent fraudulent transactions involving assets that have been provided as guarantees.

The third lesson of the crisis is that banking authorities must have adequate and timely information. A common cause of banking crises is that regulatory agencies have difficulty detecting problems of illiquidity, insolvency, loan concentration, and insufficient capital in time to prevent failures. In Venezuela, the decision to save some insolvent banks was based on incomplete and inaccurate accounting and financial information. In other cases the limited resources of the supervisory agencies prevented them from carrying out effective or timely supervision of the banks' accounts over many years. Consequently the crisis was much more severe than could have been foreseen based on the available data and information.

The fourth lesson is that the state must have financial mechanisms that allow for rapid decisionmaking at an appropriate level. One major difficulty Venezuela faced during the banking crisis was FOGADE's lack of resources: the banking system contributes only half a percent of deposits per year. This limited contribution seriously hampered FOGADE's ability to pay off depositors, which hurt the credibility of the banking system.

Today FOGADE is in a better position to meet its obligations: the banks now pay a 2 percent rate for deposit insurance, and the administration and Congress have agreed to devote a significant amount of funds to strengthening FOGADE's equity capital base. In addition, the Financial Emergency Law authorizes FOGADE to issue long-term, low-interest bonds to meet its obligations to the central bank and to banks that were taken over by the state. These debt securities have maturities of at least 20 years and interest rates of no more than 5 percent. However, because market interest rates in Venezuela are currently seven or eight times that level, these instruments—which the central bank accepts in payment of FOGADE's debt—will not be attractive enough to investors to use for open market operations in the immediate future.

FOGADE is also charged with selling assets received in payment from banks affected by the crisis. What procedure will be used, what kind of company will carry out the process, and which international agency will advise FOGADE on these matters, have not yet been determined.

The fifth lesson of the crisis is depositors in different problem banks must receive equal treatment. Due to the changing institutional, legal, and financial environment, as well as the various policies that existed earlier, depositors in Venezuela were treated unequally during the crisis. In cases where a financial institution was fully rehabilitated, every depositor was paid, including those who had shifted their funds to other banks. Some depositors in institutions in which the authorities intervened were also fully paid, even if their funds were not recorded on the bank's books or were deposited in offshore affiliates. Some depositors received payments in excess of the guaranteed amount, which was increased by Congress from 1 to 4 million bolivars, whereas others were paid only the amount guaranteed by FOGADE. This disparity of treatment introduced an element of anarchy into the deposit insurance system. It also complicated FOGADE's job of precisely calculating its obligations, imposed an extra cost on the rest of the banking community, and created suspicions, thereby undermining confidence in the system.

The sixth lesson of the crisis is that a specialized and technically proficient judicial body must effectively prosecute banking crimes. This calls for a body of judges with specialized banking knowledge, to assist Superintendency officials in the difficult process of supervision, control, and punishment of the criminal actions of some bankers. Recovering the assets held by failed banks to compensate for the enormous expenses incurred by the state is not the only reason for pursuing criminal penalties. Even more important than this reasonable objective is society's legitimate demand for an ethical financial environment.

The final lesson is that the specialized agencies that regulate and supervise the financial system—the central bank, the Superintendency, and FOGADE—must be insulated from the political debate. Because it affects so many interests, a banking crisis exposes officials to public opinion and raises their profiles to the point of notoriety. This situation is worsened when affected groups try, through politicians and the media, to intimidate those charged with these sensitive responsibilities. Officials of bank supervisory agencies then must devote excessive attention to these threats, which takes time away from the critical work of managing the crisis.

Antonio Casas is President, Central Bank of Venezuela.

United States

Richard Spillenkothen

I agree with what others have said about the need for strong, independent bank supervisors, as well as a central bank that is meaningfully involved in supervision. During the 1980s in the United States, when banks were failing at the rate of 200 a year, some of my economist colleagues asked me why supervisory authorities were allowing so many failures, and when this parade of failures would come to an end. My standard reply was, "As soon as you economists tame the business cycle and establish sustained growth with low inflation."

Whether one calls what happened in the United States in the 1980s and early 1990s a crisis or merely challenging times, bank supervisors certainly had their hands full. U.S. banks had severe difficulties with their loans to developing countries, with agricultural loans, and with commercial real estate loans. Some statistics will give an idea of the scope of the problem. Between 1985 and 1992 about 1,300 banks failed. Most were small regional or community banks, but some were large institutions. The banks that failed had combined assets of more than $200 billion, and the total cost of their failure to the Federal Deposit Insurance Corporation was about $30 billion. At different times as many as 1,600 banks were considered troubled, and problem bank assets exceeded $500 billion—15 percent of commercial bank assets at the time. In 1990 and 1991 the shares of the larger, publicly traded banks in this group were selling at about 50 percent of book value, an indication of how markets then viewed the industry's outlook.

The United States had an effective and broad safety net for the banking system, including a discount window, good supervision and regulation, and a well-designed system of deposit insurance, all of which were critical to preserving financial stability in the 1980s. Conditions in the U.S. financial sector today are strong again: Bank earnings and capital-asset ratios are healthy, and nonperforming loans are at relatively low levels. Even though the banking system faces numerous challenges— our laws and regulations are outdated and we need to review the kinds services that banks may provide in the future—still the system as a whole has regained its strength.

The problems of the 1980s had several sources. The first was the macroeconomic environment, because banks reflect the strength or weakness of the economy as a whole. Bank supervisors obviously want a banking system that is both strong and safe, so that when the economy falters, the system can help the economy absorb the shock. By the early 1980s inflationary expectations in the economy profoundly influenced the circumstances of banking. Loans were made on the expectation that the real assets securing them—whether oil, real estate, or other tangible assets— would continue to rise indefinitely in dollar value.

Paralleling these expectations was a second trend, toward excessive concentration in loan portfolios. In the early 1980s, U.S. banks held only about 15 percent of their assets in real estate. By the end of the decade that figure was close to 25 percent, if one includes both commercial and residential properties, with much of the growth occurring in the riskier commercial construction and development category.

A third important trend was increasing competition for banks from the nonbank sector. New technologies and a rapid pace of financial innovation allowed high-quality borrowers to access capital markets directly. This tended to undermine the traditional banking franchise and cut into bank margins. The loss of these customers caused banks to look for new clients in the real estate arena; it also contributed to lower lending standards and the underpricing of risk.

These same new technologies and innovations contributed to the fourth trend: an increase in both the pace and complexity of banking activity, accelerating the speed and expanding the volume of transactions in ways that greatly complicated supervision. Finally, the decline of capital-to-asset ratios and loan loss reserve coverage in the 1980s amplified the problems caused by these other developments.

What are the lessons to be derived from the U.S. experience? First, adequate diversification is critical. Defining what constitutes excessive concentration or adequate diversification in a loan portfolio is not easy, however. Some banks in Texas believed they were achieving diversification by adding real estate-backed loans to their existing loans to the oil and gas sector. But in that part of the country, much of the value of real estate is linked to the fortunes of the energy sector. Moreover, many banks have limited ability to diversify: a small bank in an Iowa farm community might wish to make loans to condominium developments in Florida, but that is hardly realistic. Supervisors need to pay greater attention to this issue of concentration. But it takes a strong and independent supervisor to confront bank managers when their real estate lending is booming, and tell them they should do less of that lucrative business.

A second lesson is to emphasize sound management in terms of controlling risk, particularly for the United States. Senior management and the boards of directors of banks should exert more control, through an independent internal risk management function, over their organization's lenders and traders. The Barings case and the situation with Daiwa Securities indicate the importance of keeping the responsibilities for trading and for risk management separate. Certainly derivatives and other new trading instruments pose special problems for supervisors. But simple mistakes in management (such as letting traders be in charge of bookkeeping) are sometimes the real source of the problem.

A third lesson is the need for effective, consolidated supervision. There should be more careful scrutiny of loans to insiders and owners of banks, and more on-site inspections. When supervisors come on site to look at bank records and deal with management face to face, they have a better chance of unearthing specific information to review that bank's operations.

A fourth lesson is that rapid growth in any area of lending activity—such as the explosive growth in real estate lending in the United States in the 1980s—is a serious matter that should be carefully monitored. Although it may be difficult for supervisors to intervene at such times, there is a critical need to moderate rapid expansion and its associated risks.

Fifth, banks need adequate capital and loan loss reserves to give them the strength and the time to solve any problems that arise. In the large bank mergers that the supervisory authorities helped engineer in the United States in the 1980s, a principal objective was to ensure that the new or surviving institution was at least as strong as the institutions it absorbed. To achieve that, we tried to avoid stretching the definition of capital and weakening its meaning. Maintaining the integrity of the capital base is important, but one cannot simply focus on capital-asset ratios. If assets are overvalued, the capital-asset ratio becomes meaningless.

Bank managers will resist acknowledging that they have a problem. This very human characteristic leads to the sixth lesson—when regulators find something amiss, they should look beyond managers' protests and deal with it immediately. Resolving bank problems takes time, and the sooner one starts, the better. The United States has implemented new statutory requirements that call for prompt corrective action when a bank's capital-asset ratio falls below a certain threshold. Regulators can compel a troubled bank to address its problems by cutting dividends, raising new capital, or selling assets. When these new requirements went into effect, there was much concern that markets would overreact. But in fact it appears that the markets had already discounted the banks' weaknesses and reacted favorably to the new requirements.

Finally, as Gerald Corrigan said, supervision is never perfect, but it can help. Supervisors should accept that they will be recognized only for their failures; their successes will remain a well-kept secrets. Those seeking fame and fortune should not become bank supervisors. But for persons who want to contribute to the stability of their countries' financial systems—which is a prerequisite for overall economic well-being—bank supervision is a good business.

Richard Spillenkothen is Director of Banking Supervision and Regulation, the Board of Governors, Federal Reserve System.

Timothy Ryan

Bank crises occur in industrial as well as developing economies, and in either situation it is essential to keep one's focus on the ultimate goal. That goal is a strengthened, more stable banking system, which developing countries need no less than industrial countries if they are to enjoy a resilient economy. Successful bank crisis management invariably involves four critical and interrelated elements. The most important is the political will to take whatever measures are necessary. Without political resolve, an effective financial resolution is almost impossible. The second element is sufficient funds to do the job. The third element is swiftness: once authorities decide what to do, they should do it quickly; delay only raises the price to be paid. The United States learned the importance of this third element at great cost: the authorities supervising the savings and loan industry procrastinated for some five years, which probably tripled the cost of the cleanup.

The fourth piece of the puzzle is revision of the standards—supervisory, regulatory, and accounting—that allowed the crisis to occur. A permanent and more durable set of standards will diminish the risk of new crises. Risk will never be eliminated, because history does repeat itself: despite the many new regulatory and supervisory standards the United States has established, we have surely not seen our last financial crisis.

An incipient banking crisis presents several basic but critical questions: What is the scale of the problem? To what extent is the banking system as a whole impaired, and how severely? What is the nature of the problem? Is it purely one of liquidity? Or is there a deeper, underlying solvency problem, in the form of delinquent loans that probably won't be repaid? Will aftereffects ripple through the rest of the economy, and if so, which sectors will be hardest hit? In the U.S. savings and loan crisis, for example, the real estate sector was most immediately affected.

These questions are necessary to identify and assess the losers in the crisis. But we must also ask, Who are going to be the winners? In resolving a banking crisis, the losers are relatively easy to identify, the winners less so; yet the winners will serve as the foundation of a stronger financial system and a stronger economy in the future. In the United States, for example, many of today's large regional banks were still relatively small local or single-state banks when the savings and loan crisis hit. Through participating in the resolution process for the failed banks and thrifts, many of those smaller but better managed banks became strong institutions in a recovering economy and leaders of a thriving banking industry. Finding the institutions under good management and involving them in the resolution of the crisis are essential: good management is the only thing that can fix a financial institution—or a financial system—that is broken. Without good managers to assume leadership, no plan or strategy, however well conceived, and no amount of money, will solve the problems.

Next, the authorities must determine the cause of the crisis and secure funds to resolve it. These funds can come from internal sources, as was the case in the United States, or from outside. Some countries can obtain the necessary funds from capital markets. Those that cannot access the markets are in the most serious difficulty, and for them the only realistic counsel is patience.

Also critical is maintaining the confidence of the electorate in the ability of regulators to carry out their work honestly and transparently. The United States and the countries of Latin America are now all democracies, in which voters what actions the government may or may not take. Therefore the voters need to understand exactly what the problem is, what is being done to solve it, why the solution serves their interests. This last point can be a hard sell: many will believe that government money is being spent to bail out a group of wealthy bankers or property owners.

A banking crisis and its resolution can exert a substantial drag on the economy as a whole. The difficult economic circumstances in the United States in the late 1980s and early 1990s were exacerbated by the problems in the banking and thrift industries. These problems then spilled over into the real estate sector. Markets failed to clear, so no one could assess the real value of properties. Banks that were paralyzed refused to make new loans, which led to the credit crunch of the early 1990s. Thus each problem feeds on the last, and eventually the macroeconomic effects can be extensive. If unaddressed, the problems continue to fester and spread—as is now happening, for example, in Japan.

The successful resolution of a banking crisis must address all of these elements simultaneously—the pieces of the puzzle must be brought together to form a complete and unbroken picture. The political dimension of a banking crisis illustrates how complex a balancing act the job can be. Although one may categorize the players into four distinct types—depositors, borrowers, shareholders, and the electorate—because some players have more than one role. Some borrowers are also depositors; some shareholders are also borrowers and may at the same time engage in other, more solvent businesses. There is thus the potential for a domino effect: if the borrowers fail, the bank fails; if the bank fails, the individual shareholders fail; and if those shareholders have other businesses, even if they are not financially related to the failed institution, those businesses may fail as well.

Last but not least, the domestic and multinational markets—are important players. They register the subtleties of a bank's circumstances and the situation of the banking industry much more quickly than the regulators do. The confidence of markets is therefore key to how quickly problems can be resolved.

I was deeply involved in the resolution of the U.S. savings and loan crisis as Director of the Office of Thrift Supervision (OTS) and a director of the Federal Deposit Insurance Corporation (FDIC) and the Resolution Trust Corporation (RTC, the public entity to which the assets of failed savings and loans were transferred by OTS for eventual sale). This was an extremely complex and extensive operation. Over a three-year period, more than 700 institutions with combined assets of more than $400 billion were shut down, at a cost to U.S. taxpayers of about $200 billion. At its peak, the operation involved more than 20,000 people on the government payroll alone, with thousands more supporting our efforts in the private sector. As part of the process, we created bulk sales procedures and new mortgage-backed securities to help us sell off the nonperforming and commercial real estate assets we had acquired, and we created real estate service companies to manage those assets. For a government agency, these may seem unusual actions, but we viewed them as simply good business: they enabled the government to solve problems quickly and effectively.

The first step in resolving the crisis was to determine the level of impairment. We analyzed each institution's loan portfolios and marked each holding to market, to determine whether equity capital was positive or negative. Next we looked at management. If the capital level was poor but management, in our judgment, was good, our typical approach was to give management more time to try to work out the problem. And in fact, some financial institutions that would have failed the capital test, but that had good management which we left in place, survived and are thriving today. Not shutting those institutions down saved U.S. taxpayers billions of dollars.

When the decision was made to close down the 700 or so institutions that failed both our capital and management tests, we began doing so as quickly as possible. In the first year we closed as many as ten or fifteen institutions per week, transferring their assets to the Resolution Trust Corporation. We knew that we could not resell those assets as quickly as RTC had acquired them. However, neither could we permit those institutions to continue under their current management: with their equity stake down to zero or negative levels, the owners, having nothing left to lose, would simply have continued to bet on ever-riskier ventures. They would have kept on losing, and eventually the government would have had to bail them out.

Therefore, rather than close the doors of these institutions (which might also have precipitated a run on the remaining healthy ones), we placed them into a government conservatorship. Then we took control away from the existing managers, forced the existing shareholders to realize their losses, and put government employees (ex-bankers in many cases) in charge. This often took place over the course of a weekend. The new managers were instructed to learn from the outgoing managers all they could about the institution's affairs in two days, and then reopen for business on Monday morning.

Some institutions placed in conservatorship were actually operated by these government-hired managers for a considerable period. But we always viewed such arrangements as transitory. We made it a fundamental rule that we would not nationalize any financial institution. Instead we directed our efforts toward getting the taken-over S&Ls ready for sale. Sometimes this meant selling the institution whole, both assets and liabilities together; other times we broke up the company and sold assets and deposits separately. Some of these sales were handled in the capital markets, which is seldom an option in developing countries; others were done through auctions or by directly identifying potential buyers.

In short, there is a range of possible responses to the problem of financial institutions in trouble. Liquidation is the answer for the weakest institutions—but only the weakest, because it is the most costly. At the other extreme, private recapitalization, with one strong private institution simply buying a weaker one, is the least expensive solution. Whatever strategy is utilized, the same elements are required: political will, sufficient funds, timely implementation, and development of a future system that can minimize (but never really eliminate) banking crises.

Timothy Ryan is Managing Director, J.P. Morgan and Company, Inc.

Part VII

Conclusions
and the Policy Debate

Ricardo Hausmann and Liliana Rojas-Suárez

Conclusions and the Policy Debate

Ricardo Hausmann and Liliana Rojas-Suárez

The conference that led to this book produced important insights on various aspects of banking crises in Latin America. Regarding the causes of banking crises, how best to resolve them, and how to avoid them when possible, the participants reached consensus on most issues. Other important areas will need further research and analysis.

The plan of the book presented four broad questions (p. xi). Here we will summarize how the writers have answered those questions, and conclude with some unresolved issues for future consideration.

1. What are the salient features of banking crises in Latin America?

Banking crises occur in both industrial and developing countries. As Michel Camdessus points out, the new challenges countries face in preventing and solving problems in the financial sector are, to some extent, the price of success: they are a consequence of economic progress and technological advances that have allowed a rapid globalization of markets. But because banks play a key role in the payments system and in economic growth, the eruption of banking crises is as serious a concern for policymakers today as ever.

Although banking crises all share common features, such crises in Latin America tend to be more severe: they last longer, they affect a larger segment of the banking industry, and their resolution costs the public more than in the industrial world. Rojas-Suárez and Weisbrod show that, on average, the cost of rescuing banks in Latin America has been more than twice that in industrial countries. Not only do banks play a more dominant role in Latin American financial systems, but certain peculiarities of banking systems in the region make them more fragile than their industrial country counterparts. In particular, deposits are more volatile and their maturity is much shorter. These features suggest that investors lack confidence that financial assets will yield positive rates of return on a sustained basis.

The fragility of Latin American banking systems is due both to economic instability and to weakness in the institutional infrastructure of financial systems. Long periods of high inflation, punctuated by occasional steep currency devaluations, have eroded investors' confidence in assets denominated in domestic currency. Weak legal standards make it difficult for creditors to assess their prospects of repayment, and underdeveloped accounting standards do not permit a transparent evaluation of the quality of banks' balance sheets or of the income statements of borrowers. Moreover, as Ruth de Krivoy emphasizes, not only are bank supervisory procedures often inadequate, but the supervisors themselves, lacking independence from other government institutions, have limited capacity to enforce those rules that exist.

In such an environment, even relatively mild shocks to the banking sector can quickly result in sharp drops in the deposit base. The evidence presented by Rojas-Suárez and Weisbrod indicates that depositors in Latin America are much more prone than their industrial country counterparts to flee the banking system when bank borrowers' capacity to pay comes into question. The evidence also supports the related conclusion that government guarantees on deposits—whether through explicit deposit insurance or through an implicit promise to rescue depositors in troubled banks—are more credible in real terms in industrial countries than in Latin America. That is, investors in industrial countries for the most part believe that the real value of their holdings will be protected even in the event of a severe crisis; in contrast, depositors in Latin America fear that they will suffer a real financial loss in any banking crisis.

Lack of confidence in Latin American financial systems is not confined to domestic asset holders. During banking crises, Latin American countries also lose access to international capital markets. That explains in part why the economic costs of solving crises are so high in the region. Large current account adjustments usually accompany periods of banking crisis in Latin America; in contrast, the external positions of industrial countries remain largely unaffected when they undergo similar episodes. This hair-trigger response of foreign investors leads Lawrence Summers to advise a cautious, conservative attitude toward capital flows: the safest course, he says, is for governments in emerging markets to treat surges in capital inflows as transitory, and then "be pleasantly surprised if they turn out not to be."

The flightiness of international capital implies that Latin American countries seeking funds to resolve banking crises are largely on their own, their sources of funding being confined to scarce domestic capital and to funds extended by the multilateral financial organizations. Another severe constraint is an absence of deep markets for nonperforming assets and failing institutions. As will be discussed below, both these constraints have played a central role in the way banking problems are resolved in Latin America.

2. What are the main causes of banking crises in the region?

Most experts agree that banking crises result from a combination of factors, and they mostly agree on what those factors are. But opinions differ greatly regarding the relative importance of those factors. At the risk of some oversimplification, the debate can be stylized as one between two comps: those who see macroeconomic conditions as the main cause, and those who emphasize weaknesses at the microeconomic level, especially poor bank management and failures in the regulatory and supervisory frameworks. This difference in emphasis leads to differences in policy prescriptions. For example, those who stress the role of macroeconomic factors recommend such policies as tightened capital and liquidity requirements, which protect banks against shocks to their deposit base or to the quality of their assets. In contrast, those who underline the role of bank management recommend improvements in supervision and in the role of market forces to provide incentives for strengthening banks. But while the debate is important, this difference is largely one of emphasis, not principle. Neither the diagnoses nor the policy conclusions offered by the two comps are mutually exclusive; in fact, most analysts agree on the importance of both macroeconomic conditions and the incentive structure created by market and regulatory forces.

Macroeconomic factors

Those who stress macroeconomic conditions point to the more volatile economic environment in Latin America. Macroeconomic shocks can threaten banks on either of two fronts: by depleting the sources of bank funding or by impairing the quality of bank assets. In the first case, shocks to fiscal accounts, whether caused by external factors or by domestic policy changes, may create expectations of inflation or devaluation which result in a sharp contraction of bank deposits, thus reducing banks' liquidity. The impact on expectations may be much larger in Latin America than in industrial countries, because the financial system that will be expected to cover the resulting deficits is relatively shallow. If, to restore liquidity, banks stop renewing credits as they come due, the sudden reduction in credit to nonfinancial enterprises may lead to a severe business contraction, adversely affecting firms' capacity to repay bank loans. As Guillermo Calvo argues, the effect of macroeconomic shocks on banks can be amplified by herd behavior. If individuals come to expect a massive reaction—for example, large withdrawals of bank deposits—to an initial shock, they, too, react in order to avoid large losses; this results in more widespread and severe bank problems than would have resulted in the absence of such behavior. A number of economists have cited the sharp decline in Argentine bank deposits that resulted from an external shock—the Mexican devaluation of December 1994—as an example of such herd behavior.

Adverse macroeconomic shocks to asset values—the second threat to which banks are vulnerable—may undermine the quality of banks' portfolios either directly (when banks themselves hold assets affected by the shock) or indirectly (when the decline in asset prices affects bank borrowers' capacity to repay loans). A decline in real estate prices that weakens the balance sheets of construction companies to which banks have extended loans is a frequent source of bank problems in both industrial and developing countries.

The underlying strength of the banking system at the moment an adverse macroeconomic shock hits is an important determinant of whether a banking crisis will ensue. If the initial capital base is small, the shock may wipe out the bank's capital. Moreover, as argued by Morris Goldstein and Pablo Guidotti, even if the bank survives initially, low capitalization gives bank managers particularly large incentives to "gamble for resurrection" by adopting riskier strategies in hopes of getting lucky and recovering, knowing that their downside risk is limited.

Gavin and Hausmann argue that this traditional mechanism, based on moral hazard, is not the only way in which systemic vulnerabilities in the banking system may emerge. They argue that fragilities may also develop during good times due to information problems rather than moral hazard.

Gavin and Hausmann note that during periods of macroeconomic boom, the demand for bank deposits tends to rise dramatically, as increased confidence in the macroeconomic outlook spurs an increase in demand for domestic assets. The increased funding allows banks to start a lending boom. During such a boom, given the limited borrowing capacity of their traditional client base, banks need to recruit new borrowers, about whom they have relatively little information. In Gavin's and Hausmann's view, "good times are bad times for learning" about the creditworthiness of firms, because the widespread availability of credit implies that borrowers can always "prove" their liquidity by borrowing from some other banks, who are themselves in search of new clients. Moreover, since lending booms are often associated with periods of economic expansion, firms appear to be more creditworthy than they will prove to be once the boom subsides. This makes it difficult for banks to distinguish good loans from bad, and results in faulty information: if banks grant loans excessively, such loans have an adverse impact on the quality of information available to other banks in the market. Also, because banks have a limited installed capacity in loan appraisal, during booms they tend to examine loans less carefully, given the excess resources available to invest. The "information externality" and the congestion problem lead to increased bank fragility during the lending boom. When the lending boom ends, as eventually it must, firms will have increased difficulty servicing their debts, because they can no longer borrow to pay existing debts, and because the downturn will impair their own capacity to repay bank loans.

To support their argument, Gavin and Hausmann show that banking crises have been preceded by lending booms, in industrial as well as in Latin American countries, and that these booms have ended one or two years before the eruption of the crisis.

A number of policymakers and economists share this cyclical view of banking crises. For example, both Eduardo Aninat and Sebastián Edwards agree that, during economic booms, euphoria about the economy's prospects leads bankers to "race ahead of the curve," expanding their portfolios beyond what the underlying economic fundamentals will sustain in the long run. In Aninat's view, the result is that the boom becomes speculative in nature, feeding upon itself rather than building on a sound economy. As economic agents realize that the boom is unsustainable, even a minor bit of adverse news may precipitate a large sell-off of assets, exposing the excessive risk that the banks have taken, as the value of the collateral that backed up bank credit declines sharply.

Guillermo Calvo also agrees with the interpretation that economic booms may lead to bank problems, but he adds an important qualification: economic expansions are more likely to affect the banking system adversely when they result from increases in consumption rather than in investment. Changes in the demand for money are more closely correlated with variations in expenditure than with changes in output; so a temporary increase in expenditure, such as a consumption boom without higher levels of investment, will bring about an unsustainable expansion of money demand. If, in contrast, the increase in expenditure largely reflects a higher level of capital accumulation, the associated changes in the demand for money can be expected to be more permanent. In this latter situation, adverse shocks need not generate sharp reductions in a country's deposit base, and there is less probability of a major disruption in the banking system. From this perspective the source of large current account deficits matters. A current account deficit generated by large increases in consumption demand is likely to be destabilizing, but one that stems from increases in investment may not be.

Microeconomic factors

Those who emphasize microeconomic factors point to poor bank management as the key element behind banking crises. Proponents of this view acknowledge the role of macroeconomic shocks in precipitating crises, but argue that such shocks only expose a preexisting weakness in bank portfolios. In fact, during most crisis episodes—even following an adverse macroeconomic shock or in the midst of a sharp recession—some banks escape the fate of their less well managed competitors.

Aristóbulo de Juan argues that poor prudential regulations and loose supervision are at the root of banking crises, because they lay the basis for poor bank management. David Folkerts-Landau supports the need for an effective supervisory infrastructure: without it, managers have enormous incentives to gamble with their depositors' money, given the previously noted moral hazard problem. When returns are good, banks collect large profits; but if problem loans lead to solvency problems, banks have limited liability and can often expect to be bailed out.

One indication of poor bank management is poor lending practices. These include undue concentration of lending in a single sector or geographic area; lending to financially connected entities; mismatching of loans by term or by currency; and poor loan recovery. For many who see bad management as a major cause of banking crises, including Angel Rojo and Carlos Santistevan, *loan concentration* is a major factor, especially in countries where banks and large industrial interests are closely intertwined. Another sign of unsound management is *poor internal controls*, reflecting inadequate internal audit procedures or insufficient provision of timely information needed for decisionmaking. A third is the practice of *concealing problems* from supervisors by rolling over nonperforming loans. By not classifying these loans as bad, banks avoid having to set aside loss provisions for them. This manipulation of income and balance sheet accounts allows banks to show on paper a much larger stock of capital than they actually possess.

According to de Juan, improper supervision of banks ends ultimately in an overt banking crisis by way of a three-stage process. In the first stage, a bank with problem loans takes on additional risk by continuing to lend to the worst borrowers; obviously, default by such borrowers would expose the bank's difficulties to the regulators. But as the cash flow from these accumulating bad loans dwindles, the bank faces liquidity problems. Consequently, the bank offers higher interest rates to attract new deposits. This sends a signal to some market participants about the bank's problems and may lead to a sell-off of the bank's shares, which aggravates the problem. In the final stage, the bank becomes illiquid and the authorities are called to the rescue. As Rojo notes, this terminal stage can be postponed but will eventually occur, often triggered by a macroeconomic shock.

While there is agreement that well-supervised capital adequacy requirements can effectively address the moral hazard problem, those that view the problem as caused by an information externality question the effectiveness of supervision by arguing that regulators probably have even less information than bankers do. Banking records are not at all like the computer programs in which appearances automatically correspond with reality; in supervision, as Gavin and Hausmann note, "it's what you *don't* see, that gets you." They caution policymakers not to assume that supervision alone will protect the economy from the risk of a major banking crisis.

3. How can governments manage banking crises effectively?

Whatever the causes of a banking crisis, policymakers throughout the world face the same dilemma of how to deal with it. One piece of good news is that experience with banking crisis management has brought to light some basic principles that may contribute to a successful resolution; the corresponding bad news is that even when these principles are followed, the resolution of banking crises remains arduous and painful. On two of these principles, there is now general agreement. First, those who have benefited from banks' risktaking must bear a large portion of the cost of restructuring the banking system. This implies that if anyone is to lose their stake, the bank shareholders should be first in line, and delinquent borrowers should not be given favorable treatment. This principle is especially important in cases when authorities decide not to close down a troubled institution. As Miguel Mancera concisely puts it, the basic philosophy here is one of "saving the banks, not the bank owners." A corollary is that if a bank with serious solvency problems remains open, its management must be changed. This policy prescription is particularly important for those who, as discussed above, attribute banking problems largely to poor bank management. Some note, however, that although bad management must be removed, ensuring better management may be difficult, especially in countries that have a weak base of human capital. Moreover, government appointees may lack experience and may abuse their power because they also face incentive problems.

The second principle is that action must be taken promptly to prevent severely impaired institutions from continuing to expand their activities, especially when the expectation is that public funds will ultimately bear the increased risk. In other words, this principle aims at avoiding the moral hazard associated with banks "gambling for resurrection." In recalling their experiences with banking crisis resolution in Argentina, Sweden, and the U.S. savings and loan industry, Roque Fernández, Stefan Ingves, and Timothy Ryan strongly emphasize the importance of these two principles.

Some debate remains concerning a third principle: that society must muster the political will to allocate noninflationary sources of public funds toward bank restructuring operations. Whereas Ingves and Ryan argue that such political commitment was essential to the success of the bank rescue operations in which they were involved, Fernández questions not only the use of public resources for bank restructuring but even the usefulness of publicly discussing problems in the financial sector. In his view, the release of information may further aggravate the problem, since mistrust and misunderstanding may arise. Instead, he argues that a central bank should not disclose in detail the rules it will apply in solving bank problems, but rather allow itself some room to maneuver by maintaining a degree of "constructive ambiguity" in its relationship with banks.

If there is considerable agreement about the principles to apply in dealing with banking crises, why has crisis resolution in Latin America been more costly and difficult to implement than in industrial countries? The answer may be that Latin America faces much more stringent constraints in applying these basic principles than do industrial countries. Rojas-Suárez and Weisbrod identify three major constraints. First, funds with which to solve banking problems are extremely scarce. Because of the features of Latin American financial markets described above, private international sources of capital vanish at the first sign of problems. To finance bank restructuring without causing inflation, governments must reduce expenditures in other areas, making adjustment still more painful. Pablo Guidotti also recognizes the constraints imposed by scarcity of funds, arguing that for governments in emerging markets the relevant issue "is not unwillingness, but rather, inability to provide the required liquidity assistance."

Ready access to resources from multilateral organizations may become crucial in such an environment. Michel Camdessus, in his analysis of the Mexican dilemma, underlines the importance of this source of finance to developing countries when private capital flows dry up at the outbreak of a crisis: "On January 31, 1995, this was the problem: If the IMF did not contribute quickly and substantially to a major international package for Mexico . . . [the country] may have had no other solution than a moratorium on foreign debt or a reimposition of trade and exchange restrictions." This is very different from what happened when Sweden had to resolve a major banking crisis: since international capital markets were still available, the Swedish authorities could finance the resolution of the crisis without a major burst of inflation or a deepening recession.

A second constraint is the lack of markets in which to sell financial institutions or their financial assets. In his review of the savings and loan crisis in the United States, Ryan notes that the Resolution Trust Corporation had several options for disposing of the assets of failed institutions: to sell the whole institution or to break the company up and sell its assets and liabilities separately in the capital markets. These alternatives are simply not available to most Latin American countries.

The third constraint is lack of regulatory knowhow and independence. For experienced policymakers in industrial countries, such as Gerald Corrigan, the existence of an adequate regulatory framework to provide the tools, authority, and flexibility to deal with banking problems is essential for effective crisis management. A well-established legal and administrative framework allows policymakers to assign clear responsibilities to the various institutions charged with dealing with the crisis, and it also insulates those institutions from political pressures. As Antonio Casas observes, the lack of adequate legal tools to deal with systemic crises impeded efforts to manage the 1994 banking crisis in Venezuela.

Does the presence of these constraints imply that restructuring programs in Latin America have little chance of success? Fortunately, the answer is no. As Rojas-Suárez and Weisbrod explain, a country can resolve its banking difficulties even under the most severe constraints if it adheres to the basic principles outlined above and adapts them to local conditions. A well-known example in Latin America is that of Chile in the early 1980s. Proper crisis management in Chile included designing ingenious mechanisms to extend the maturities of viable loans, as well as imposing severe penalties on bank stockholders. A strong fiscal effort complemented the restructuring program. Chilean authorities used the opportunity provided by the crisis to strengthen supervision and improve the quality of bank management. So by 1996, almost a decade and a half after its banking problems first surfaced, Chile had one of the most healthy and resilient banking systems in the region. These lessons are not lost on other countries in the region. For example, both Argentina and Mexico, where severe banking problems erupted in early 1995, are fully exploiting the opportunity to strengthen their banking systems.

4. How can banking crises be prevented?

Not surprisingly, the list of policy recommendations to avoid banking crises is long and covers all the dimensions discussed thus far. Some of these recommendations remain matters of debate, but there are two general points of consensus. First, if they are to withstand the pressures associated with the globalization of international capital markets and the volatility of capital flows, banks in developing countries must be sound. Second, both a sound macroeconomic environment and a strong bank regulatory and supervisory framework are essential to ensure bank safety. The disagreement is over some of the more specific recommendations. The rest of this section summarizes the state of that debate.

Macroeconomic policies

Because large macroeconomic misalignments harm the banking system, there is full agreement that a sustainable fiscal stance and a monetary policy aimed at achieving long-term price stability are both essential to maintaining the soundness of banks. Another high priority is avoiding grossly overvalued currencies and excessive current account deficits. In reviewing their country experiences, all the policymakers who participated in the conference agreed with this prescription.

A key feature of Latin American economies is the much greater macroeconomic volatility under which their banking systems must operate. This means that Latin American banks must cope with much larger shocks to their liquidity and asset quality, and are much more likely to experience macroeconomic conditions conducive to a destabilizing lending boom. The policy dilemma, therefore, is how to avoid lending booms without unduly restricting the financial intermediation necessary for economic growth. Discussions in this area generally concern the following four questions.

- *What is the appropriate conduct of monetary policy?*

A central bank may intervene in various ways to control the expansion of credit growth. This issue has become particularly important now that volatile capital flows severely complicate the conduct of monetary policy in Latin America. Although the debate over active versus passive monetary policy remains unresolved, several participants (including Gavin and Hausmann, Calvo, and Roberto Zahler) support an active monetary policy. Believing that an effective regulatory and supervisory system is not sufficient to control excessive credit growth, they recommend the active use of reserve or liquidity requirements and open market operations to prevent an unduly rapid expansion of bank credit when the economy enters a boom period. Rather than maintain a fixed ratio over time, authorities would change liquidity requirements, so as to "lean against the wind" of credit booms, and to ensure that banks can avoid a dangerous degree of illiquidity when the boom turns sour. By the same token, liquidity requirements can be relaxed if the demand for deposits abruptly declines, thus ensuring that the reduction in deposit demand does not translate into an abrupt and disruptive contraction of bank credit. Some argue that such a policy reduced the recessionary impact of the fall in demand for Argentine bank deposits after the "tequila" shock.

• *What is the appropriate choice of exchange rate regime?*

The state of the banking system is recognized to be an important factor in the choice of exchange rate regime. Thus the consensus has shifted toward greater flexibility in exchange rate policy. Supporters of this view argue that adverse external shocks will have a more devastating effect on a fragile banking system under fixed than under flexible exchange rates. For example, Gavin and Hausmann, among others, argue that, under fixed exchange rates, a shock leading to a reduction in international reserves will result in a reduced money supply and higher domestic interest rates, putting pressure on bank borrowers from the associated contraction in bank credit and the higher cost of servicing bank debt. In contrast, under flexible exchange rates the same shock will lead to a depreciation of the currency and an increase in the domestic price level. As a result, the real value of both bank loans and liabilities will decline, avoiding increased stress on borrowers while maintaining banks' capacity to pay depositors. Guillermo Ortiz and Sebastián Edwards agree with this view but recognize the importance of a fixed exchange rate as a mechanism for establishing government credibility during the initial stages of a stabilization program. In their view, the policy dilemma—which is not yet resolved— is deciding when to move away from the exchange rate anchor and toward more flexible exchange rates.

Calvo and Zahler offer a more cautious view about the advantages of flexible rates. Calvo argues that if the problem is to avoid a contractionary reduction in credit following an adverse external shock, the solution could take place in the context of a fixed exchange rate system by lowering banks' reserve requirements. This would require, of course, that the required reserves be high enough going into the crisis to provide adequate liquidity to draw upon. Zahler does not view the choice of flexible exchange rates as problem-free. He argues that if authorities in a country with a flexible exchange rate system decide to fight inflationary pressures by increasing interest rates, the stresses on domestic banks will be the same as under fixed rates. In his view, weak banking systems impose severe constraints on the achievement of central bank policy goals—constraints that will prevail whether exchange rates are flexible or fixed.

• *How should international reserves be managed?*

The discussion of the appropriate stock of international reserves in Latin American countries that opt for a managed exchange rate regime has been strongly influenced by developments in domestic banking systems. Although, as Edwards recalls, the traditional literature focuses on trade flows to determine the optimal stock of reserves, sharp outflows of capital have often followed from increased perceptions of banking difficulties. A new wave of thought relates the appropriate stock of international reserves to the total stock of domestic liquid assets. A rule of thumb for countries with fragile banking systems, suggested by Calvo, is that the stock of a country's foreign exchange reserves should not be less that some proportion of the stock of the domestic monetary aggregate M2.

• *Should capital controls be used to deal with volatile capital flows?*

Since lending booms in Latin America have often been associated with large capital inflows, which tend to reverse themselves sharply at the slightest deterioration of perceptions about economic conditions, discussions about the desirability of capital controls have reemerged in the region. There is still no consensus on this issue, however. Although some draw a connection between Chile's and Colombia's use of such controls on short-term flows and their financial stability, others emphasize the disruptions and inefficiencies that controls generate. Still others claim that the discussion is pointless, because with the current state of financial technology and degree of global integration, controls are easily evaded and therefore largely ineffective.

Microeconomic policies and issues of regulation and supervision

Those who think that inadequate bank management—a microeconomic factor—lies at the core of banking problems, believe the basic prescription for crisis avoidance is to design an adequate regulatory and supervisory framework. While agreeing that the maintenance of sound macroeconomic policies is essential to achieve bank stability, supporters of the microeconomic approach differ from those who focus on macroeconomic policies in that they do not favor the use of policies based on management of aggregates, such as reserve requirements. Their argument is that such a policy taxes all banks equally, without differentiating among the risk characteristics of individual banks. Since in every crisis episode a number of banks have remained solvent and have actually contributed to resolving the crisis, such a "tax" may prove unnecessarily burdensome to bank activity and economic growth. Notwithstanding these reservations, it is also recognized that there are cases in which reserve requirements may be the only policy tool at hand to deal with a risky expansion of credit. These are the cases in which regulatory and supervisory practices lack the necessary development to deal with bank problems. In these situations the usual recommendation is that reserve or liquidity requirements may be used while supervisory systems are being strengthened.

The list of policy recommendations dealing with regulatory and supervisory issues is long. These policies are discussed in detail by de Juan and de Krivoy. Among them are, first, the implementation of appropriate accounting systems to properly identify bank problems. Stringent rules for proper classification and valuation of assets need to be an essential component of accounting standards. Since, as Santistevan and Folkerts-Landau argue, most banking crises originate in the loan portfolio, the focus of bank supervision should be to assess the true value of loan portfolios. A second policy recommendation calls for regulations limiting loan concentration and related lending. As de Krivoy emphasizes, proper compliance with these rules can only be achieved through frequent and comprehensive on-site inspections of banks. A third recommendation is improvement of the legal system, including establishment of clear bankruptcy procedures to ease loan recoveries. A fourth is improvement in bank disclosure procedures: proper information should be available not only to the supervisors but also to the public, to allow the discipline of market forces to operate. As Fernando de Santibañez observes, those banking systems that provide reliable information are the most resilient to shocks. A fifth recommendation is to improve the overall bank monitoring system by allowing for external auditors and private rating agencies to complement the role of official supervisors. A final recommendation is stricter criteria for granting licenses to those seeking to enter the banking industry.

While there is consensus on most policy recommendations regarding regulatory and supervisory practices, a few areas remain open to debate. This debate can be organized around the following four questions.

• *What is the right mix between stringent regulation and supervision and market discipline?*

Debate on this issue has recently gained prominence, with the claim by some market observers that bankers will always be ahead of supervisors in detecting problems. The issue here is whether regulatory and supervisory procedures should be made even more strict or whether, on the contrary, they should be made more lax, allowing banks to fail and letting the markets force banks to strengthen their own mechanisms of internal control and management. As Rojo argues, the optimal level of supervision can be determined only by assessing the costs and benefits associated with it. While the potential benefits of supervision—the reduction of bank fragility—are well known, its costs have been less thoroughly discussed. Not only is it costly for governments to finance a large team of supervisors, but it is also costly for banks to maintain capital levels in excess of what they would have chosen to maintain. Rojo's solution to this dilemma entails establishing a supervisory system that allows for failure of badly managed banks but will prevent a local crisis from spreading throughout the system. De Juan takes a more skeptical attitude toward market discipline. While agreeing that it is a good supplement to bank supervision, he argues that the two key assumptions to guarantee the proper functioning of market discipline, namely, appropriate disclosure and government's willingness to close problem banks, do not hold in most countries.

• *Are the capital adequacy ratios established by the Basle Committee adequate for Latin America?*

Although a few participants argue that high capital-asset ratios impose unnecessary costs on banks, most agreed that capital requirements for Latin America should be greater than the 8 percent capital-to-risk-weighted-assets ratio established by the Basle regulations. The principal argument is that the 8 percent ratio, although appropriate for banks in industrial countries, is not suitable for banks operating in Latin America, given the greater economic volatility they face. Andrew Crockett agrees and adds that, even in some industrial countries, supervisors require higher capital ratios than those recommended by the Basle Committee. There is a consensus that, whatever the ratio chosen, it should take into account the overall portfolio risk of banks, that is, not only credit risk but also market risks (exchange rate and interest rate risks) and loan concentration risk.

In this context, Richard Spillenkothen raises a note of caution: capital-asset ratios have no meaning if assets are overvalued. A first step toward improving the capital base of a bank is to ensure that capital is measured correctly: real and not accounting capital is what counts for bank solvency.

- *Which institution should be in charge of bank supervision?*

Although there is complete agreement that the effectiveness of supervisory procedures depends on the independence of bank supervisors from political pressures, opinions differ about where the supervisory function should be placed. Among others, Ruth de Krivoy, Manuel Guitián, and David Folkerts-Landau argue that the central bank should be assigned that role. The central bank cannot achieve its ultimate goal—the achievement of price stability and the effective operation of the payments system—if it cannot act directly to prevent a banking crisis. From this perspective, locating supervisory powers within the central bank helps ensure its independence. Andrés Bianchi disagrees. He argues that if the central bank were obliged to take drastic action, such as closing banks, in the event of a crisis, the political pressures that would have been exerted on a separate supervisory agency would now turn against the central bank, compromising its independence. From Bianchi's perspective the right alternative is to strengthen existing supervisory bodies.

Unresolved Issues

Perhaps one of the most important contributions of this book is to identify issues that have yet to be resolved if effective management of banking systems is to prevail in Latin America. At a minimum, the following four issues must be addressed.

- Concerning the adequacy of capital-asset ratios, should the bank regulations that are effective in industrial countries be implemented in Latin America, or should policymakers within the region design rules and practices appropriate for its particular features?
- What should a bank supervisor in Latin America do after discovering that a bank is not fulfilling existing regulations, such as capital-asset ratios? As the discussions indicate, financial constraints make it harder to close a problem bank in Latin America than in the industrial countries. Can an approach based on early intervention and resolution, like the U.S. FDIC Improvement Act, solve this problem?

- What is the appropriate design of deposit insurance? Although policymakers in Latin America generally agree that the creation of a financial safety net is a worthwhile objective, the reform of current systems is complicated by remaining fragilities in financial institutions. The question here is what accompanying changes in regulations need to be undertaken to establish soundly financed deposit insurance systems without raising concerns about the capacity of banks to make good on their liabilities.

- To what extent should Latin America banking systems become more international in their operations? Although the advantages of greater diversification are clear, further globalization of the region's banks may pose risks to the stability of domestic financial systems. These risks, clearly emphasized by Enrique Iglesias and Paul Volcker, underscore the need for international coordination in the design of regulatory and supervisory practices of financial institutions.

These and other issues provide ample motivation for further research by those concerned with the achievement of economic and financial stability in Latin America. We hope this book will contribute to reaching that goal.